Modernities and the Popular Melodrama

Modernities and the Popular Melodrama

The Suchitra–Uttam Yug in Bengali Cinema

Smita Banerjee

Orient BlackSwan

MODERNITIES AND THE POPULAR MELODRAMA:
THE SUCHITRA–UTTAM YUG IN BENGALI CINEMA

ORIENT BLACKSWAN PRIVATE LIMITED

Registered Office
3-6-752 Himayatnagar, Hyderabad 500 029, Telangana, India
e-mail: centraloffice@orientblackswan.com

Other Offices
Bengaluru, Chennai, Guwahati, Hyderabad, Kolkata,
Mumbai, New Delhi, Noida, Patna

First published by Orient Blackswan Private Limited 2023

ISBN 978-93-5442-452-6

Typeset in
Adobe Jenson Pro 11.5/13
by Le Studio Graphique, Gurgaon 122 007

041768

Printed in India at
Kensington Printing & Packaging, Noida 201 301

Published by
Orient Blackswan Private Limited
3-6-752 Himayatnagar, Hyderabad 500 029, Telangana, India
e-mail: info@orientblackswan.com

For my parents

Contents

Figures

Abbreviations

CFS	Calcutta Film Society
CSDS	Centre for the Study of Developing Societies
CSSSC	Centre for Studies in Social Sciences, Calcutta
DVD	Digital Video Disc
JNU	Jawaharlal Nehru University, Delhi
SRFTI	Satyajit Ray Film and Television Institute, Kolkata
TRP	Television Rating Point
VCD	Video Compact Disc
WBJFA	West Bengal Film Journalists' Association

Publisher's Acknowledgements

For permission to reproduce copyrighted material in this book, the publishers would like to thank the following:

BioScope: South Asian Screen Studies, for permission to reproduce the essay 'Evolution of *Dada* Uttam Kumar: Performing Masculinity and the Disillusioned *Bhadralok Mahanayak* in the 1970s' Popular Melodramas', Volume 10, Issue 1 (June 2019): 1–25. Extracts from this essay have been reproduced in various chapters of this book. Permission granted by Sage Journals.

John Wiley and Sons, Inc., for permission to reproduce extracts from the chapter 'Performing the *Bhadramahila*: Suchitra Sen and Popular Bangla Cinema', in *A Companion to Indian Cinema* (2022), edited by Neepa Majumdar and Ranjani Mazumdar: 219–238. Extracts from this chapter have been reproduced in various chapters of this book. Permission granted by John Wiley and Sons, Inc.

Denise Jans, for the photograph used on the title page. Permission granted by Unsplash.com.

Acknowledgements

A first book accrues many debts. I would like to thank all my teachers, family, friends, colleagues, and strangers who became interested in my research project over the years and helped in the writing of this book.

I would like to express my gratitude to my doctoral supervisor, Ira Bhaskar, for her patience, erudite scholarship, her faith in my abilities and unstinting support towards my research journey and its culmination in this book.

My thanks to Ranjani Mazumdar for her intellectual engagement, unfailing enthusiasm and for all her help, which remained constant in enabling my research journey.

I take this opportunity to thank Christine Gledhill and Richard Allen for their insightful and engaging comments as the external examiners for my dissertation, which proved immensely helpful in writing this book.

Two research grants facilitated my archival work in Kolkata: the Sarai IFS (2007) Fellowship granted by the Centre for the Study of Developing Societies (CSDS) and the Spear Grant (2009) from the School of Arts and Aesthetics (SAA), Jawaharlal Nehru University (JNU), Delhi.

Kamalika and Ranjana at the Centre for Studies in Social Sciences, Calcutta (CSSSC) archive in Kolkata, Abhijit da, and others were immensely helpful. I am grateful to Moinak Biswas for sharing his work. I thank Sanjay Mukherjee, Subhajit Chatterjee and Arijit Mukherjee of the Jadavpur Film Studies Department, the Media Lab staff and project coordinators, and the library staff, who were extremely kind and facilitated the archival work.

Sanjay da at the Temar Lane Little Magazine Library, the Librarian and staff of Baagbazaar Reading Library, and art curator and collector Sounak Chacraverti, all welcomed me and my research queries and provided invaluable contacts and material. G. K. Ray, senior journalist and Suchitra Sen's biographer, was instrumental in helping me with queries. Aparna Sen, Partha Sen, and Monojit Lahiri took time off their busy schedules to speak with me. Sova Sen, Samik Bandopadhyaya, and Ratna Ghoshal helped me with their reminiscences on Bengali cinema.

My consulting editor at Orient Blackswan, Roopa Sharma, Nilanjana Majumdar and Proteeti Banerjee from the editorial team, and Sanna Jain for her meticulous copy-editing, deserve my gratitude for their patience and support. I also thank the anonymous reviewer whose incisive comments helped immeasurably in the revisions to the manuscript.

Shikha Jhingan, Bindu Menon, and Aarti Wani, my PhD batchmates and friends, as well as Spandan, Anugyan and the 2006–07 MPhil batch, SAA, JNU, whose courses I audited, have been unfailing in their support. Thanks to Shohini Ghosh for her constant encouragement and for sharing her collection of material on the two stars who have dominated my intellectual field for over a decade, and to Kaushik Bhaumik for his suggestions. Sumangala Damodaran deserves huge thanks for reading the chapter drafts.

To my extended family in Kolkata and friends who were there to make me feel at home, and new friends who stepped in when everything seemed impossible, especially Tanaji, whose cinephile enthusiasm is a huge boon. I am thankful to Neelambari for the indexing and Abhishek for helping with film images.

My friends, Hephzibah, Mukul, and Preet, who have been part of my life and academic journey. Sumangala, Asmita, Shobha, Geetha, Mahesh, Saumya, Krish, Shakun, and Alok (who left us too soon), for believing that I could do this.

Last but not the least, I thank my family, Manju, Shankho, Dipanwita, and Aatreyi, whose love for all things filmy makes me feel special. Chini, who had to spend half her life waiting for her mother to finish her PhD, and then be more patient with her while she was writing the book. And this is for my father, who is not around to share this moment but as Chini says, he is up there and still with us….

Preface

Quest for the Stars, Travel for the Archive

This journey in search of the stars began way back in 2006, as part of the Centre for the Study of Developing Societies Independent Fellowship (CSDS Sarai IFS) project.[1] I travelled to Kolkata in search of material on the experience of urban modernity in the cinema of the 1950s–60s. As I traversed the city, I discovered a curious absent presence of Suchitra and Uttam, not only in their overwhelming visibility in media texts, especially their ubiquitous presence on television or satellite channels, but also on the streets, in the cultural memory of people—not, perhaps, amongst the culturally intellectual pursuers of serious cinema, but the small-time booksellers on College Street, the photocopiers in different parts of the city, the shops where I would enter in search of VCDs and DVDs. Back then, I could only get poor-quality DVD rips, or VCDs, usually sold by vendors around the Chandni Metro station in Kolkata.

I was initially stumped by the complete lack of any organised archive. The National Library proved more labyrinthine and mysterious than any Marquesan archive and after numerous futile attempts at entering, I finally gave up. The Satyajit Ray Film and Television Institute (SRFTI), the state-run Rupkala Kendra, the ambitious new state government project to convert the old Radha Studios into a film archive, launched with great fanfare and a commemorative exhibition in May 2007, all confronted me with a huge lack. They had nothing on the popular cinema, no publicity material, no clue about older film magazines, no books. In fact, at this particular exhibition at the older Radha Studio, I could see a few photographs of the only superstar that Bengali popular cinema had seen! Of course, the Jadavpur University's film studies department had some tangential material that I was able to use.

More recently, their Media Lab has added some highly valuable resources, especially the popular film magazines of the late 1940s and 1950s, which I was able to access. It seems easier to obtain material pertaining to the earlier decade, as Aurora and Bharatlaxmi studios, as well as the Sarkar family (who owned New Theatres) have made some serious attempts to preserve their film publicity material. The Bangiya Sahitya Parishat and the Centre for Studies in Social Sciences, Calcutta (CSSSC) also have some excellent journals pertaining to performance arts and early cinema from the 1920s to the 1940s. The CSSSC has widened its archiving ambit to include film publicity booklets, which proved invaluable for my research, as did their newspaper archives, which are digitised.

However, the 1950s, which is unquestioningly accepted both in popular and critical circles as the most important and exciting phase for Bengali cinema—being the decade of the celebrated trio, Satyajit Ray, Ritwik Ghatak and Mrinal Sen, along with witnessing the emergence of the star duo of Suchitra–Uttam, and the financial recuperation of the industry after the Bengal Famine, World War II and the Partition—seemed to be missing from the critical template of serious archival engagement. Most people were either amused or flabbergasted at my research project. As I continued in my pursuits, I encountered the varied terrain of discourses surrounding cinema. The pursuers of 'serious' 'Art Cinema' guided me to various people involved with the Film Societies. The polemical critical template of the Film Society discourse, embodied in the Calcutta Film Society's valourisation of realist cinema with its realist agenda, was clearly not interested in the industrial model.

I was directed to the Little Magazine library on College Street to see if I could get some material on my area of interest: popular cinema. This particular one, located at Temar Lane, is highly regarded as the owner/librarian is a well-known figure in the city's research community. In fact, he has single-handedly managed to collect all kinds of Little Magazines published across the state. The Library is housed in a small room and has shelves stacked to the ceiling in the narrow alley of the staircase, but is well-catalogued. It is not open access; there is a minimal membership fee and one is allowed photocopies, which are a huge boon in a city where many students and researchers still use long hand notes. The journals on cinema are only two pitiful stacks but are crammed with popular magazines such as the elusive *Rupmancha,* as well as some now-defunct Film Society Journals, *Chitrbhavna, Chalachinta,* etc. I was also told that the Nandan library did have a few copies of old film magazines such as *Rupmancha* and *Chitrabaani,* but I was not given access to those as they were in the process of digitising their collection, which did not materialise during the three years that I searched for my archive.

College Street[2] presented me with a problem of plenty. I was able to collect some sixteen-odd biographies of the two stars, which are available on the streets as well as in reputed and respectable book stores such as Dey's and Ananda's, or with dedicated film book publishers such as the independent Bani Shilpa. Most of these are written by old cine journalists who covered the film beat for newspapers such as *Jugantor* or *Dainik Basumati,* or popular magazines such as *Prosad, Ultoroth,* etc. However, these biographies, which rely on the circuits of gossip and rumour about the two stars, are hardly taken seriously by either contributors to the Film Society Journals or by most film scholars who remain sceptical about the nature and validity of the material.[3] The biography writers, some of whom I tracked down and met, on their part, seemed either unaware of film studies interventions, even work done on the popular, or were as dismissive and disdainful as the film society circuit is of them.[4] It was quite fascinating to encounter this carefully preserved and disparate terrain of engagement of these two sides with the popular. This lack of interface between the two domains presented me with a peculiar methodological problem. How was I to suture the two? Were they even to be brought together as critical interventions with equal status as material, or would I too follow the trend and consign a rich and immensely colourful plethora of texts to the ghetto of the popular/sensational? The travel for the archive and the stars is the story that is this book.

NOTES

1. This project was meant to collect and collate material for studying the representation of the woman in certain city films of the 1950s–60s. The archival work done for this project has been very useful for my book.

2. This city site off Presidency College and Calcutta University campus is host to lanes, by-lanes and alleys of bookstores and was the key to my archival work, as myriad book shop assistants patiently scoured old film books and helped me.

3. Although this seems to be changing at present, as some of the young researchers especially affiliated to the Film Studies discipline do use these biographies as sources, as their writings in the newer kinds of Little Magazines show.

4. I was able to meet and interact extensively with G. K. Ray, who has authored four books on Suchitra, and Himanshu Chatterjee, who has written two books on the stars. I had telephonic conversations with Ashishtaru Mukherjee and Ranjan Bandopadhyaya. Mukherjee has written two books on the stars and is quite active in the fan activities organised by Shilpi Sansad. Bandopadhyaya was a film critic for *Desh* and is actively associated with populist film criticism and writing. He is the author of a novella on Suchitra Sen that I discuss towards the end of Chapter Five.

Introduction

This book maps the star story of two Bengali superstars, Suchitra Sen (1931–2014) and Uttam Kumar (1926–1980). Known and feted as the ultimate romantic screen couple, they have become metonyms for love and modern romance. The journey of the 'self' in this particular romantic context has been mapped through their films of the 1950s, the formative period of their career in which they had their biggest hits (Biswas 2002; Chatterjee 2007; Gooptu 2010). More recently, others have attempted to analyse their films to provide illuminating discussions on stereotypes (Kundu 2004), or to reflect upon questions about cinematic and cultural modernity (Chowdhury 2012; 2021), or to understand the social and cultural ramifications of Partition in Bengal (Mehta and Mukerjea Leonard 2014; Sarkar 2010). It was the decade of the 1950s that saw Suchitra and Uttam act in twenty-two films, beginning from the 1953 production *Saare Chuattor* to *Chaoa Paoa* in 1959.[1] Most of these films went on to become hits and super hits. In industry parlance, they were referred to as 'made for each other'. They acted in thirty films opposite each other, from the beginning of the 1950s until 1975, when they appeared for the last time in *Priya Bandhabi*. Suchitra's corpus is limited to around sixty films over her career, while Uttam acted in 202 released films. According to a survey, Suchitra delivered twenty-one super hits, eighteen hits, eight average runs, and six flops out of the fifty-three Bengali films that she acted in (Gupto 2003: 167). Uttam delivered seventy-five silver jubilees, ten golden jubilees, and three of his films had platinum runs (Bhowmick 2001: 15).[2] Besides these numbers, most of his films and the romantic films with Suchitra had repeat releases and did good business.

However, it is to be noted that both Uttam and Suchitra were equally successful in films where they appeared opposite other stars, and these films were vehicles for their individual star selves and exploited their star value further. While their couple films were marketed as the Suchitra–Uttam films,[3] the others came to be known either as Suchitra starrers or Uttam starrers, each getting top billing as the star who would ensure assured box-office returns. The fact that they both earned the status of *mahanayak/nayika* is not merely denotative of their superstar status and commercial success; it is also indicative of a particular space in the popular imaginary which has accumulated and accreted far beyond its constitutive moment.[4] These two stars, as vectors of economic, cultural, and symbolic capital, are extremely significant within the history of Bengali cinema. My endeavour will be to unpack the nature and materiality of these layers of capital to signpost the varied and contingent subjectivities that emerged in the course of their filmic careers across the two decades and beyond.[5] I also examine this accretion of symbolic and cultural capital in the contemporary via the mode of retro histories, aided in large measure by media circulation and the nostalgia industry. But the media frenzy cannot be explained away only in terms of the demands of the nostalgia industry, which requires easily identifiable objects that can mediate a particular kind of relationship to the past that is paradoxically brought into being in the present. So in a sense this book narrates both the 'then' and the 'now'. I consider their stardom as a construct that has 'endured' (Bolton and Wright 2016)[6] across time, and analyse the contours of this *longue durée* of their star texts.

Nonetheless, this book is not a grand history of popular Bengali cinema of these two decades; it attempts to recover traces, sediments, and fragments of Bengali modernities of these two decades via the films starring Suchitra and Uttam. Like all fragments, it is incomplete and partial, but at the same time, it represents a powerful intervention in the imagination and struggle towards the realisation of the modern selfhoods of the Bengali middle class. To fully examine these aspects of popular Bengali cinema, it takes into account the context of the national against which the regional is played out. The book will engage with the specific social and political concerns as they intersect, inform, or define the cinematic as these emerge in the two decades from the 1950s to the 1970s. It will also focus on understanding the star texts of these figures through different periods as this particular formation has an afterlife, influencing the popular cinematic discourse even in the contemporary. Uttam passed away in 1980, and Suchitra retired from the industry in 1978 and died in 2014; it is imperative to situate the trajectory of the star texts from their constitutive moment to the present to understand the contours of this star-induced imaginary that still inhabits the popular emotive spaces of Bengal. Given the above, the book is organised into five chapters; the first two chapters analyse the Suchitra–Uttam films as the romantic couple films with love and conjugality as the overarching frames, while the next two chapters look at their individual star vehicles. The last chapter analyses their star texts as they appear in media sites and imaginative literature from the 1980s until the present.

The Beginning of the Star Story

Two statements speak of one event, namely the Suchitra–Uttam 'romance', which acquired the position of a metonym for love, not only in its own time but with continued symbolic value within the popular Bengali imagination even years later. For Sudipto Kaviraj (2007), they represented what falling in love meant for Bengalis. 'They taught us how to romance', asserts Monojit Lahiri, ad man and self-confessed Uttam Kumar fan, and brother-in-law of actor/director Aparna Sen (personal interaction, New Delhi, 2010).

That they were a phenomenon with a strong box office draw, and subsequently a part of the public imaginary, is a foregone conclusion. Is it the number of hit films that they had, or that they came to be identified with a specific kind of product identification in industry parlance, the Suchitra–Uttam film, much like the Raj–Nargis film, standing in for what Neepa Majumdar has called 'the star-centric generic specificity of Indian cinema'? Majumdar observes that in the Indian context, stars and their stardom stand in for genre, that is, they are the primary markers of product differentiation: 'Dominating the cinema at all levels, from the economic structuring of the film industry to the formulaic nuances of textual strategies, stardom... came to take over almost exclusively, the function of product identification that genres have had in Hollywood cinema' (Majumdar 2009: 11). Unlike Hollywood, in the Indian context, it is the star who becomes the mode of generic identification, and in the process lends her/his self to narrative, product, and symbolic value and, as Majumdar points out, 'the rise of [the] star system also led to a greater emphasis on the star as genre than on genre per se' (ibid.: 131). Both these stars have functioned in this sense in the Bengali film industry: credit sequences of their films and advertisements would prominently name the stars, which would signal the generic specifics of a Suchitra–Uttam film. They appeared in the late 1940s and went on to become the superstars, *mahanayika/mahanayak*, as they are popularly referred to. Initially unsuccessful with flops and relative obscurity, they took the industry by storm in 1954 with the super hit *Agnipariksha*, which set the stage for this duo to become the most popular romantic couple on the Bengali screen, and rule the industry for over two decades (Banerjee 2009). Moreover, Suchitra and Uttam have been credited with reviving the fortunes of the Bengali industry after the decline of the studio era (Raha 1991: 36).[7] From 1954, they delivered hits with unfailing regularity, and by the time *Sagarika* was due for release in 1956 (which I discuss in Chapter One as significant for their romantic iconicity in the 1950s), their star presence had reached an unprecedented popularity.

The earlier studio period in Bengal had its fair share of popular film-star duos as well, like Pramathesh Barua–Kanan Devi, Durgadas–Jamuna, etc., but none came close to the kind of superstar status that Uttam and Suchitra achieved (Ghosh 1997).[8] This earlier studio period in Bengal is identified with the iconic presence of New Theatres in particular (Gooptu 2010),[9] though in the 1950s, the preeminent status of New Theatres had suffered a severe jolt with the box office disaster of *Bakul* and other films made in double language versions. The falling fortunes of New Theatres added to a sense of despair. By 1955, New Theatres had virtually become a non-player as the owners only used the technical and production facilities for hire (Raha 1991). The other studios in operation in Bengal, Auroras, Bharatlaxmi, Technicians, and production outfits such as Murlidhar Productions were found to be floundering in the changed circumstances. There was a palpable sense of imagined loss and perceived threat as industry watchers felt that Bombay cinema would erode the status of Bengali popular cinema (Banerjee 2009).[10] The industry sought newer ways of re-establishing its primacy and the star pair became one of the key reasons enabling this recuperation for the industry and the Bengali public imaginary.

In the deeply troubled and de-centred post-independence Bengal, the euphoria of independence was accompanied by the trauma of Partition, which to my mind provided the most relevant space for the star texts of both Suchitra and Uttam to take deep root and fashion their personas and presence in the public imaginary. I am not suggesting that the popular cinema of this time participated directly in narrating the trauma of Partition. In fact, as work on the Partition has underlined, there was a silence around the traumatic event for at least three decades. Yet, as has been suggested, the shadow of this catastrophe was present in the traces of displacement, and the dislocated figures that inhabited filmic spaces (Biswas 2002; Sarkar 2010).[11] It is in this context that the primacy of Uttam's star figure is resituated in terms of the narrative and cinematic investment in a particular kind of middle-class figure who contained within himself aspirational dreams and the various narratives of possibilities despite the trauma of Partition (Bhowmick 2001; Dasgupta 2010). Gledhill cites Dyer to make a similar point in a different context: '[The] rise of particular stars can be traced to their condensation of values felt to be under threat or in flux at a particular moment in time' (1991: 217). For popular Bengali cinema of the 1950s, it is the figure of the two stars that became the most visible cultural, economic, and structural component that enabled the recovery from the crisis caused by the above economic and social transformations. One of the reasons given for Uttam's rise in the 1950s is his appeal to the educated middle-class audience and the narratives of love and recuperation that his films dealt with. The values of education, hard work and decency made his persona acceptable to the *bhadralok*[12] imaginary (Dasgupta 2010). It remained so for the rest of his career as well.

Suchitra too fashioned her star text in the mould of the urban elite *bhadramahila* and was known for essaying roles featuring the strong, independent, modern woman (Biswas 2002).

In the 1960s and 1970s, while popular Bengali cinema continued to feel threatened by Bombay cinema, it was the box-office guarantee of these two stars that was the most significant factor to substantially stymie the inroads of Hindi cinema. The 1960s especially saw the Bengal film industry face stiff competition from Bombay, as its star-studded spectacles and the lure of better production values resulted in Hindi films being better produced and accepted for their technical competence as opposed to popular Bengali films. The Bengali industry was plagued by the sorry state of film finance and lack of infrastructural facilities. Added to this was the general atmosphere of gloom, especially the deteriorating social conditions in Kolkata, the general strikes of the 1960s, and the eruption of violence in the late 1960s with the Naxal movement (for more details, see the discussion in Chapter 4). Accounts of the state of the industry in these two decades all seem to radiate a sense of despair at government apathy, the inability of the state to provide better institutional support to the commercial industry, and the lack of upgradation of studio and production facilities. Bengali popular cinema continued to rely on its adaptations of literary texts and the two stars to create products that could hold their own against Hindi films (Raha 1991; Sanyal 2008). Placed against this scenario of almost dystopic gloom, the Moscow Film Festival award for Best Actress to Suchitra for *Saat Paake Bandha* (1963), the Filmfare award for *Mamata* (1966), Uttam's international recognition for *Nayak* (the award-winning film by auteur Satyajit Ray, 1966) and the National award for *Chiriakhana* (again a Ray film, 1967), the Filmfare award for *Amanush* (1974), and Suchitra's Padmashri in 1972 provided some significant moments for the popular to anchor itself in the two stars even further.[13] I discuss this aspect of the consolidation of their stardom in Chapters Three and Four to contextualise their star texts across these two decades.

This consolidation in the 1960s differed from the 1950s as the two stars established their status with awards, which managed to deflect the dominant criticism against them—that they had created a star monopoly and excessively invested in romantic melodramas in the formative period of their careers. It was with Uttam's death in 1980 and Suchitra's retirement in 1978 that the cinematic career of this couple came to a literal end. This 'end', however, did not end the imaginary of the 'star romance' or its significance within the popular, or even in the narratives of the popular in the accounts of the 1980s–90s and in the present. The deaths of the stars led to a narrative of lament at the passing of the *bhadralok* imaginary, which had been a significant marker of popular cinema in these two decades. I analyse this lament and the re-emergence of the star texts and their romance in the contemporary period in Chapter Five to mark the accretion of their iconicity.

Modernity, Melodrama, and Popular Bengali Cinema

The constitutive feature of Indian modernity is read as being communitarian in nature, as opposed to the narrative of individuation in the West.[14] The modernity thesis, which had fashioned itself in the colonial period and which was the bedrock on which the nationalist imaginary had mapped itself out, continued in varied formations in the post-independence period as well. Partha Chatterjee has argued that in the nationalist imaginary, this impulse to define Indian modernity as a counter to Western modular forms rested on a separation of the outer and the inner, the material and the spiritual. These negotiations were primarily projected onto the figure of the new woman, and her subjectivity was directed and circumscribed by the concerns of the new patriarchy (Chatterjee 1993). The particular concern of post-independence modernity in the Indian context has been the renegotiation of tradition and modernity, not as binaries but as deeply imbricated with each other. It can be productively understood as a continuous process across time that does not replace tradition with modernity (Kothari 1968). Gyan Prakash has rightly pointed out that our reading of the Indian modern needs to move away from the binaries of West versus East or modern versus tradition. According to him, these are not either/or choices that informed the discourse of Indian modernity:

> Indian modernity has always existed as an internally divided process.... uncertainties and estrangements point to its sources of creativity and to possibilities of new arrangements and new accommodations... messy history cannot be tidied up... difference does not cancel identity, hybridity does not dissolve opposition, capital does not erase community, but rather one enables the other's reformulation. It is thus that Indian modernity emerged as Janus faced; crafted in the image of Europe, it is also ineluctably different; founded in the capital community opposition, it is also the undoing of that polarity. (Prakash 1999: 234)

This double-faced modernity, where the traditional and the modern are intertwined in selves that co-exist with their other, is best exemplified in the layers of self-fashioning that my work uncovers as it examines star texts across the characters, the films, the extra-filmic, and the popular responses to this fragment of cinematic modernity across time and space. The concerns of the new patriarchy, the new woman, issues of love, romance, and conjugality, and the myriad enactments of social and individual roles that both men and women stage are some issues that I will address.

Resituating the terms of our engagement with varied communitarian modernities can be a useful trope through which to decode the regional particularities that need to be factored into our readings of the cinematic Indian modern. It has been suggested that the more appropriate term would be 'vernacular modernity', which can aid a decoding of the particular modern cinematic enunciation seen in the romantic films starring Uttam and Suchitra (Biswas 2002). On the other hand, our engagement with the region and its specific self-imaginary should not lapse into a narrow parochialism—that of investing the region with a discrete and enclosed cinematic history, or even a monolithic identity, that can stand for the entire cinema practice or impulses. Biswas has cogently argued that any engagement with regional cinematic practices needs to be carefully calibrated in terms of the theoretical template being deployed (cited in Bhattacharya 2011: 4).[15] My endeavour is to map the varied formations of the modern that the Suchitra–Uttam films articulated and to track the responses to these formations in the reception circuits[16] and journalistic discourses. The narrative that I chart can have different contours if one reads the relays and flows across the national, the regional, as also global transactions of forms and cinematic practices.[17] Cinema works with a range of adapted and refracted influences that may not always be positioned in sharp binaries of self and other. These transactions are complex in nature and have to be uncovered to see how these regional film texts and star texts set out to create a particular product that was a refashioned cinematic self, functioning as a regional variant of the Bombay film and their star vehicles.

In the discursive space of cinema criticism, within the time frame of these two decades, a certain kind of Bengali chauvinism and pride in the notion of 'cultured Bengali-ness' (Gooptu 2010) was at odds, but nevertheless intersected, with the Suchitra–Uttam filmic romances and their stardom. Therefore, any claims about their uncontested representative status, as well as the use of the *bhadralok/bhadramahila* paradigm to read their star texts, need to be carefully calibrated in the varied discursive spaces that this cinema occupied, in terms of its historical, social, and aesthetic locations.[18] Further, it needs to be clarified that these filmic romances cannot be used as a monolithic or simplistic model for the urban modern in this period. Also, in the larger context of Indian popular cinema, the relation of the modern with the melodramatic mode and the question of genre was a complicated one. The popular Indian melodrama was usually critiqued as a form that perpetuated an ossified tradition, and was considered conservative and status quoist. It was generally marginalised in favour of the realist, auteur cinema and the Indian New Wave. Cinema criticism also favoured the art-house model. Bengal was no exception to this critical template. Writings emerging from the journals of the Calcutta Film Society (CFS)[19] found the commercial cinema of the period lacking in narrative coherence, as it was seen to be an inchoate form that catered to the lowest common denominator. Indian popular melodrama was also critiqued for being a dispersed product, which did not follow the generic classification of the Hollywood film.[20] The Suchitra–Uttam romances, as well as their individual films, were consigned to a critical ghetto.[21] Their films were regarded as sentimental melodramas fit for weeping, maudlin audiences who had to be rescued from this spectre of mass culture that was debasing their taste. The critical discourse emanating from the Film Society journals and the Little Magazines carried this charge against the popular, especially when seen in relation to Uttam, as he was considered a 'one-man industry' well into the 1970s. It is important to signpost this hostile reception in the context of any 'recovery' of the love films and the popular in the present (Chatterjee 2010: 70). This particular critique of the popular will be addressed to lay out the critical terrain of the reception circuit, which is important to assess the formation of the star text and its collision with the entire corpus of critical opinion, including Film Society discourse, as well as popular film magazines and newspapers, to productively engage with its acceptability as a valued or debased cultural construct.

It was only in the 1980s that the intervention of Indian film studies scholars helped in recuperating the specificities of the popular form and enabled new work in the field (Chakrabarty 1993; Mazumdar 2007; Prasad 1998; Rajadhyaksha 1987; Vasudevan 2000, 2010). These critical interventions have provided the template against which it is now possible to read the popular film as a mode that involves transactions of the melodramatic, the realist, the modern, and both local and global codes of film practices. These interventions arise from within the broad disciplinary frameworks and global discourses of Cinema Studies. One of the most notable of these for the study of popular Indian film has been the reconstitution of Melodrama Studies. Countering the criticism levelled against melodrama as a mode of excess and sentimentality that operates only in 'woman's films', Gledhill and others have argued that it operates as the 'foundational mode' of Hollywood cinema (Gledhill 1987a, 2000; Williams 1998). This cinema studies intervention drew on Peter Brooks' seminal work, which had offered valuable insights into the emergence of melodrama as a modern aesthetic mode.[22] Melodrama as a modern secular form is considered particularly useful as it offers subversive possibilities within its apparently conservative formal structures. As a form that brings into focus the drama of personality in its staging of the personal and the private, this mode is significant as it unpacks the interface of the trope of modernity and its attendant crises. The fissures and gaps engendered by the modern in its loss of the 'traditional sacred' are ably expressed in all its forms by this mode. I use Melodrama Studies as a point of entry to unpack the specific uses that it is being put to in Bengali films to render the experience of modern urban subjectivities and their self-fashioning that find an expressive voice through this mode.

The relation of cinematic melodrama to realism is of particular significance to my reading of the Suchitra–Uttam romance and their individual star texts. In particular, I refer to the staging and articulation of the everyday, and melodrama's ability to situate the ethical in the everyday, as well as its ability to foreground the lived experiences of the individual coping with the social in her/his attempt to carve out a niche, and achieve emotional and psychic fulfilment. The realisation of these subjectivities and their desires are articulated via melodrama as the predominant expressive mode. Emotion has been considered a key feature of melodrama; it is this constitutive specificity that bestows upon this form the capability and flexibility to respond to varied experiences of cultural modernity across the globe. As Bhaskar argues,

> As one of the most popular and enduring cultural forms through which contemporary social and political crises are represented and negotiated cinematically melodrama's 'capacity to respond to questions of modernity' (Gledhill 2002: 232) accounts for its pervasive influence in different cinemas of the world. (2012: 162)

She cites Gledhill to argue that the focus on personality and its centrality to the melodramatic project is crucial for understanding how this form projects a drama of the personal, which stands in for the social. My intervention draws on this template, but extends it to the star text. This interconnection between the star text and the melodramatic text has been a seminal intervention by Gledhill. Majumdar, too, uses Gledhill to explicate the 'conceptual links between melodrama and stardom' which, paraphrasing Gledhill, she says

> ...include an exteriorized and hyperbolic concept of the 'person', one that is dependent on spectacle and excess, and the

> translation of social issues into private, emotional ones. Both melodrama and stardom are invested in meaning displayed as iconic presence whose moral significance is immediately legible. (Majumdar 2009: 139)

In this sense, stars are particular kinds of individuals who offer insights into the melodramatic imaginaries of the selfhoods of modern individuals, and are therefore important signs of the 'modern' in a representative as well as a personal sense. They are what King terms 'signs of culture in the host culture' (1991: 170). To invoke Dube's argument from another context, '(stars can be read as)… subjects of modernity… historical actors who have been active participants in the processes of modernity, both subject to processes but also subjects shaping these processes' (2009: 9). I argue that for the two decades of the 1950s–70s, the star text and the film text can provide us an entry into the realm of this cinematic, melodramatic, modern Bengali *bhadralok* self-imaginary.

According to Bhaskar, the capacity of the melodramatic form to capture and narrate an 'intense experience of crisis linked to modernity makes it a powerful expressive register that exemplifies particular concerns of the local cinematic culture' (2012: 162). She extends Gledhill's emphasis on 'personality' and the 'person' as the source of 'desire and motivation', 'morality and ethics', preparing the way for 'the psychologisation of characters and performance of twentieth century popular culture' (Gledhill 1991: 209), to 'suggest that the expression of intense emotion communicates a charge of subjectivity arising from the externalization of the interior self that is normally unexpressed' (Bhaskar 2012: 163). She moves away from melodrama's normative association with a feminine form to suggest that in the

> …expressionistic foregrounding of emotion, melodrama also enacts subjectivization, not as the realization of gender, but rather as the embodiment of the individual's most intense condition of felt selfhood. This is because at the root of melodrama as expressive form is the emotional self, the self that in its expression takes different cultural forms. (ibid.)

I enter this terrain via Bhaskar's intervention to demonstrate how the two stars, Suchitra and Uttam, complete with their individual personas, are central to this intensification of an affective and emotional selfhood and its myriad manifestations in the popular cinema of these two decades. This intensification of affect and emotion, so central to the self-fashioning of individuals, does not obfuscate the presence of reason or thought. Bhaskar has cited the specific intervention in contemporary Emotion Studies that is particularly useful in reading affect productively (ibid.). This relationship needs to be kept in sight, given that I have mentioned that the popular Bengali melodrama was castigated for its display of excessive sentimentalism.[23] Bhaskar has demonstrated how the interface of emotion, subjectivity, and the particular inflections of melodramatic language are central to the Indian cinematic form. She refers to two key ideas in melodrama debates that are integral to the Indian context: the 'high emotionalism' (Brooks 1984: 12) of melodrama, which acquires a particular form in the Indian context, and her refutation of Heilman's point that melodrama deals with 'nonpsychologised monopathic characters' (as cited in ibid.; see also Bhaskar 2012: 162). I argue, following Bhaskar, that it is this reliance on emotion, affect, and sentiment that gives voice to desires and articulates deep-seated selfhoods that attain affective fulfilment via these films. The popularity of the films that I discuss rests on this affective encounter, and the evocation of states that can evoke pathos[24] and create scenarios of affective empathy with their audiences.

Following Bhaskar, I also read the use of songs productively as a specific narrative trope which foregrounds the expressive desires of individual subjectivities. She has insightfully pointed out that the song and its narrative function must not be understood as extraneous to, or as a para-narrative element in, Indian melodramas;[25] rather, its staging, especially in romantic melodramas, 'expresses the central meaning of the sequence—meanings that have to do with emotional intelligibility and the exteriorizing of inner subjective states' (Bhaskar 2012: 166). The deployment of songs that render the subject's most intensely felt experience, which seems otherwise impossible to articulate in everyday language and its idioms, is a crucial feature that I will use to engage with the particularities of this form. My reading of these films demonstrates the intensification of the individual's emotive negotiation via certain expressive registers, both in the diegetic and in the extra-filmic. This intensification is what constitutes the emotional charge of these enactments, and this staging deploys certain cinematic techniques, via states of performative and gestural excess and the use of a dense *mise en scène*, that visually, aurally, and sensuously narrate and embody these states. I will also analyse how the varied formal properties of the woman's film and domestic melodrama are deployed in these films, and use local cultural idioms to instantiate and impress the symbolic articulation of repressed desires or states of intense suffering. One of the crucial insights that melodrama studies has provided is into the operation of 'excess' in the melodramatic universe. In the diegetic world, this mode of 'excess' is located in the dense *mise en scène* of repressed desires that are brought out in the open via melodramatic enunciation. This excess of affect defines the characters across varied forms of selfhood—the lovers, the married couple, the doomed lover, the sacrificing mother, the divorced woman, the male 'intruder-redeemer figure' (Schatz 1981), the decrepit putative elder brother figure, and the insane elder brother—that are central to this journey of the filmic imaginary that I chart. Further, I argue that this excess, which is a constitutive feature of the melodramatic text, cannot be contained either within the diegesis, despite the status quoist resolution, nor resolved in its own historical moment of emergence. This *longue durée* needs to be excavated in order to ask questions about the particular desires that were embodied in these cinematic self-fashionings.

This particular relationship of emotion and the melodramatic form that over-intensifies emotions has been critiqued by Marcia Landy (1996). Her critique is mounted especially to foreground the contemporary validation of melodrama as an emotive form able to capture historical experiences associated with traumatic events. I, however, choose to read the power and charge of the emotive and the melodramatic as it emerges in the popular film as significant. The specificity of the films that I analyse lies in this display of emotion, which exemplifies the individual's intense subjectivity. These stagings of the deeply personal and the emotional allow the form to give voice to desires that desperately seek release and fulfilment.

Melodramatic enunciation in these films is not necessarily tied to an exploration of Manichean conflict but is articulated as textual conflict, where the form opens up a space for the staging of this conflict across the body of the text. The tremendous appeal of this conflictual staging of selves attests to the power of melodrama, the predominant mode and genre that provides the narrative terrain on which to lay out all the contradictions of individual and social being, and allows for the display of affect, articulating the individual's drive to realise the possibility of love and selfhood. It is this power of form, content, and the star that was of immense significance in the accretion of the star persona and its staging of the post-independence cinematic modern.

I also locate my investment in the star text, the formulation of star subjectivity and its self-fashioning as a particular kind of 'emotion travel' that uses melodrama to narrate its story. Giuliana Bruno argues that the 'Latin root of emotion speaks clearly about a "moving" force, a stemming as it does from *emovere*, an active verb composed of *movere* to move and *e*, "out"' (2002: 7). Drawing from her insightful analysis of film, I investigate the travel of emotions and desires that these two stars articulate through their films and their star texts 'of affect', in which 'motion indeed produces emotion and that, correlatively emotion contains a movement' (ibid.). My mapping of self-fashioning explores the varied articulations of the desires and the journeys that this fragment of popular cinema has undertaken. These desires and journeys also imbricate themselves in the socio-political history of the region and are an important component of the relation between the genre and the intended audience and community. This relation is the zone where social history finds form in the melodramatic text. Chatterjee paraphrases this relationship between the figure of the star and the form by drawing on recent work on stardom and melodrama studies. He observes that '…[the critics] suggest that melodramatic representations of the social universe enact and therefore validate the very mode in which a larger social history evolves under changing or altered political conditions' (2007: 159).[26]

The enactment and fashioning of subjectivities that I unravel function under certain specific social conditions that existed between the 1950s and the 1970s, alerting us to the evolving political conditions of post-independence Bengal and its urban middle-class coordinates.

SELF-FASHIONING AND SUBJECTIVITIES: THE STAR TEXT

Greenblatt's (2004) pioneering work on the idea of Renaissance self-fashioning provides an enabling theoretical and methodological template to think about the formation of selves and subjectivities in other historical moments. Writing about the fashioning of the poet's persona in England in the sixteenth century, Greenblatt's theoretical formulation draws our attention to two significant ideas: one, that the individual self is fashioned and remade in conjunction with the cultural milieu; and second, that these selves are never homogeneous or finished enterprises.[27] This varied engagement helps to foreground the myriad levels of self-fashioning by the two stars whom I examine. These do not necessarily affirm each other; rather, they intersect, collide, and produce a slippery terrain of gaps and fissures that create polymorphous subjectivities that cannot be pinned down to one homogeneous construct. Drawing on Greenblatt, the term, as I employ it, works in the following manner: at the level of characters essayed by Suchitra–Uttam as the star duo, both as a couple and as individual stars; at the level of their star texts and the fashioning of their personas; and at the level of lending themselves to fashion a particular cinematic self of the popular industry. The stars function as objects of desire with their fan following and huge popularity, yet they are subjects on whom the varied and contradictory impulses of the allure and anxieties of modernity are located. Representational works and their effects are useful not only for articulating subject positions but, following Greenblatt, I reiterate that they also allow us to move beyond the subject's location in ideology. In their encounters with historical forces, these representations continuously refashion and reshape the imaginaries produced by these encounters. These cultural imaginaries can often accumulate as symbolic manifestations of selves and subjectivities that are neither cohesive nor homogeneous.

They are contested, contradictory, fractured imaginaries that nevertheless have resonance for communities and their sense of collective identities.

Subjectivities, in both the individual and the communitarian sense, are important as they are in a dialogic relation, impacting and feeding off each other in the processes of construction and negotiation of images and their cultural ramifications. Subjectivities are different from identities as they 'imply always a degree of thought and self consciousness about identity, at the same time allowing a myriad of limitations and often unknowable and unavoidable constraints on our ability to fully comprehend identity' (Hall 2004: 3). This notion of subjectivity formulates the social and the individual as the production and organisation of knowledge about itself. This method enables a move away from simplistic assumptions about the relationship of either influences or causal links between social history and cultural constructs. Further, the idea of self-fashioning, or of fashioning subjectivities, is located in the imaginary of the characters essayed by the two stars, as well as their appeal as stars. Moreover, the allure of stardom enables and aids the fashioning of the modern. I see both cinema and the star text as participating in this fashioning of a modern, urban imaginary of the self.

Modern Bengali *Bhadralok* Imaginary and the Stars

The subjectivities visible in popular Bengali cinema in the two decades under consideration are manifested in terms of a specific kind of cinematic modern, constructed through the prism of the Bengali urban middle class, the *bhadralok/bhadramahila* paradigm. I will uncover these imaginaries over the course of this book. This particular inflection of the Bengali cinematic modern articulates a specific discourse of the regional modern within its specific cultural location. This experience of modernity, which carries over from ideas of urban middle-class experience, has been studied as an explication of the *bhadralok* identity central to the experience of colonial modernity in Bengal, as I have explained above. The term denotes a particular sensibility that defined the educated middle class. What defines the meaning of this term is a certain value system: it resides in a broad behavioural pattern of genteelness, civility, and a cultured, refined response to life and the social. It is imperative to point out that this class-specific discourse, in its enactment of the dreams, desires, and aspirations of the *bhadralok*, is an imaginary construct, carrying within itself 'a sociological shorthand' as well as retaining a 'broad charismatic authority' (Sarkar 1997: 169). The category itself is heterogeneous, comprising people from diverse social and economic strata (Bhattacharya 2005; Ghosh 2004). What binds the self-imagination of this class is a belief in the value of education and work. According to Sarkar, this class was so invested in the values of education and *chakri* or 'job/work' because the colonial administration denied them all other avenues of social mobility (cited in Bhattacharya 2005: 26). In the cinema of the post-independence period, I explore this articulation of the discourse on the *bhadralok* and its female counterpart, the *bhadramahila*, as seen in the films featuring Uttam and Suchitra.

The other significant trope of *bhadralok* subjectivity is the urban coordinate, the imaginary of the city. Studies of the Bengali *bhadralok* have generally focused on the journey of the male to the city as an important marker of this self. This journey facilitated the acquisition of education and initiated the *bhadralok* figure's participation in the formal structures of civil society (Bhattacharya 2005). Others have commented on the availability of informal social practices, such as the *adda*, that defined the male *bhadralok* in an urban milieu (Chakrabarty 2000: 204–05). I link this urban imaginary—central to the self-definition of the *bhadralok* imaginary—to the films featuring the two stars to see how this journey unfolds specifically in the two decades under consideration, via the trope of subjectivities defining themselves through their investment in education and work, as well as their emotional and affective encounters. Additionally, I also examine this journey as a spatial trajectory of gendered selves moving from the 1950s to the 1970s. This movement charts the changing coordinates of the self and its spatial location with the shifts that Kolkata witnessed from the 1950s to the 1970s. At the same time, it is important to point out that this urban imaginary is not necessarily tied to the 'real' city of Kolkata, but rather that there is a particular urban imaginary of gender and its spatial locations and relationships that I wish to foreground. Cinematically, this imaginary is rendered not so much through actual location shots as through a certain iconography of urban homes and spaces of the modern, such as educational institutions or professional spaces, that define characters.

Biswas has studied the male citizen's journey to the city via the Uttam characters (2010). I extend Biswas' argument to include the journey of the Bengali *bhadramahila* via Suchitra. I am influenced by Swati Chattopadhyaya (2005), who has charted the urban cartography of colonial Kolkata and locates gender spatially as her intervention. My intervention in this terrain to read the self-fashioning of the Bengali *bhadramahila* is undertaken with the full acknowledgement that Suchitra's social location and profession participates in a deeply fraught gender transaction, and cannot be used as a template for all sections of women belonging to this category. But I argue that her star text and its self-fashioning, as well as her star vehicles and her romantic iconicity with Uttam, can enable us to map the uneven terrain of positions that informs gendered modernities and their spatial locations. Moreover, I argue that both stars exhibit a particular charismatic aura that is located in their class and spatial locations. Hence, I read the star text as a symbolic working of middle-class urban aspiration, desire, lifestyle, and excess, located within the charismatic zone of enchantment.

Stars and Subjectivities/Star Personas

Stars and their self-fashioning are important because they are social phenomena, to use Richard Dyer's oft-cited argument which has acquired a normative status in cinema studies. To begin with, I will briefly discuss some tropes about the 'star text' by drawing on some of the key ideas he works with (Dyer 1979). Stars are images that are produced and consumed within a given social and cultural matrix and network of relationships. They are, of course, media images, created and circulated via various media texts, publicity, advertising, promotional material, newspaper reportage, fashion, etc. These discourses evoke or construct the star for the viewers/readers as they overlap, intersect, and feed into each other. Following Dyer, we know that the star figure becomes the vehicle to condense the affects of a certain 'persona' created for consumption by both filmic and extra-filmic registers. This star persona is always both a character and an excess, circulating across the narratives of multiple film and media texts, often drawing criticism for being stereotyped images.[28] I choose to engage with these stereotypes, not as ideologically constraining but as essential tools to decode images and their resonances. These stereotypes are not always pejorative; they can reinforce ideology but also alert us to our 'understanding of ideological processes that constantly define and redefine basic notions—like "male" and "female"—and the realities they reflect' (Byars 1991: 72). Dyer has argued that stereotypes can and do function as positive images that speak for and to the specific culture they are located in (1993: 11–12). Drawing from the theoretical discourse of stardom, we know that a star is always more than an actor, moving and circulating across a range of contexts and domains, articulating a conception of the 'imaginary' of the 'self'. This 'imaginary' of the 'self' operates through intertextual relays of social and cultural signification, a fluid sign of the filmic and non-filmic in the larger social matrix. Despite Neepa Majumdar's reading of Dyer as an inadequate blueprint for the study of Indian cinema,[29] I think Dyer's methodology can be useful in plotting the adequacy of the star text, as it participates in the relays of self-fashioning in ways that can be useful to survey possible points of acceptance or rejection of images and their significances. My narrative of cinematic self-fashioning therefore locates itself at the intersection of the star text and the films.

Furthermore, this book foregrounds the multiple axes of self-fashioning that I have briefly introduced above, as it argues that the modern cinematic urban imaginary was staged through the bodies of the two stars, Suchitra and Uttam. Therefore the site/sight of the stars is equally important to understanding this mode of self-fashioning. I will use the discourse of star biography, the axes of their social/personal locations and personas, which informed the construction of their *bhadramahila/bhadralok* identity, to analyse this self-fashioning. The stars as icons of desire, in terms of their body, beauty, fashion, dress, make-up, etc., are significant to this self-fashioning. Therefore, the figure of the star and the space of the couple, along with the centrality of the individual star texts of Suchitra and Uttam, will be significant to examine the formation of this particular cinematic modern. And it is imperative to keep in focus that for this particular staging of the cultural modern in the 1950s, the star figures with all their newness—in terms of the two young people and the industry's investment in them—was novel as well. Uttam had reportedly acknowledged that before Suchitra was cast opposite him, he had failed to connect with his audiences, since his earlier leading ladies, like Bharati Debi or Manju Dey, could not match his romantic image (Bosu 1998). Suchitra and Uttam became complementary to each other in terms of their respective personas. Their looks, bodies, voices, acting, and pleasing personalities were given full expression in their romantic narratives. This star pair became successful as they were able to create a sense of empathy and emotional connectedness with their audiences through the narratives of love and romance that they enacted. They came to stand in for symbols of middle-class love, romance, and desires that were aspirational for their audiences. Uttam's soft-spoken dialogue and fresh, youthful looks, along with Suchitra's beauty and glamour, were used effectively to articulate the varied experiences of falling in love, unrequited love, unfulfilled desires, and the culmination of their love in the formation of the heterosexual couple or, alternatively, the impossibility of achieving affective union. The larger question would then be: What does this circulation of 'aura' and 'personality', to borrow Benjamin's idea (2008 [1969]), mean for the contemporary? And why is this particular star couple the object of this looking back?

Since I am interested in these two stars who achieved remarkable popularity, uncovering the particular 'relationship between popularity and stardom' (Majumdar 2009: 12) is a significant endeavour that allows me to reveal the layered and complicated manner in which these star selves intersected with fame and commercial success. If one of the desires inherent in the star figure is realisable financial value, then does box office draw ensure uncontested cultural acceptance? The star body is one of the most visible objects that conjoin the values of hard labour with fame and monetary acclaim. Despite the opaque nature of film finance in the Indian context and the remuneration available to stars, the two stars in question did manage to use their star value to maximise their economic capital. The question to ask is: Did this maximisation of their labour, which made them safe box-office returns, translate into unqualified acceptance in the cultural and critical domain? The selves that were enacted as characters could carry the charge of spectatorial desires and aspirations, albeit with some anxiety, as I demonstrate in my reading of the films; but what of the star's selfhood as economic capital? I draw on Clark, who suggests that a method that rests on star texts only as images and performative aesthetic valuations needs to be positioned along the axis of star subject and labour in order to decode the complex manner in which star bodies fashion themselves and function within given social and historical locations. She rightly points out that a 'a cultural studies approach to star studies... would introduce the notion of struggle into the scenes of actor's labor... the fragmented and fought-over position of the actor as a subject of film labor and film representation' (Clark 1995: 3).

Following Clark, I argue that the levels of discomfort, the unease and critique directed at the two stars in their time foreground this contestation over the meaning and position of the actor/star. I cite this in my analysis of the critiques that informed discussions over the meanings of films, and the star value as well as the star's spatial location within discourse. The advocacy of the actor's subjectivity in star biographies, the critique of star monopoly, and the circulation of gossip and rumour are struggles to ascribe meaning to these stars and their texts. The texts themselves keep evolving and mutating over the two decades that I investigate, opening out new conduits of self-fashioning. As such, narrative and character analyses are complementary to and positioned within the discursive regime of stardom as a framing principle.

In the context of Bombay cinema, Majumdar identifies a particular critique of the star's economic value as the 'stardom racket' (2009: 13). One of the major fallouts of star monopoly was the star being seen as an assured investment. Stars become assured guarantees against investments, or at least are perceived as such, and hence they command astronomical sums as fees. They are also blamed proportionately for failures if the film fares poorly. Perhaps, as Majumdar remarks, this critique and the allure of popularity have to do with the ambivalent space accorded to popular cinema as 'guilty pleasure' (ibid.: 12). By the 1950s, if 'excess' was the predominant trope for stardom, as Majumdar remarks in her study (ibid.: 125), a similar drive was visible in the context of Uttam and Suchitra in Bengal.[30] Fame, popularity, and economic capital seemed inversely proportional to critical acceptance. In between 1954–56, the duo had appeared in thirteen films. Both superstars were held responsible for dominating the field. However, in one particular study concerning the deplorable dearth of good stars to replace the duo, Kaalish Mukherjee, editor of *Rupmancha*, carried out an analytical survey of the star power of both superstars and concluded that unless the industry made concerted attempts to train and manufacture stars, spectators would have no choice but to keep watching the two, however monotonous the experience might be.[31]

There is, however, a crucial temporal dimension to this accumulation of fame and popularity. In the 1960s, the critical template had changed a bit, largely because of the various awards that the duo had won and due to Satyajit Ray's casting of Uttam in two of his films (*Nayak* and *Chiriyakhana*). The critical clamour against Uttam resurfaced in the 1970s, especially as film society discourses took on a radical and more overtly political turn. Suchitra had by then reduced her workload, and perhaps that is why she did not face too much criticism. As I have already remarked in the discussion on melodrama, the person and the operation of excess in the discursive template is central to both the melodramatic form and the star text. My analysis views these two stars as inhabiting an excess. This excess is not limited to the hyperbolic display of emotions in the filmic text; it spills out into the extra-filmic as well.[32] I discuss this spilling over of the excess associated with the star text in my analysis of the excess of sensuality associated with Suchitra. The imperatives of commerce, star value and use, as well as a discourse of 'morality and excess' (Majumdar 2009), all came together to stake out a space that created a deeply contested modernity. This contestation was not limited to the surface of the film text, but also participated in the articulation of the contested realm of the star's private self. A crucial insight that Dyer's works provides is the centrality of the 'private' in the star persona. The notion of the person, the individual, is equally central to the modern. The other constitutive feature of modernity is the separation of the public and private domains. The modern subject emerges only when the interiorised private self is brought into the public realm via written outpourings. It needs an audience for its self to be staged in public. This contest was mapped onto the star body and its negotiation of 'interiority', and it is to this aspect that I now turn.

MODERNITY AND THE PRIVATE: STARS AS MODERN SELVES

Dipesh Chakrabarty has called attention to the absence in Indian self-narratives of the intimate private life that is central to the emergence of the modern bourgeois individual. A specific problem with using the idea of modernity vis-à-vis the self in the Indian context is the inadequate nature of articulation of the private in the discourse of the self, which is certainly not in the mode of confessional autobiography prevalent in the West (Chakrabarty 1996: 230). Citing Nirad Chaudhuri's autobiography, Chakrabarty points out the rhetorical use of bracketing in Chaudhuri's description of his intimate experience of the first night of marriage. There is a self-conscious screening-off that is deployed, and the writer, who is otherwise modern in every sense of the term, makes the excuse that since this is in the past, his memory is not so accurate. Thus, despite the proliferation of forms, both fictional and non-fictional, that narrate the self in the Indian context, these narratives are marked by a bracketing-off of the intimate, the private, and the sexual (ibid.).[33] All narrative forms that express the self 'seldom yield pictures of an endlessly interiorized subject' (ibid).[34] Others have provided aesthetic and cultural explanations for the use of reticence in the Indian context.[35] Udaya Kumar (2008) makes an interesting intervention in this discourse of autobiographical writing and the bracketing of the private in the context of male public figures. These silences about the private are read usually as arising out of some kind of deference to social norms:

> This kind of view assumes a prior existence of a fully expressive autobiographical desire in the author, upon which the normative structures of society come to enact their constraining work. This is problematic for social norms are seen as external to—rather than shaping—subjects and their desire for self-articulation. If we are to understand practices of self-narration in India in positive terms, we need to move away from this model and engage more centrally with their avowedly public character.... paradigms of spectacle and performance may be more relevant to the study of self narratives than models of authentic expressiveness. (2008: 420)

In her analysis of stardom, Majumdar takes on board this particular methodological gap in the use of the star text to decode the modern subject in the Indian context, and suggests that the display of 'reticence' in self writings and the use of 'innuendo' in journalistic discourse about stars, the parallel of the literary wink, can be an enabling trope to decode the discourse of the private (2009: 45). In this sense, 'interiority' and subjectivity need to be uncovered in sites that can and do signpost the private through indirections and suggestive remarks, or get plotted onto fictional, imaginative reconstructions.

As I discovered in my research, the general trope of star discourse, especially in film magazines, did deploy the displacement of interiority onto other sites, and used innuendo as one of the rhetorical styles to bring the private into the public. Many of the star biographies and autobiographies that I uncovered in the course of my research are marked by 'reticence', which Majumdar states are governed by the 'urge to control' (ibid.). In her introduction to Durga Khote's translated autobiography, Gayatri Chatterjee (see Khote 2006) has lucidly analysed this particular impulse to gloss over uncomfortable or unpleasant experiences that Khote had to encounter in her professional life. This glossing over could be attributed to Khote's personal status as an elite woman who was extremely self-conscious about her social position, 'both natal and marital' (ibid.: xvii). She has further argued that other autobiographies, such as those written by Hansa Wadkar and Leela Chitnis, in contrast, appear to be more forthcoming about their troubled professional dealings (ibid.: xxvi–xxvii). The pertinent point remains that autobiographies cannot be conflated into a unified generic category. We need to factor in the varied impulses inherent in these self-narratives as well as analyse their reception and target audience. As Udaya Kumar remarks,

> We may also need to be more cautious about regarding autobiographies as a unified genre with a distinctive identity. Are we right in approaching with the same set of generic protocols, an entire range of personal narratives which perform widely varying functions? Should we not rather consider such narratives as belonging to different discursive forms with distinctive objects? (2008: 421).

In the context of Bengal, this urge is visible in the autobiographies written by both male and female actors.[36] In my readings of these auto/biographies, I found that the personal and the intimate were almost always screened off, at least in the self-narratives of older veteran actors. The material considered unfit for articulation in public[37] was elided, or dismissed as professional hazards of the industry that are to be taken in stride. To cite one example: Kanan Devi does not name the people who exploited her when she came into the industry; she does not even name her first husband (they had a *gandharva vivaha*[38]), who was a wastrel (Devi 1973).[39]

In fact, the very form of these two modes, the auto/biography, seems to go against the production of the private of public figures, at least in the Indian context, as has been aptly argued by Udaya Kumar (2008). As a form, the desire in auto/biography is to hold up for its readers an exemplary life, a 'public persona', and hence details of scandals and gossip are considered of no use in this agenda. Since cinema always had to defend itself against charges of immorality, the star auto/biographies or life-stories were especially careful in their revelation of private details of the protagonists. Suchitra's refusal to give interviews, her seclusion, and the concerted attempts by her family to control the availability of current information on her private retired life still seem to deploy this reticent mode. Uttam's text, in contrast, is not so invested in deploying this mode. He has one published autobiography (Chattopadhyay and Ghosh 1980).[40] These personal outpourings need to be read against the grain in order to productively read the impulses inherent in the projection of images and selves.[41] Therefore, the question remains: Is it only filmic space that can allow us to unpack the nature of the intimate and the private in this modern form of self-fashioning?[42] Or is it possible to suggest that the extra-filmic, not perhaps the official sites, but the unofficial, especially the oral circuits of memory and gossip, can be used in this enterprise?[43] These unofficial archives are important tools for my enterprise. My aim is not to give salience to salacious material while reviewing the variety of gossip that circulated. My larger aim is to decode the nature and materiality of this circulation, to scrutinise the varied texts of the self that emerged at different times, and the possible meanings those articulations and negotiations could have in relation to the fashioning of modern selves and their staging of desire and intimacy. I shall discuss the theoretical template of gossip in Chapter Five to contextualise the star text and its position within this narrative of romance, desire, and the emergence of the private into the public.

This book employs formal narrative analysis vis-à-vis the content to examine the notion of selves through the trope of love and work, and uses the changing contours of the star text as it participates in this process. I use formal plot analysis to substantiate the unravelling of the selves and follow Gledhill's intervention to accord primacy to this neglected area of cinema studies. Byars cites Gledhill, who argues that '[a] mainstream feature film is not constituted simply by a series of looks; it is above all fiction, deploying a range of strategies' (cited in Byars 1991: 107). I do not wish to limit my reading to unravelling the usual 'feminist fascination' with the 'gaze'. Rather, I deploy the feminist lens to read both female and male subjectivities as they appear in the films starring the duo as a couple and as individual stars. It is this construction of the star persona residing in the characters and the person that needs to be considered in all its variations, so as to capture the forms of engagement central to this fragment of popular Bengali cinema. Drawing from these interventions, I argue that it is precisely the operation of a mode of excess that becomes a productive trope to frame questions about the cinematic Bengali modern across the two decades.

My methodology involves invoking the biographical/historical template, where I use the two stars as texts to analyse the varied kinds of self-fashioning taking place in the popular Bengali film in the 1950s–70s. In this sense, perhaps one can use the term 'melodrama work' as the particularities of the deployment of melodramatic address, which can allow us to enter the domain of self-fashioning that is crucial to this enterprise in these two decades. The critical discourse on popular cinema, stardom, and the two stars in particular will inform the unpacking of the specificities of the imaginary self-fashioning that emerged in the region across this period.

I use archival material primarily from two magazines, *Rupmancha* and *Desh*, and two newspapers, *Jugantor* and *Anandbazaar*.[44] This comprises film reviews as well as news reports pertaining to the stars and the industry. Other magazines, such as *Ultoroth* and *Prosad*, also form part of my material. I use Little Magazines, film society journals, as well as interactions with some of the biography writers as my primary sources. Along with this, I also use star biographies, accounts of their filmic careers and star personas, and film publicity booklets and reminiscences that keep appearing in popular media sites. Most of these circuits of memory and gossip around the two star texts had started appearing in the 1950s and 1960s. In Bengal during these decades, the popular film magazines were themselves evolving. Many newer kinds of magazines, which relied on the sensational for coverage, were responsible for relaying salacious material and rumours as their staple.[45] Unfortunately, most of these have long ceased publication.[46] But I was able to find some references to them in interviews of film magazine photographers and small-time writers who used to be part of these magazines during the two decades, and are quoted in many of the star biographies published from the late 1970s to the present. Many biographies of the two stars also use and quote material or reminiscences of cine journalists and photographers associated with these defunct popular film magazines. I fully understand the problematic nature of these disclosures, since it is difficult to confer the status of factual evidence to this material. Most of them cannot be verified with any certainty.[47] My efforts at corroboration were rebuffed for obvious reasons. Considering that there is currently a complete sanitisation and hagiography around the two stars, the impulse to erase all forms of scandalous detail is understandable. But I suggest that these fragments are necessary components in fully comprehending the relationship between the public and the private. I argue that it is the star body that carries traces of a fragmentary but still invaluable entry to signpost the emergence of the intimate into the public.

The films are important, but so is the extra-filmic. This extra-filmic cannot be limited to its immediate context; it is to be found now in the contemporary, in varied kinds of circulations, and I focus on some of these in Chapter Five, 'Afterlives'. I discuss two books, an autobiography of Uttam and a biography of Suchitra, in the chapter to signpost the fashioning of the star self central to the formation and embodiment of cultural desires that are made visible through the star body. Methodologically, my attempt brings together varied and disparate material on the same interpretive plane: the filmic, the extra-filmic, circuits of memory, and oral gossip. This allows me to take into consideration the contested, ambivalent, and marginalised body of knowledge that has limited normative legitimacy. But to follow Dyer is to know that these are not to be taken as truth, but as segments that allow entry to the star text and to the larger social and cultural matrix of subjectivities that speak to that time and to other times as well, with changes, erasures, accretions, additions, and deletions.

The book has five chapters. The first four can be understood in clusters of two; the first two chapters deal with the stars as a romantic couple while the next two analyse the individual star texts of Suchitra and Uttam. The last chapter provides an overview of their stardom and the contemporary discourses surrounding their iconicity. The timeline refers to specific moments in the post-independence period of the 1950s–70s, where I assess the cinematic journeys of middle-class protagonists through the euphoric experience of a new sense of subjectivity and selfhood in the 1950s in Chapter One, 'Screen Romance: The Suchitra–Uttam Love Films'. I analyse the staging of love and romance as seen in the constitutive romantic phase of the star couple, to the unravelling disquiet of the 1960s and through the disillusioned 1970s. The transformative possibilities of exuberant selfhoods in the romantic films starring the star duo, seen in a marked romance of the self with—and in—the urban in the 1950s, gives way to a different sense of disengagement of the self in the 1960s. The eruption of violence in the social polity of Bengal in the 1970s created its own cinematic moment of rupture and breakdown, visible in the few romantic films that Suchitra and Uttam appeared in together in this decade. I investigate this fissure in the social through an examination of certain films wherein the narrative foregrounds discord in marriage in Chapter Two, 'The New Woman: Marital Sagas'.

Subsequently, I look at certain configurations of the woman as the lonely *bhadramahila* in Chapter Three, 'The Female Star: the Lonely *Bhadramahila*', and then move on to read the crisis of the self in certain male melodramas narrating the crisis of the middle-class lover and husband in Chapter Four, 'Disenchanting Modernity: The Crisis of the *Bhadralok*'. In Chapter Five, 'Afterlives', I contextualise the star texts and their extra-filmic appearance in different media sites to foreground the materiality of their iconicity. The discourse of nostalgia that seems to haunt the star text is located in this passing of the popular cinematic time defined by the two stars. I argue that these fictional extra-filmic sites are important cultural sites: they enable the popular to create its storehouse of affect, which resonates with unfulfilled desires and finds articulations that give them a plenitude of meaning that might have been undesirable or unsanctioned in its first moment of appearance. My engagement with the trope of self-fashioning of filmic characters essayed by these two stars within the films I have chosen is located in this discursive grid. I deploy textual analyses of the films to excavate issues of gender and self-fashioning of the star text, while the use of the reception circuit illuminates the template of regional self-fashioning that the local, popular film culture aspired to.

Notes

1. In fact, the decade of the 1950s–60s is usually referred to as the 'Uttam–Suchitra yug' (the Uttam–Suchitra era), so much so that even films that did not star the two were clubbed under this rubric. Biswas identifies the following features as constitutive of popular film practice of this decade: the idea of romance and the couple space, middle-class values, and a dependence on literary narratives (2000: 122).

2. A silver jubilee run means that the film, on its first release, would have run for twenty-five weeks at a stretch; a golden jubilee film would have had a run of fifty weeks; and platinum, of more than seventy-five weeks. It also needs to be noted that in these two decades, that is, 1950–70, Bengali films had a chain release in at least three single screens simultaneously.

3. I use this placing as it corresponds to the credit sequences and publicity campaigns specific to the couple films that the two stars appeared in. I depart from the normative practice of designating the pair as Uttam–Suchitra. I shall explain my position when I discuss Suchitra's professional status in Chapter Five.

4. They function as 'mythic icons' in the Barthesian sense, both denotatively and connotatively. Denotative would imply a 'first system while connotative would mean the second system'. The connotative plane is constituted by the denotative, that is, the first order of signifying system (Allen 2007: 50–51). The accumulation of both denotative and connotative meanings constitutes the iconicity of the star text. My book attempts to unravel the multiplicity of such possible meanings inherent in this particular star text.

5. I am influenced by Pierre Bourdieu's idea of the varied kinds of social capital that define selves and their class locations. He defines four such capitals—economic, cultural, social, and symbolic—which are essential in the formations of subjectivities and identities (Bourdieu 1986).

6. In their volume on stars and their stardom, Bolton and Wright argue (2016) that star studies needs to understand and analyse both stardoms that have faded and those that have endured. This analysis opens up possibilities for productive engagement with images and their cultural and symbolic values; they also enable nuanced readings of how star texts continue to be refashioned, especially those that occur posthumously.

7. This phenomenon of the rise of the stars is not specific to Bengal; the decline of the studio period was also seen in Bombay (Barnouw and Krishnaswamy 1980).

8. It is important to keep in mind that the later star pairs of Soumitra Chatterjee–Aparna Sen in the 1970s, Prosenjit Chatterjee–Debashree Roy in the 1980s–90s, and Jeet–Koyel in the present do not inspire the kind of phenomenal recall value that this star pair still enjoys.

9. Gooptu (2010) argues that the New Theatres is an iconic marker of Bengali cinema's pre-eminent status in the Studio period. According to her, this studio was able to create a space for itself in the all-India market and gave stiff competition to Bombay. Hence, it symbolised 'Bengali-ness' or the *bhadralok* worldview that is specific to Bengali identity. In view of some recent archival work on Bharatlaxmi and Aurora, initiated by the Jadavpur Media Lab, the narrative of primacy accorded to New Theatres may have to be modified. The special volume on Aurora Studios situates it as an important player involved in the all-India market along with New Theatres in 1920–50 (Bhattacharya 2009). It is interesting to note, though, that it is the 1950s–60s decade of the Suchitra–Uttam romantic films that began to be referred to as the 'golden period' of popular Bengali cinema in the 1980s–90s discourse. I shall discuss this shift in Chapter Five.

10. The following factors were responsible for the imagined threat to the industry: the loss of the East Pakistan market due to the partition of the country; the crisis of raw stock and censorship issues discussed by the Film Committee Report of 1952; and the experience of social and emotional trauma occasioned by human suffering and the refugee problem due to the Partition (Banerjee 2009: 39).

11. See Salma Siddique (2022) for a detailed analysis of the traffic of émigré film personnel between Bombay and Lahore, which offers a counter to this discourse of the 'trope of silence and erasure' about the Partition. This book provides interesting insights into the biographies and films of the actors, actresses, producers, and directors from both sides of the divided nation and seeks to uncover this unmapped history that segues the two nations and their creative energies as a collective endeavour. However, the other node of this traffic, the East Pakistan and Bengali film traffic between Kolkata and Dhaka, is not included in Siddique's investigation. She has mentioned the work done by Lotte Hoek (2014) on Urdu language cinema produced in then East Pakistan, which remains the only available resource to map this traffic between the two industries located in the East:

> The work of Lotte Hoek in mapping cross-wing film-making between East and West Pakistan between the 1950s and 1960s awaits a pre-history that

> examines the partition of Bengali cinema. While important for a comprehensive understanding of partition and film production in the subcontinent, the distinctiveness of the Bengali case makes it a separate part of the larger story. (Siddique 2022: 17)

12. *Bhadralok* indicates the idea of a

> 'respectable' Bengali middle class—a large body of hierarchical heterogeneous, upwardly mobile cultural community of professionals, bureaucrats and civil servants who emerged as an off shoot of the colonial administration and acted as an intermediary between the British rulers and the common people. Although designated a 'middle class' they came from the higher caste groups representing the upper class and comprised the respectable society in colonial Bengal. *Bhadramahila* would mean the female members of the family. (Banerjee 2006: 17)

Education and culture are two primary acquisitions of this group, although Bhattacharya suggests that we should not conflate the term with a specific class. Therefore, the deployment of the term 'new middle classes', as has been done by Sudipta Kaviraj and Partha Chatterjee, is problematic, because this group was socially heterogeneous and came from different class and caste locations, though the Brahmins and Kayasthas were the dominant members. According to her, this category should be regarded as a sentiment or ethic (Bhattacharya 2005: 52). As she says, this ethic was significant for self-definition and was held for various reasons by individuals from different class positions, whereas the term has been mistakenly read to indicate a social whole, or even a single class. Social commentators of nineteenth-century Britain made the same mistake about the category of the 'gentleman'. She says that the 'Rentier class, rich *bania*, educated middle class, low petty bourgeoisie' all could lay claim to being the *bhadralok*. She continues thus,

> Self definitions are curious artifacts. Besides serving as sociological shorthand for the past they also retain a broad charismatic authority. '*Bhadralok*' is one such definition. Sumit Sarkar gives us near precise definition. In their own perception this was a middle class (*madhyasreni, madhyabittya*), *bhadralok* world which situated itself below the aristocracy but above the lesser folk engaged in manual labor and generally differentiated itself from the lower castes or the Muslim. (cited in Bhattacharya 2005: 24–25)

13. Satyajit Ray was another icon who had managed both national and international fame, but for the popular industry, the two stars were the most important cultural capital to shore up its self-imaginary.

14. Javed Alam's argument of locating Indian modernity within different contingent moments of 'discreet modernity' as against the overarching and

homogenising trope of 'entrenched modernity' is an important intervention. See the Introduction in *Living with Modernity* (Alam 1999). Partha Chatterjee's argument is crucial in understanding this position on the particularity of Indian modernity (Chatterjee 1993). Saurabh Dube agrees that Chatterjee's positing the 'independent narrative of community' as against the 'grand narrative of capital' in his thesis on the limits of the modern nation-state creates sharp binaries between the trope of Western modernity and our indigenous traditions. However problematic this sharp separation might be, Dube rightly points out that by 'locating narratives of community within regimes of modernity', Chatterjee is not 'reifying these as instances of romanticized tradition' but is facilitating our understanding of community, modernity, state, and nation, not as 'empirical categories but as entities that carry critical epistemological connotations and moral ontological attributes' (Dube 2004: 18).

15. Biswas is referring to Gooptu's (2010) deployment of the 'Bengali-ness' of the *bhadralok* as an overarching frame to study the history of Bengali cinema. I discuss her intervention in Chapter One.

16. Reception circuits include film reviews, readers' letters in film magazines of the time, film publicity in newspapers and magazines, as well as later reappearances of their star texts, more recently through popular biographies.

17. For instance, many of the films starring the two stars were remade in Hindi. *Sagarika* was remade as *Prem Patra* (1962) by Bimal Roy, *Saat Paake Bandha* as *Kora Kagaz* (1974), *Uttar Phalguni* as *Mamata* (1966), etc. Even *Saptapadi* was to be made into Hindi, but was eventually shelved. The journey of the two stars to Bombay for work and Uttam's Hindi production *Choti Si Mulaquat* (1967) has to be kept in mind to unravel the relays between Kolkata and Bombay.

18. Gooptu's idea of the love films denoting the display of 'Bengali-ness', as seen in the ethical male and the idealised female, also subscribes to this view (Gooptu 2010). I have subscribed to this view earlier, when I was arguing about Suchitra's star text in the early part of her career. See my article, 'Mahanayika Madam' (2009). However, I am revising my position in the light of further research that I conducted to unravel the responses to the 'romantic' films of the two stars.

19. The Calcutta Film Society was established in 1947 with Chidananda Dasgupta and Satyajit Ray as the main organisers.

20. Vasudevan (2010) provides a cogent summary of this 1950s critical template. He calls this the 'good film' discourse that governed the notion of cinema's space and place in the immediate period after independence.

Rochona Majumdar (2012) has analysed the film society discourse in Bengal to demarcate the differences in the critical agendas governing film sense in the 1950s and 1970s.

21. Mary Ann Doane has commented on the ambivalent status of Hollywood love films, which were supposed to have catered to female audiences and was not given enough critical attention (1987: 96). In the context of the Suchitra–Uttam romances, the critical charge was formulated on a different axis, which I shall discuss in Chapter One.

22. Brooks (1984) argues that melodrama as a distinct form evolved in the post-enlightenment world in which the 'traditional sacred' had lost its moorings. Melodrama becomes the bourgeois form that is able to express the inexpressible as the individual grapples with a world devoid of traditional certainties. It responds to the psychic needs of the bourgeoisie in which the social expresses itself as the personal.

23. I have referred to this critical slant of film criticism in the section on popular melodrama above.

24. Elsaesser (1987) discusses the centrality of pathos by invoking the ways in which characters experience suffering due to their social circumstances. These circumstances overwhelm their lives and make them victims of a tragedy that they cannot surmount, yet they attempt to face it heroically (1987: 66).

25. This idea of designating the song as external to the narrative has been read as dictated by its use as an interlude to segment the running text (Sangari 2011: 275). Sangari points out that both Prasad and Vasudevan argue that this externalisation of the song is occasioned by the disaggregated nature of the form of popular cinema and its dispersed production circuit (Prasad 1998: 29–52; Vasudevan 2000: 10, cited in Sangari 2011: 275).

26. Gledhill's lucid introduction to her edited volume, *Stardom: The Industry of Desire* (1991: 1), encapsulates this relationship between the melodramatic project and stardom; both enterprises rely on the ideology of individualism.

27. Greenblatt demonstrates how men of letters and poets such as More, Wyatt, Sidney, Spenser, Shakespeare, and Marlowe created their selves and fashioned themselves in Renaissance England. His method involves placing the literary text and the extra-literary to read these self-fashionings.

28. Thomas Harris says, in 'The Building of Popular Images', 'A star is accepted by the public in terms of a certain set of personality traits which permeate his or her films'. This stereotyped image is an essential component of the star text that enables audience identification as well as recall value for the star. Over a period of time, these images and performances get identified as specific mannerisms or character traits associated with individual stars

(Harris 1991: 40). Edward Morin's sociological study of stars and their evolution, as well as the method of constructing a star, with the aid of beauty, make-up and typology, and its essentially feminine attribute, is also important for a larger understanding of reading stars and their images (Morin 1961).

29. Majumdar (2009) remarks that in the context of early Indian cinema, we constantly encounter incomplete or nonexistent archives. She does have a valid objection. Even in my research area and the period of study, I encountered a completely dispersed and inadequate archive, since popular cinema in Bengal was not considered worthy of preservation and archiving. It is now slowly becoming a part of serious engagement, especially due to the efforts of the Jadavpur Film Studies department and the Cinema Studies department at the School of Arts & Aesthetics, JNU.

30. Majumdar (2009) identifies the twin axes of gender and class as significant for reading star discourse in the 1920s–40s, while for the 1950s she deploys morality, excess, and frontality as tropes that can be used productively to read stardom discourse in Bombay cinema.

31. *Rupmancha* (February–March, 1956: 58).

32. Gledhill has argued that melodramatic excess exists in a paradoxical relationship to the real world. So does the star persona: 'If the excessive moment in melodrama infuses ordinary characters with excitement and significance, stars represent ordinary people whose ordinary desires become extraordinary through the intensity stardom imparts to them' (1991: 213).

33.'Many of the public and private rituals of modern individualism became visible in India during the nineteenth century…the sudden flourishing of genres that help express the modern self: the novel, the biography, the autobiography and history' (Chakrabarty 1996: 230).

34.'This bourgeois private self is not born unless one discovers the pleasures of the private. Indian public life may mimic on paper the bourgeois legal fiction of citizenship, but what about the history of the bourgeoisie private and its history?' (ibid.).

35. Majumdar quotes Orsini to give a possible explanation of the bracketing of the personal and the private. According to Orsini, this bracketing of the private could be explained by the cultural expectations governing respectable behaviour in the Indian context, especially in relation to women. Orsini is using the autobiography of the noted Hindi woman writer, Mahadevi Verma, to make this point (cited in Majumdar 2009: 45).

36. For instance, actors Bikash Ray and Kamal Mitra's autobiographies, *Ami* (1985) and *Flashback* (1989), deploy a 'reticent' mode. In contrast, Supriya Debi's autobiography, *Amar Jibon Amar Uttam* (1999), is an xception to this reticent mode. This book is full of personal, private details

of her affair and the intense jealousy—as well as traumatic love life—that she shared with Uttam. Perhaps the fact that she had been publicly a part of his life and had a long relationship with him made it possible for her to use intimate details of her live-in relationship. It is also to be noted that this autobiography was serialised in a women's magazine, *Sananda*, which is known for its liberal feminist orientation. Actor Aparna Sen edited this magazine for a long time. Madhabi Mukherjee's autobiography, *My Life, My Love* (1999), published in English by Stanford University, is quite candid about her troubled relationship with her father, who abandoned her mother and took a second wife, as well as about Madhabi's estranged marriage to fellow actor Nirmal Mukherjee. However, it is cautious in describing her differences with Satyajit Ray.

37. According to G. K. Ray (1992), one of the reasons cited by Suchitra herself, who refused to write her life story, was the inability to bare all. She confided to him that 'I cannot tell lies. If I reveal the truth about my life and profession then that would mean shredding too many reputations'.

38. '*Gandharva vivaha*' is a form of Hindu marriage where the couple mutually decide to marry and where familial or parental consent is not needed or may be unavailable.

39. In contrast, Kanan Devi gives almost all details of her second marriage to Haridas Bhattacharya. In fact, I found references in a *Rupmancha* advertisement in which she had committed to provide exclusive pictures of this marriage only to them and no other magazine.

40. I shall discuss this particular autobiography, *Amar Ami* (*Me Myself*), in Chapter Five.

41. For instance, Uttam's serialised autobiography, published in *Nabakallol* in 1961, has been used by Gooptu (2010) to read his star persona as displaying an ethical *bhadralok* self. This text does project this persona, but as I discovered in my research, in late 1959–60, Supriya figured consistently in photo shoots with Uttam in intimate poses. There were rumours about their affair and eventually, in 1963, they started living together. Readers' letters in *Rupmancha* repeatedly asked about the break-up of his marriage to Gauri Devi. It can be speculated that Uttam needed to project himself as the middle-class 'good' person who was also a family man, particularly around this time in his career and life. In Chapter Five, I will address this issue in further detail.

42. Chatterjee's unpublished dissertation examines a history of desire in literature, from Tagore to the 1950s Uttam-Suchitra melodramas (Chatterjee 2007).

43. A possible methodology is suggested by Majumdar (2009) in her use of 'innuendo' and in her chapter 'Real and Imagined Stars'. She uses court cases, imaginative literature, and other sites where the gossip about stars circulated to plot the split nature of this articulation.

44. *Rupmancha* was primarily a film and performing arts magazine, begun in 1941 by Kaalish Mukherjee. Mukherjee modelled himself as a crusader of public taste. He wanted to educate his readers to become the ideal film spectator who would be well-informed about photography and the technology of cinema. His feature, 'Kalapaharer Kalpajog', solicited audience and reader reactions on cinema and the film-viewing experience, including projection, seats, and the general theatre infrastructure of cinema halls. This feature seemed to have generated a lot of response, going by the kinds of letters that I found all through the issues, from the mid-1950s to the mid-1960s. *Desh* started in 1933 and is a well-known literary magazine published by the Anandbazaar group. *Ultoroth* started in 1951 and *Prosad* started in the late 1950s; both were very popular. *Rupmancha* ceased publication in the 1970s, while the other magazines continue to be published till date. *Anandbazaar* and *Jugantor* are well-known newspapers in Bengali.

45. Despite the presence of rumours in film magazines, prominent editors such as Kaalish Mukherjee, the editor of *Rupmancha*, in his editorials and replies to readers in the 1950s, and Prosad Sinha in his editorials of *Ultoroth* deplored the use of gossip in journalistic discourses.

46. I refer to magazines such as *Cine Advance*, *Notun Khabar*, *Saat Rongo*, *Cinema Jagat*, etc. However, I must admit that despite repeated attempts, I could only find very few surviving copies of many of these magazines. I had to rely on many published references to these in the biographies. I was able to acquire two published volumes of Robi Bosu's *Saat Rongo*, a collection of his writings from the magazine of the same name he edited.

47. Many of these photographers, such as Dhiren Deb, the photographer who clicked the famous 'No kiss' picture of Suchitra (I discuss this photograph in Chapter Five), Hemen Mitra, with whom she had a longstanding tiff and who once asked her to move out of a group photo he was clicking, have passed away. See Sumon Gupto's account of Dhiren Deb's interview in *Je Jon achen Nirjane* (One who is in isolation), or Himanshu Chattopadhyaya's account of the tiff that Suchitra had with Hemen Mitra in *Tollywood er Greta Garbo*. In many conversations with G. K. Ray, the old cine journalist who has authored four books on Suchitra, I was able to piece together some corroboration for many incidents referred to in the various biographies.

1

Screen Romance

The Suchitra–Uttam Love Films

Introduction

In this chapter, I map the discourse around modern love and romance as it emerged in the popular Bengali cinema of the 1950s–60s, specifically in the romantic films starring Suchitra and Uttam. I will focus on three big hits of this pair, *Sagarika* (1956), *Suryotoron* (1958), and *Saptapadi* (1961). The films ran for twenty-four, twelve, and fifteen weeks, respectively. I use these as texts to unravel the emerging romantic subjectivities which in different ways consolidated the romantic iconicity of the pair.

Sagarika[1] explores an ideal of individuated modern love in which the proactive, independent, and educated 'new woman' Sagarika/Suchitra, a medical student, takes on the role of a companionate lover to nurture and nurse her injured blind lover, Arun/Uttam, a surgeon, to health and successful eye surgery. This film is significant as it constructed a cluster of cinematic framings, advertisement, and publicity that was responsible for creating a novel template of the star pair's screen romance.

Suryotoron[2] is the story of a talented young architect Somnath/Uttam, who eschews heavy classical baroque designs and practices the Bauhaus style, a minimalist, modernist trend of urban planning. It explores love as an ethical choice, where the woman Anita/Suchitra is driven to create a community housing project for the poor people of a slum. Placing this slum at the centre, the film articulates anxieties about poverty, urban housing, lack of cleanliness and hygiene, and poor infrastructural support for slum dwellers. To realise her dream project, Anita is willing to harm her father's business reputation; she is not averse to marrying Rajsekhar, her father's business rival, who wants to ruin him as an act of revenge, but she is open about her attraction to Somnath even when engaged to Rajsekhar. The film ends with Rajsekhar's suicide, and his money, which he has left to Anita, enables her to build a new 'Suryotoron', sun tower, designed by Somnath.

Saptapadi (1961)[3] traces the love and separation of two young lovers, Krishnendu Mukherjee, a Hindu Brahmin, and Rina Brown, an Anglo-Indian woman, who are divided along racial and religious lines. The film raises issues of religion, caste, inter-racial liaisons, and inter-caste marriages. They can only be united after both undergo a tortuous process of self-negotiation that helps them realise the ethical and moral dimensions of romantic love, which can transcend the familial, personal, and the religious to forge the romantic couple.

How do these films open up a terrain where feminine subjectivity collides with the social? Is it through the figure of the new woman, the *bhadramahila* in *Sagarika*, and the actualisation of her desires; through a particular relationship of space and gender in *Suryotoron*; or through the enactment of religious conversion as the lovers confront familial prohibitions across religious divides in *Saptapadi*? What are the specific coordinates of the star text and its self-fashioning that can be mapped in the constitutive moment of this star pair? How was the star pair's romantic aura constructed using novel methods of film publicity, advertising, and film journalism? How does the romantic star text shape and intersect with the imaginary of the region and its cinema? These are issues that concern my engagement in this chapter. Before explicating these issues, I turn to a summation of arguments that contextualise the 1950s romantic films cluster and its cinematic terrain.

New Romantic Love: The Suchitra–Uttam Filmic Romances

It has been suggested that unlike the Hindi socials of the period, in the Suchitra–Uttam films the romance track was not a subplot. It was the plot itself (Biswas 2002; Chatterjee 2007; Gooptu 2010).[4] Biswas uses the term 'new melodrama' to designate this cluster of films, arguing that they deploy 'space as cinematic substance' to create the imaginary of a modern, middle-class Bengali self, or the imaginary of the male citizen self's journey into urban modernity,[5] which differs from the family-oriented Studio Socials of the 1930s and 1940s. In the popular film of the 1950s, 'class and profession will increasingly define characters' (Biswas 2002: 104). In the Suchitra–Uttam films, we see these two filmic characters encountering each other in the course of their professional or educational pursuits. Both the stars are repeatedly cast as educated working professionals, doctors, engineers, teachers, architects: a wide array of middle-class professions that signpost the aspirational trajectory of middle-class Bengalis.[6] Further, the space of the couple is imagined as an in-between symbolic space created outside the familial and the authoritative. Biswas (2002) identifies the early hits such as *Agniparikshа* and *Dhuli* (though Uttam was not Suchitra's lead in the latter film) as a phase where the transition from the family-oriented social to the formation of the couple was imagined, but did not realise its full symbolic potential. He considers *Harano Sur* (1957) as deploying a completely new cinematic language to narrate the creation of the romantic couple (ibid.).[7]

Drawing from Biswas's work, Subhajit Chatterjee has identified the relocation of the romantic affect of the couple in the formal strategies of the framing and creation of narratives of urban coupling that led to a new *mise en scène* of desire. These 'new socials' imagine an insular romance that is bracketed off from the patriarchal gaze or forms of social or familial control. Deploying a new historicist template, Chatterjee (2007) argues that the Uttam–Suchitra[8] romances were participating in the discursive regimes of the 1950s, as well as legal reforms around the question of women's issues about love and marriage. Both Biswas and Chatterjee suggest that socially, these love films delineated love as a private transaction, and not dependent on or rooted in familial relations. In many films, the stars appeared as orphans; parental presences remained tangential to the emotive economy of the films. The other two motifs that dominate these filmic narratives are: Uttam as a dislocated figure, and Suchitra as the modern woman with stable urban roots, who demonstrates a search for companionship along with a zeal for independence (Chatterjee 2010: 74).

Sarkar (2010) has suggested that these romantic melodramas capitalised on Suchitra's '*adhunika*', the modern stylised persona, to stage love. He locates the social and historical value of these films in the vicarious pleasures that they offered to the audiences, who could imagine a plush lifestyle via these romances. Gooptu's intervention situates the filmic love of Uttam–Suchitra within the template of 'a cultured Bengali-ness', where the stars were able to fashion an imaginary of the 'ethical male and an idealised female companion' to demarcate the specificity of the Bengali love films. Placing the lovers at the centre, these film narratives articulate a lover's discourse that has been identified as expressing a 'romantic charge and the centrality of the couple' (Gooptu 2010: 168). Furthermore, she argues that this idea of cultured Bengali-ness was also bolstered by the 'good story' staple, and that both these constituents were able to counter the threat of Bombay cinema by creating a regional self-imaginary.

The 'good story' staple needs explication as it was a crucial marker that popular Bengali cinema used as its differentiating category. In the specific instance of the romantic films starring Suchitra and Uttam, these literary borrowings were taken from the works of Saratchandra[9] and other modern Bengali writers such as Ashapurna Devi (1909–95), Prabhavati Devi Saraswati (1905–72), Pratibha Bosu (1915–06), Tarashankar Bandopadhyaya (1898–71), Achintya Kumar Sengupto (1903–76), and Ashutosh Mukherjee (1922–89), among others. They were highly regarded for their depictions of varied modern experiences of love and romance rooted in the familial and social. Since these writers were extremely popular and well-respected, their writings adapted for the screen aided the cultural currency of the films. The adaptations would acknowledge the literary borrowing by mentioning the writer's name prominently in the film's publicity advertisements and song booklets. The films that I discuss in this chapter and in the rest of this book, with the exception of *Sagarika* and *Suryotoron*, adaptations from the corpus of writers mentioned above.[10]

While the above arguments are valid, it is pertinent to state that the romantic and affective charge of these love films was severely critiqued in the reception circuit. The use of erotic display focusing on Suchitra's screen image—which added to the accretion of the romantic iconicity of the star pair—came into conflict with the demands of decorous screen behaviour, which was central to Bengali middle-class notions of 'respectability'. As I demonstrate in my analysis of the star text in this chapter, it is important to take into account the hostile reception circuit, which occludes any simplistic slotting of the love films as signposting an idealised *bhadralok* imaginary. It is also important to analyse the displacement of the erotic excess into the performative, in terms of the filmic, aural, or visual registers, which spill over mostly via the woman/star and the extra-filmic, underscoring the operation of emotive excess associated with the star persona and the melodramatic genre. This distinctive feature of the love film cluster is visible across the Suchitra–Uttam romantic films. We see this aspect of emotive excess, where the contrary pull of tradition and individual choice is played out, through Taposhi in the first hit of this cycle, *Agnipariksha*.[11] Sometimes this struggle resulted in a neurotic breakdown, as we see in *Shilpi* or in *Pathey Holo Deri*. The prevalence of near states of neurosis and breakdown has been read by Gooptu as a manifestation of the absent presence of Partition trauma that appears in this guise (2010: 161). In other films, we see an independent and proactive woman who is capable of taking on a tradition that would hinder her from being with her lover, as we see in *Sagarika* or in *Shilpi* (where, despite being an upper-caste woman, she wants to be known as Anjana Pal, as her lover is from the lower caste of clay potters). In *Bipasha*, when her lover disappears on the eve of marriage, she puts vermillion in her hair parting to denote her married status, instead of being condemned to the state of *lagnabhrashtha*.[12] Or, as seen in *Indrani*, she can be the one to propose and declare that she will not need a priest to bless her marriage as she will have a registered marriage.

Despite different plot configurations, the emotive performative and proactive excess was continuously mapped onto the woman's characters. I have already referred to other critical positions regarding this new woman and the possibility of opening the fields of 'feminine subjectivity'. It is worth noting that in these films, tradition and modernity do not necessarily appear as oppositional binaries displaced onto or split between other characters. It is usually the Suchitra character who carries the potentially liberatory impulses of modernity while experiencing other forms of attachment that may be social or traditional. The woman, then, becomes the body through whom certain narrative blockages resulting from the conflict between past and present, tradition and modernity, or individual desire versus social and familial constraints are worked out and resolved, while she realises her subjectivity by negotiating varied subject positions of professional and emotional selfhoods. The staging of the inexpressible, the ineffable and psychic desires, and the attempt to recover that which is lost or repressed and is tied to the past is of course ably articulated through the melodramatic mode (Gledhill 1987b: 28–30).

In comparison, the male counterpart seems to be 'feminised' (Biswas 2000). Often, Uttam was cast as an emotionally passive figure, as in *Agnipariksha,* ill or ailing as in *Saap Mochon,* with a deep debilitating secret of illegitimacy as in *Sobar Upare* or *Bipasha,* blind as in *Sagarika,* or with amnesia, as in *Harano Sur.* Suchitra, meanwhile, successfully enacted roles of a strong, determined, and driven modern middle-class woman, who achieves emotional completion through the fulfillment of the love-relationship. While most of these interventions have identified the Uttam figure as fundamentally impaired in some way, I do not think that his physical or emotional impairment in these films can be simply categorised as indicating feminisation or an inert male figure. Uttam's androgynous masculinity[13] was not effete, as the Pramathesh Barua kind of masculine figure was. He is markedly different from the overtly sentimentalised, emotional Devdas figure. The masculinity embodied in his roles opposite Suchitra was not constructed as that of a virile aggressive male.[14] His diffidence, reticence, and almost seemingly passive acceptance of the strong, proactive female characters essayed by Suchitra do not indicate a weak feminised self. Rather, it seems to me that the constitutive feature of the characterisation of the Uttam figure is his emotional sensitivity to the woman, and the delicate manner in which he chooses to conduct his relationships. He is configured as an idealised new male figure who can be imagined as a complementary companion for the new woman. This new male was significantly different from the imaginary of the colonised male as womanly or effeminate, as created by the British colonial discourse. Scholars have drawn our attention to the self-fashioning undertaken by the Bengali *bhadralok* to counter the British colonial discourse (Chowdhury 1998; Sinha 1995).[15] Others have commented upon the binaries of 'traditional' forms of pre-colonial masculine identities that were less rigid and more fluid (Nandy 1983), and analysed the prevalence of ideas associated with Lord Krishna and his masculinity, especially as seen in Bankim Chandra Chattopadhaya's writings (Kaviraj 1995).[16] Such ideas can be used productively to reflect upon the varied kinds of masculine subjectivities that converge in the post-independence period and can demarcate the contours of the new male typified by Uttam's gentle and genteel physicality.

I enter this terrain within the critical discursive regime summarised above, but extend the template of the Suchitra–Uttam filmic romances in the following manner: I argue that these films participate in unravelling the cinematic staging of love across two grids. One locates the specificity of the love as it is articulated in *Sagarika* and participates in quite an innovative fashion in the modern discourse of *prem* (love), within the film text and outside of it. The other frame locates the staging of love as it intersects with the social in *Suryotoron* and *Saptapadi*, where the lovers have to negotiate their *bildungsroman* by confronting and surmounting various prohibitions. My intervention does not take away the value of the couple space as symbolic (Biswas 2000, 2002; Chatterjee 2007, 2010; Gooptu 2010; Sarkar 2010), but argues that the inscription of the social is crucial for understanding how this cinematic love was participating in and contributing to the post-independence moment when the region could lay claim to its specific love stories. The construction of the eroticised *bhadramahila* woman/star and her 'feminine subjectivity' allows for an explication of the narratorial investment in the star couple, and additionally enables a productive engagement with the reception circuits that were also instrumental in fashioning the star texts of the pair.

Clearly, the industry sought to capitalise and maximise star value by fashioning a product that seemed to be a regional variant of Bombay star vehicles, as I have remarked in the Introduction. The sensuous woman star and the romantic charge coded through on-screen physical intimacy led to objections which panned the films aping Bombay and *videshi* culture.[17] There is a marked difference in the actual cinematic signs of physical intimacy and the film magazine responses, which I discuss in the concluding section of this chapter. I think this huge gap arose out of the tremendous glamorous screen presence of this female star. This screen presence was of course aided by Suchitra's physical beauty, her makeup, her dresses, and the use of technology to capitalise on her image, which also evoked extreme negative reactions in the audiences. Perhaps the fascination and condemnation can be explained by thinking of cinema as a 'guilty pleasure', a medium that thrives on both voyeurism and fetishisation, especially of the female star's body.[18] It is also important to keep in mind that in this period, she was actually among the film personnel from Kolkata who were part of Bombay cinema, and that this movement of the woman star created its own trajectory of anxiety and dissonance.

This charge of romance was also mounted through explicit and titillating film publicity campaigns that hinted at the possibility of the stars being romantically involved.[19] It is true that these love films did not channel back the rumoured love affair onto the screen in the manner of the Bombay films (Majumdar 2009; Wani 2016). For the publicity of *Sagarika*, the possibility of romance[20] was salaciously coded by using the real names of the two stars to advertise the torrid love, *ugra pranaya*, that would send shivers down the body, *shira upshira bhore uthook*;[21] one tagline declared that the film would ensure that the 'terrible winter would be warmed by the aggressive flow of love'. Another referred to the new depiction of the 'Suchitra–Uttam leela'.[22] Chatterjee surmises that it was the apparent 'adult theme' of *Sagarika* that led to a slew of angry letters in the film magazines and newspapers (2010: 69).[23]

I argue that *Sagarika*, which had a record run of twenty-four weeks on release, brings to the fore all the formal, stylistic, and material constituents of the Suchitra–Uttam screen romance and gives it the charge that carries over into subsequent films of the romantic cycle. For instance, the next release, *Ekti Raat*, used the trope of extra-marital love and transgressive desire (the characters were married, but were forced by circumstances to spend the night in an inn as spouses and enacted intimate night scenes and erotic songs) and was at the receiving end of criticism and moral censure. At a promotional event, a scene from *Ekti Raat* depicting Uttam leaning over a sheer nightgown-clad Suchitra was severely criticised in an editorial comment.[24]

It is significant that many of these love films staged the romance as transgressive, with the lovers affianced to other characters. The plot would unravel the attraction and showcase their unruly desires. The love films continued to feed on the oral circuits of gossip and titillation and created an off-screen life of the 'affair', which was repeated in advertising and promotional events. This gossip about the romantic involvement of the two stars[25] has not been corroborated, except in one interview of Uttam that appeared in Robi Bosu's *Saat Rongo*.[26] The Q&A in film magazines enquired about the 'real love affair' of the stars. The editors would evade direct answers and draw attention to the married status of both stars, and the necessity of good acting that looked convincing on screen.

I now turn to a discussion of the films and the narrative framings that allow an unpacking of 'feminine subjectivity', which I consider significant for the star pair's romantic iconicity. This unpacking enables us to frame some possible connections between star persona, star value, and its complicated relationship to questions of popular and/or critical acceptance.

Sagarika (1956): The Limit Film of the Screen Lovers

While agreeing with film scholars on the centrality of *Agnipariksha*[27] in analysing the Suchitra–Uttam romance, I suggest, however, that it is important only insofar as it was the first big hit of the pair. To my mind, this film, and others such as *Maraner Pore, Sadanander Mela, Grihapravesh,* and *Annapurnar Mandir* (June, July, August, November 1954), and *Saanjher Pradeep, Saap Mochon, Sobar Upare* (January, May, December 1955), display a similarity in generic codes that worked out the varied conflicts between tradition and modernity faced by the romantic couple in actualising their love, wherein the woman figure actively participated in resolving the conflicts, as I have mentioned above. The trope of 'feminine subjectivity' works alongside the other social concerns dominant in the plot, which are eventually resolved to form the romantic couple. My analysis will focus on the following issues: the cinematic staging of love, which showcases love as physical desire and ethical *prem,* and its performative enactment via Sagarika's transgressive desire for a man engaged to her cousin; the definition of love as a private exchange of value only between two people who have an exclusive bond that is interiorised, and then depicted cinematically through the close-ups of eyes and letters; the play on sight and blindness and touch; and the figuration of the woman as a feminine nurturer figure.

In *Sagarika,* we see two kinds of love: love as an affective bond, *prem,* a highly individualistic emotional and ethical modern love, and love as physical attraction, where one is dazzled by the beloved's beauty, with the ethical and erotic complementing each other. It is worth recalling Sudipta Kaviraj's (2007) formulation of the 'popular middle class modern Bengali love' to understand this ethical dimension of love seen in modern Bengali literature, beginning with Tagore. He argues that this trope involved a paradigm shift in aesthetic ideals as modern writers felt the need to distance themselves from the explicitly sensual and sexual pre-modern *shringaric* [the erotic] ideal of love, and instead imagined a new ideal of *prem,* an ethical, emotional, and aesthetic ideal of romantic love, one focused on the *antar,* the inner self. These modern selves imagined their individual destinies through romantic love, while the emotional bond and companionship which two individuated souls feel for one another was considered both precious and unique. This new love also involved a certain impulse towards democracy, as it imagined love across various barriers. In Bengali culture, as elsewhere in India, there is a strong historical connection between this emerging literary aesthetic and a new social ethic of individuality and domesticity (ibid.: 161–82). The choice of a romantic partner based on ideas of compatibility and shared interests is a significant trope in creating the individual's *bildungsroman* in modernity. Kaviraj's analysis is an interesting entry point into the debate around the figure of the romantic couple on screen in 1950s films.

Statistically, of the twenty-two films that the pair starred in, fifteen can be termed as modern love stories that were not derived from either Tagore or Saratchandra. The bond between the couple in these films was projected as affective and psychic, which was also an exchange of friendship, affection, and feelings (Biswas 2002: 117; Chatterjee 2007: 284). It is true that in terms of narrative and character, we see them as being governed by the values of middle-class ethics, *bhadrata*, or refined and moral behaviour, and a sense of 'cultured Bengaliness' (Gooptu 2010). This is certainly in keeping with the value of authenticity that is important for star value. But it is also true that cinematically, the framing and staging of this modern *prem* did not eschew the physical, the erotic, and the sensual, and was also positioned in conflict with varied social and religious proscriptions.

Arun's attraction to Sagarika is compared to a disease, to a sailboat sailing in tumultuous waters; he himself compares his attraction to 'seeing' for the first time. The declaration of the dazzling aspect of Sagarika's beauty, which creates the intense sensation of love, is acknowledged by Arun thus: 'till now I only walked, never saw; for the first time I have seen what can manifest if the bones and sinews that are my domain [he is training to be a surgeon] can be transformed with *rup* and *lavanya* [physical beauty, grace and charm]'. This clear articulation of the man's desire for the woman's physical charm had not been seen in previous films of the romance cycle. Needless to say, this dimension had already been a part of newspaper advertisements for this film. The publicity booklet and one newspaper advertisement carried a stylised picture of Uttam and Suchitra's dreamy close-ups, with their eyes half-closed and superimposed on a sailboat. This, of course, signalled the magical, dreamy world of romance that the film would evoke for the spectators,[28] but this leitmotif of sailing, stormy waters, boats, was consistently referenced in the film itself, in the dialogues, in the actual shot of the steam ship sailing with Arun on it, transporting him to England, or in a picture of a sailboat visible in the frame when Sagar experiences her tormented desire for her faraway lover.

It is important to note that this idea and depiction of the power of physical attraction and love is tied to the body of the woman/star Suchitra. The eroticisation of her body, the site/sight of the glamorous woman whom we see in this film remained and circulated with variations across films and outside of films to create and unleash anxieties about her sensuous image. Cinematically, it was the use of the soft-lit close-ups of her illuminated face and other compositions that framed her through the use of 'graded soft light, wind, window frames, flowing curtains, telephoto lensing' (Biswas 2002: 115) that became the hallmark of her romantic/screen iconicity. This particular filmic persona was ably supported by Uttam, whose body had a certain 'delicateness... a musical but sharp diction... and his easy but graceful non aggressive yet assertive walk' (ibid.: 105), which enabled this star pair to embody a coupling that was cinematically complementary.

However, in the reception circuit it was the display of Suchitra's glamour and sensual screen presence that gave rise to certain uneasy anxieties about the lack of 'respectable on-screen behaviour' as befitting a Bengali *bhadramahila* and 'unprincipled modernity' in the depiction of romantic love that alert us to the varied relays of subjectivity that shaped the romantic couple star text. Her sensual image, which used bodily exhibitionism, was continuously repeated with variations in *Ekti Raat*, *Suryotoron*, and *Shilpi*, and even made its way into the Saratchandra adaptation, *Chandranath*.[29] *Chandranath* was criticised for showing Saryu's sensuality and the scenes between her and Chandranath were found to be 'too full of sex appeal'.[30] While it is true that physical beauty is a given for stars,[31] the level of scrutiny directed at Suchitra's sensuous and beautiful screen image is quite phenomenal. Therefore, when Biswas suggests that this figuration of the new woman in the 1950s melodrama via Suchitra is giving voice to a modern woman who is not like the 'guilty construction' of the modern woman of the socials (2002: 122), his claim is not completely borne out either by the narrative and figurative economy or by the responses to this articulation.[32] To my mind, Suchitra's text inhabits a different strata of performative, gestural, and figurative 'excesses', which are not only located within the diegesis but which also spill over continuously into the extra-diegetic as well.[33] In these modern love stories, she is not punished, but she remains an excess that causes anxieties that are inscribed on her 'body', both in the filmic and the 'non-filmic' space. I shall discuss the discursive regime of the reception circuit in the conclusion to this chapter.[34] I now turn to an analysis of the cinematic staging of love in *Sagarika* to explicate the romantic charge that this film embodied.

Arun and Sagarika's love blossoms through an epistolary exchange after he departs for higher studies in England. As Sagarika reads his letter, we see a close-up of her eyes. This is followed by a shot of the letter in close-up, but the framing is deliberately projected as a rectangular band, with the lines expressing Arun's feelings illuminated while the rest of the page is in shadow. The use of technology to navigate the enchanting zone of intimacy is quite forceful. The epistolary exchange is stylised, with close-ups of the woman's face in the upper and lower corners of the frame along with a blooming lotus, which seems coy by today's standards.

Figure 1.1: Blossoming Love, *Sagarika*

The lotus, of course,[35] is the symbol of their love; the lovers engaged in writing, separated by geography, come together in the same visual plane because of cinema. The usual editing pattern of shot–reverse shot is dispensed with in favour of trick photography. I think the scenes that used trick photography[36] to continuously foreground the love visually were one reason for the long run of this film, as well as for the furore against this blatant display of modern *prem*. The play on sight and blindness that the advertisements had announced cinematically highlights the intensely personal confessions and the developing exclusive bond between the two lovers.

This close-up of eyes is repeated towards the end when Arun is being operated upon and Sagarika is outside the operation theatre. As we see his eyes being prised open with surgical clamps, the shot of a close-up of her eyes wide open suggests that she too experiences the procedure on her body. The love bond is not only interiorised, but it is also cinematically enacted on the lovers' body—it is both interiorised and exteriorised. This doubling is considered significant for the melodramatic form (Bhaskar 2012). The physicality of romantic love and the site of the lover's body to actualise that desire need to be understood to decode the charge of love that *Sagarika* embodied.

The scenes that portray Sagar experiencing an internal tussle as her feelings of love run counter to her kinship ties, which she is guilty of transgressing, give form to the deeply felt emotional crisis that she experiences. Arun thinks he is writing to his fiancé, but Sagar knows she is lying to him by pretending to be his fiancé. She is also lying to her cousin and being untrue to herself. In the first instance, we see her gazing at the letter, followed by a cut to her distressed expression in close-up: 'No no I cannot do this, what have I done, what a dilemma, you tell me how will I write to you? No, no this should not be happening.' This is followed by a purely performative sequence in her bedroom where she sits on a chair. We see Sagar clutching a book to her chest, with her face inclined towards the table on which Basanti, her cousin, has placed Arun's letter. A series of shot–reverse shots alternate between her close-up and the letter. The first frames Sagar's intense frown as she tries to hold herself back. In the next shot, we see her expression relaxing and then she starts reading the letter. Arun acknowledges that her letter appeared as a symbol of a delicate touch of reassurance and her immeasurable love in the foreign land. This admission propels her to answer the letter. She keeps touching the letter and the ecstatic expression on her face denotes the affective and emotive bond that she experiences. We can almost prefigure the second trope that will define this love, that of touch. This love incessantly reiterates the tactile and sensory experience of desire through dialogue, formal compositions, and the emotive and performative economy. The intensity of her love, which is tied to her deepest desires, is externalised as objects and staged via a dense *mise en scène* highlighting the excess of feeling and its melodramatic staging, captured via her close-ups. In some of these scenes, we see her touching her throat, face, and Arun's photograph while she speaks of her 'overflowing love', 'her immersion in her yearning'. She declares, as we see her holding his photo: 'I do not have any right to talk about it, that's the biggest truth of my life, I know I will never be able to land, yet I sailed my boat towards the storm and gave the oars to you, now I have no option but to drown.'

In other films of the cluster, we see similar articulations that play on the physical attraction of love quite emphatically. In *Suryotoron* and *Saptapadi*, the lover's touch is deployed slightly differently, and, in contrast to the yearning and pining for the lover's touch that we encounter in *Sagarika*, we initially see an antagonistic attraction between the two protagonists in the other two films. Both *Suryotoron* and *Saptapadi* portray Suchitra as a proud and haughty modern urban woman who is finally transformed by her love. Suchitra was sometimes cast as the rich, spoilt urban woman, as in *Ekti Raat* or *Chaoa Paoa*, which depicted flirtatious and playful love. Despite different plot configurations and characterisations, the romance cluster repeatedly staged varied intimate scenes involving the two stars. Sometimes the lovers' intimate close-ups could be layered over with virile and aggressive sexual tension, as was seen in *Suryotoron*. In one sequence, Somnath enters Anita's bedroom at night and threatens to crush her pride by spreading the news that a low-class worker was found to have spent the night with the factory owner's daughter. This threat carries an implication of her depraved sexual attraction for the low-class man. He grabs her by her arm and throws her forcefully onto the couch. He leaves without carrying out his threat, and we see her touch her upper arm where he had held her. This was an inversion of the lover's embrace, as we see the blackened face of the proletariat male over the beautiful woman. This fraught encounter is quite different from the normative, idealised, gentle love associated with the star pair. The healing lover's touch from *Sagarika* morphs into a violent, aggressive, and angry one in this film. The threat of rape and sexual violence was something that spectators were not used to in the trajectory of romance popularised by the two stars.[37]

Saptapadi, too, uses the lover's touch by having the characters enact Desdemona's death scene from *Othello*, which allows the pair to touch and caress while performing the play. Framed in a tight close-up, the scene bristles with intensity of feeling as the two protagonists continue to hold the pose even after the play has ended. The framing, which was used in publicity booklets and newspaper advertisements, portrayed them gazing at each other longingly, with Krishnendu leaning over a prone Rina. We see Rina touching her throat where he had placed his hands, as if she could not forget the feel of them. In a number of scenes we see Rina touch Krishnendu in intimate gestures to comfort, console, and make her desire evident. The lover's touch acquires significance as the love in this film is inter-religious, and the caste and religious taboos of touch need to be surmounted by the lovers. These love films consistently used close-ups of the two stars, cheek to cheek (*Sagarika*), Uttam's face over Suchitra's upturned face (*Saptapadi*), in the diegetic as well as posters, publicity advertisements, and booklets, with unfailing regularity to denote the staging of the romance. It was as eagerly anticipated as the embrace that constituted the happy ending. Sometimes, the promotional material was designed as envelopes with an image of the embracing couple (I was able to trace an envelope for *Indrani*, which carried the star pair's embracing photo also used for the film booklet and advertisement).

It is precisely this zone that is necessary for understanding the particular charge of emotive and iconic performativity that was the Suchitra–Uttam romance. The use of the freeze shot of close-ups or reflections in mirrors in all three films (as well as others of the cluster) was also repeated to create tableau effects. The use of highly stylised tonal photography and a constant play of shadow and light became an effective strategy that added to the intensity of the scenes. Biswas has commented on these techniques, and this particular schema is very effective in creating the polarised moral universe that is of course central to the melodramatic world (Biswas 2000: 123).

Touch, caresses, and specific framings and shot compositions can be tracked consistently in their love films, which maximised star use but also led to a critical backlash in the reception circuit, discussed later in this chapter.

Figure 1.2: Desiring Woman, *Indrani*

Let me briefly discuss an interesting intimate scene of a 'near kiss'[38] in *Indrani* (1958). We see the married pair, Indrani and Sudarshan (see the discussion in Chapter Two), in their bedroom. As we see the couple discussing their relocation to the woman's place of work, she moves, holds his collar, and pulls his face down to hers while she sits. The framing focuses on the couple in close-up with Sudarshan kneeling over her, her upturned face looking at him while her hands clutch him and then move over his arms. The camera now suddenly shifts and frames the couple from behind Indrani's head as he still kneels over her. The tight frame sees her head engulfing his face, his left cheek only partially visible, her hands placed on his shoulders. The composition seems suggestive of the woman kissing or caressing the man. He slowly moves his face into the space of her head, so that it is covered a bit more. The couple holds the pose for a few seconds and we cut back to the previous composition where the camera frames them from the side, with her sitting and he kneeling over her with her hands on his chest. It is evident that love here is not merely psychic, but equally tactile. The motif of physical touch and desire is an important trope that signifies this modern love; I have already discussed other formal compositions from their films that signified the performance of love between the star pair.

Arun's return in *Sagarika* plays out the trope of 'the lover's touch', which becomes the blind man's guide, and also suggests the scandalous possibility of the unmarried lovers spending day and night together. This figuration of the new woman who would be the ideal companion in every possible way, the nurturer of her impaired or traumatised lover, is not unique to this film, as I have mentioned earlier. The audiences had already been introduced to this figure in *Sobar Upare* and *Saap Mochon*, two earlier Suchitra–Uttam romances, and such notions circulated across other texts such as *Shilpi, Harano Sur*, and *Bipasha*. In *Sobar Upare*, she not only helps him in his quest to exonerate his father who had been wrongly accused, but as he experiences a breakdown, questioning his paternity, she also reassures him that his illegitimacy does not matter; he can create his own family lineage. In *Saap Mochon*, she rushes with a doctor to her ailing lover, who is ill as a result of a family curse. Conversely, in some of the romances, the woman experiences a nervous disorder, for instance in *Shilpi*, or her breakdown in *Pathey Holo Deri* where Mallika is nursed back to health by her lover, or *Saptapadi*, where Rina becomes an alcoholic and is saved by her lover's surgery after an injury. This role reversal nevertheless enabled the two lovers to be constantly shown in each other's company, providing enough cinematic opportunities for the staging of the lover's touch.

However, in no other film do we see the protracted segment over which this nurturing feminine figure is staged in quite the same manner as *Sagarika*. Arun is uncomfortable with Sagarika moving in to look after him as they are unmarried, and he worries about salacious gossip and rumours. In a crucial scene, Sagar tells him that she is safest with him, as her love is true and strong enough to ride over all societal disapproval. It is interesting that the narrative seems unconcerned about the impropriety of the two unmarried young lovers staying together, and it is the woman who is confident enough of her love to be able to live with and care for her lover without being troubled by social norms. The placement of a romantic song in this segment, '*ei modhu raat shudhu tomar amar*', 'this honeyed night is yours and mine', as she puts her lover to bed, is laden with her desire, which is transposed onto the song. The film ends with Arun recovering his eyesight, lying helpless and vulnerable on the hospital bed, wanting to see Basanti, his dream woman. In the climax, Sagarika leaves the room so he can be united with Basanti, but Arun realises by 'touching' Basanti that she is not his beloved. Of course, Arun had to lose his 'sight' to 'see' his real companion. He experiences her 'touch' and it is this tactile physical interaction that supplants his earlier attraction to her *rup* and *lavanya* to one of *prem*. We have seen Sagarika hold, touch, lead Arun all through the period of his convalescence. As Arun experiences intense anguish on touching the real Basanti, he cries out for 'his Basanti'. The brisk editing with shot–reverse shot that reveals Sagar crying for her lost love in the corridor is particularly well-mounted. The camera tracks her as she rushes in on hearing that Arun might lose his sight again if he is too traumatised. The film ends with a lover's embrace as we see her hold her lover in a passionate hug, tears streaming from her eyes.[39]

This charged staging of love foregrounds the affirmative possibility of nurturing love and the enactment of choice, portrayed through a highly stylised and melodramatic staging which showcased the intensely individualistic and deeply felt subjectivity of modern lovers. The constant cinematic enunciation of love and physical desire adds to the emotive charge of the experience. The opening of the 'feminine subjectivity' and romantic charge of these love films is tied to the realisation of the lover's *bildungsroman*, the trope for modern *prem* that I have borrowed from Kaviraj's (2007) intervention. In the Suchitra–Uttam romances, this *bildungsroman* emerges also as an urban encounter, tied to the spatial mobility of the lovers, especially the woman, as well as the social and ethical choices that the lovers enact to fashion their subjectivities. These choices also bring forth the melodramatic trope of displacing the social and the political onto the personal. It is therefore important to track the relationship of space and gender that these films articulate to see how the feminine subjectivity was unfolding spatially, narrating the *bhadramahila's* negotiation of work and space.

URBAN LOVE ENCOUNTERS: THE SPATIAL IMAGINARY OF LOVE

The two filmic characters essayed by Suchitra and Uttam often encountered each other in the course of their professional or educational pursuits, or during travels in new spaces, which provided the topoi of spaces of the urban modern, creating a map of possible romantic and affective encounters. The marking of these physical spaces is important as they were an intrinsic part of urban modernity, insofar as they are anonymous spaces uncontaminated by traditional stratifications and caste/class divisions. In this sense, they are truly democratic. The discourse of love itself is tied to the experience of the city and its spaces, as previously discussed in connection with the experiences of the *bhadralok* journey to the city. This cartography drew on certain specific city spaces which were tied to modern cross-gender encounters, which had become possible due to the emergence of newer public spaces available for modern selves. The class or the mess, the hostel room, the college common room, staircases, restaurants, hospital wards, offices, public parks, city streets, buses, trains, cross-connections over the phone, all provided contexts for the characters to meet and become lovers. In this cluster of films, these spaces were used to allow the lovers' paths to intersect and for love to blossom, which eventually shifted shape in the turbulent 1970s, as I show in my discussion in Chapter Four. It is also the everydayness of these spaces, the ordinariness of the shared looks, the fleeting glances, the tentative acknowledging of their love that made these romances part of the generic cluster that became their screen trademark.

College social functions, rehearsals, cinema, theatre, parties, clubs, and football matches in *Sagarika,* the playgrounds in *Saptapadi,* and public meetings in *Suryotoron,* as well as slums, radio talks, radio singing, and vacations provide a map of newer social actions related to professional, educational, or recreational pursuits. Education and work therefore became the two significant coordinates of this self-fashioning, enabling the lovers to define themselves vis-à-vis the two crucial signifiers of urban middle-class characters. The two youthful songs in *Sagarika* and *Saptapadi*: '*amra medical college e pori*' ('we are students of the medical college'; *Sagarika*), and the *kali kirtan,* a devotional song sung in praise of the goddess Kali by Krishnendu and his friends to drown out the noise of Rina's party in *Saptapadi,* are placed because they signify this new interactive possibility.

These filmic romances deploy a particular template of urban space[40] and gender.[41] If, as Biswas has suggested, the 'new melodrama' was quick to respond to the large number of women entering the job market (2002: 121–123), and as Gooptu believes, these films see the new woman as the active independent woman (2010: 166), then what does this imply in terms of the spatial negotiations that we encounter? It is true that we see Suchitra repeatedly cast in the roles of the working professional woman, doctor, teacher, medical student. But what remains significant is her traversing urban spaces, as she travels for her education, her classes, to meet with her lover, or for work. She seems constantly on the move. She drives, she rides in taxis, she is equally at ease in the palatial mansion, the classroom, parties, and various forms of public transactions that are dependent on cross-gender interactions. If these melodramas enact the journey of the male citizen stepping into modernity, then they are equally invested in staging the travel of the new woman, portrayed by Suchitra, as she negotiates varied forms of urban experiences that become enabling and transformative. Biswas rightly points out that it '...would be impossible to find any other actress being persistently cast as the professional woman... (showing) new mobility within the public space... who was endowed with the license of crossing the threshold of the home with ease' (2002: 123).

SURYOTORON: LOVE AND THE VISION OF SOCIAL UTOPIA

Suryotoron has a spatial imaginary tied to the protagonist—a woman who is a social crusader. She is continuously on the move, in the city and the slum. She wants to transform the working-class living environment of the urban poor.

FIGURE 1.3: Social Crusader, *Suryotoron*

Her radio programmes highlight the sharply polarised access to civic life and infrastructural support that the urban poor is excluded from. This pressing concern of urban living is not an ahistorical liberal humanist one, but is deeply tied to the actual lived experience that the city was witness to in the 1950s. 'By the 1950s, Kolkata's civic facilities were under severe strain and grossly inadequate' (M. Chatterjee 1990: 142). This 'severe strain' was occasioned by the influx of refugees, primarily in three major phases.

The first was during 1946–49; the second wave was due to the fresh communal clashes in 1949 in Khulna (in present Bangladesh, then East Pakistan), and again during 1951–58, comprising mostly of the educated middle classes who were forced to take up land in the south of the city. The refugee colonies existed side by side with urban elitist middle-class neighbourhoods (N. Chatterjee 1990). *Suryotoron* does not, of course, blame the refugees as the cause of the decaying and inadequate civic facilities, but I would argue that the slum and Anita's traversing of it can be placed against the enormity of the problem that the city was experiencing. Anita's radio talk provides documentary evidence of the various inadequacies that urban slum-dwellers experience on a daily basis: the lack of hygiene, of clean drinking water, poor sanitation, and rented tenements over which they have no rights. Anita, of course, blames the cartel of selfish landholders and their vested interests, which do not allow any possibility of betterment and change in the actual living conditions of the urban poor and middle classes.

A crucial marker of the Nehruvian model of development was the vision of the state as the controller and manager of production and redistribution of industrial development, as well as the redistribution of wealth. In this enterprise, private capitalist endeavours were considered to 'worsen economic inequality' (Kaviraj 2010: 223). In *Suryotoron*, all the private players, mainly architects and builders, epitomise the worst examples of greed and corruption. The film stages these anxieties through the discussions that Anita has with her father, a businessman who has inherited the ownership of the slum. The father represents the model of old wealth: he does not consider it necessary to improve living conditions in the slum. He is only concerned with the 'commissions' that he can wrangle from the various public-sector projects. He also places the responsibility for reform and development on the state, arguing that the individual cannot take on its role and responsibilities. Anita challenges this ideology and sets out to demonstrate how she can make even a limited change within the domain of her father's personal slum by creating the dream tower, Suryotoron.

The dream tower, in effect, becomes the story of modern post-independence Kolkata. It is this cityscape that is transformed through Anita's dream, Rajsekhar's money and sacrifice, and Somnath's architectural vision. The film publicity posters, booklet, and newspaper advertisements had the towering building in frame to the right and the lovers' faces in a smaller framing in the left corner. The film publicity itself signalled the dream tower as central to the idea of the romantic couple and their realisation of their romance, and the formation of the couple as an affective unit. It is central to the kind of self-fashioning that the lovers would signify for the social. This vision is integral to the imaginary of the vertical post-independence city that addresses the problem of using space more productively. Somnath designs a thirty-storied living complex which has a school, a swimming pool, and playground for children.[42] This architectural design draws on the Bauhaus form that can be identified with a particular socialist vision of using space optimally and productively with minimalist design, providing the residents with clean and airy living spaces.

The last sequence opens on the terrace at dawn, framing the two lovers looking at the first rays of the sun breaking through the clouds. Anita turns happily to Somnath, finally able to express her deep contentment at the realisation of her greatest dream. He turns to face her, and his left hand covers her hand, placed over the railing—the gesture making clear that he senses her need for reassurance. We see a crowd of happy people, the erstwhile slum dwellers, walking into the tower, the smiling couple exchange contented and loving gazes, and Anita extends her hand as Somnath holds it while they walk inside together. The shot dissolves to the high-rise standing tall and proud like its visionary and the creator. The film is invested in staking out the transformation of the lovers' selves as participants in the modern civic and public domain, where the state is no longer a stakeholder in this vision of urban modernity. In *Indrani*, too, we see something similar as the lovers help create a commune for displaced Partition survivors. It can be argued that this was perhaps signalling a move from governmentality to governance, in which the lovers will be the transformative locus. *Saptapadi* also imagines such a transformation as the lovers negotiate a religious divide.

Saptapadi: Love and Religion

This film participates in the discourse about religious identity through a clash between the ideological and religious position articulated by Krishnendu's father and the negation of that position through Krishnendu's conversion to Christianity. The Kali-worshipping father cannot accept the son's desire to marry outside his religious and racial community. Marriage based on inter-racial love is a source of conflict and threat, as it would bring the 'other' into the realm of the private familial space, a space that is the locus of all that is sacred. This clash is also generational. The father remains trapped in the image of Kali, the Hindu goddess central to his sense of self. Nandy critiques secularism as an idea imposed from above, untenable in a society governed by different notions of tolerance for 'others'. This tolerance is, of course, located within the ideas emanating from Hindu civilisation (Nandy 1999), which in this film is not demonstrated by the Brahmin father. One crucial plank of modern India was the Nehruvian vision of India as a secular nation. This vision was different in nature from the secular imaginary that evolved in the West, which was an '... ethics of behaviour and a prescription for political organisation...a separation between religion and politics...and for the individual it delineated the world into private and public arenas with activities appropriate to both' (Tejani 2007: 1).

India adopted secularism as a core constitutional principle. This was one of the important elements of nationalist self-conception and was tied to debates on citizenship in the post-independence state. Communalism, which was its other and which indicated the public presence of religion, could have no place in the modern nation (ibid.: 2). The vision of India as a secular state was central to the imaginary of India as a liberal democracy. According to Tejani,

> ...the Indian vision was not simply a separation of political from religious institutions, or creating a peculiarly Indian ethics of tolerance...rather it represented a formulation of nationalism that involved dovetailing liberal discourses around individual representation with definitions of the democratic majority as broadly Hindu. Moreover, secularism became one of the pillars

> of Indian nationalist thought because the architects of the new nation state—overwhelmingly middle class, upper-caste Hindu men—saw it as providing a counterpoint to challenges posed from the margins by Muslim and Dalit communities. (ibid.: 14–15)

The film, however, enacts a different transformation via Krishnendu's conversion. This transformative enactment is a move away from the Hindu majoritarian vision that underpins the idea of Indian secularism discussed above to the more forgiving and inclusive vision of religion that he embraces. This gesture is at the heart of the self-negotiation required for this love to achieve fulfillment. I shall discuss the conversion sequence and the last chance encounter of the estranged lovers which propels their reconciliation. Mr Brown, Rina's father, demands Krishnendu's conversion as a precondition for his marriage to Rina. Krishnendu's acquiescence to this proviso is enacted as a simple instrumental necessity, as he professes to be a non-believer. He informs Rina of his decision and knows that she too knows in her heart that she is his wife (modern love as a relationship of two souls, the *antar*, as Kaviraj has argued). From his rhetorical statement, we cut to a shot of a letter with his voiceover informing his father of his decision to marry. He signs it as 'the disobedient son'. We see the father's hand crushing the letter and moving to fling open the door. We see the Kali idol in frame; it has been shown before when we saw the father kneel in prayer before his goddess. Now we see him standing on frame right, face suffused with anger at his son's audacity. The aural track resonates with the clanging sound of cymbals and bells, underscoring his rage. The loud clash of bells ringing changes suddenly to the pealing of cathedral bells, with an accompanying dissolve to a shot of a church steeple. The camera slowly moves down to frame the imposing gothic façade of the cathedral and the left pan sees Krishnendu standing in the same right corner in which we had seen his father in the previous scene. His standing in the same place in the succeeding shot is meant to denote the shift from the older generation to the new modern generation, which will be able to live by its personal sense of right and wrong instead of being cowed down by rigid religious prescriptions. He is now dressed in a suit, whereas in the early parts of the film he was dressed mostly in the Bengali style, in dhoti and shirt. He had earlier donned a leather jacket and trousers during a song sequence when the lovers were riding a bike, signifying the modern mode of transport and the articulation of this modern imaginary. He moves into the church and we see him entering Rina's house. The entire sequence uses the ringing of church bells on the aural register. We have moved from the Kali-worshipping father to the newly converted Christian male who sees his religious conversion as a mere instrument through which to realise his romantic desire, only to be turned away by Rina. Rina feels compromised as she turns out to be the illegitimate daughter of Mr Brown and his Indian maid. She refuses to marry Krishnendu, becomes an alcoholic, and goes into a self-destructive spree since her certainties about her identity are shattered by the revelation of her illegitimacy. She falls victim to her personal fears and becomes an emotional wreck. Krishnendu becomes a missionary doctor and devotes himself to serving the poor.

Various plot twists stage their separation and their encounters as nurse and missionary doctor during World War II. The last sequence begins in a hospital room with an injured Rina. She is informed that she has had a successful surgery, performed by Reverend Krishnendu, who has taken responsibility for her as his wife. He comes to her bedside and puts his hand over her hair and forehead; we are now again in the domain of the lover's touch. He gives her his father's letter, which we had seen him read earlier. We know the father is repentant and contrite and accepts Rina's greatness and humane qualities, which have raised her to the status of a *Devi* [a goddess] in his eyes. The sanction, which had been absent until this moment, is now available. It is staged in the framing of the letter clutched prominently in Rina's hands. As Rina's tears fall and she clutches that letter, the camera cuts to a shot of the open window, from which we see a church in the distance. The aural register reverberates with the sound of a hymn and pealing church bells.

FIGURE 1.4: Inclusive Love, *Saptapadi*

With a dissolve we see Krishnendu walking out, carrying Rina in his arms to the sound of the ringing bells and the church in the distance. The filmic romance ends happily, unlike the doomed lovers of Shakespeare's *Othello*, which is at the centre of the film and the novella from which the film was adapted.[43] It is to be noted that the producers had inserted an advertisement signed by the author, consenting to and applauding the happy ending that the film had staged. This seemed to have been a regular practice, as I chanced upon many such statements applauding the film versions and the necessary changes made to the literary text.[44] This was possibly mounted to deflect criticisms against screen adaptations, especially with reference to the proverbial happy endings.

The ending thus signals a shift from the Hindu majoritarian position that Tejani refers to as the bedrock of the statist, secularist vision. This view was a hegemonic imposition undertaken by the state and subscribed to by the majority, as Nandy (1999) has argued. But at the same time, Nandy's advocacy of the ideal of traditional religious tolerance, which we do not see in the films discussed above, is actually built on a critique of modernity. This critique is mounted on the premise that the modern nation-state and its insistence on the value of scientific rationality is an anomaly in a traditional society. But what transpires when the traditional self has to give way to the modern? How does the 'modern' self negotiate a self that can conjoin the religious and the personal? What the film therefore signposts for us is a vision of modern individual choice that has not only rejected the traditionalist view espoused by the father—who seemed to find it problematic to accept the racial and religious 'other'—but also moves away from the statist view of the secular. It has done so by embracing a personal space for a religion that is always the 'other', the much-maligned religious affiliation of the colonial masters! The last shot, where we see the two lovers moving into the painted *mise en scène,* can be read as another instance of the symbolic space of the couple, which has been formed outside of the familial, but is definitely not outside the religious. We know that Rina is illegitimate; the only religion that can perhaps accept her is Christ's tolerant and humane vision. The personal then rejects the majoritarian Hindu secularist vision, as well as negates the shame of illegitimate birth. In rejecting the social, the personal renegotiates its subjectivity to embrace a different vision of an inclusive social, which seems to be the particular emotive charge of the cinematic text and drives its highly symbolic resolution.

In different ways, all three films stage the emergence of individual subjectivities, with their unrealised selves coming to the fore through the actualisation of their love. Vasudevan aptly summarises Biswas's reading of *Harano Sur* when he says that this film envisages '...a more modern occult, a dark underside of perception of individual sensibility and interiority' (2000: 13). The three films that I have discussed do not necessarily have the 'dark underside' of *Harano Sur,* involving the play of lost memory. The social is not absent, though; here, it is the couple who mandate the social. The particularity of this post-independence modernity is enacted through the articulation of repressed desires, which are given form and expression through varied melodramatic strategies of the hyperbolic staging of love. This is seen in *Sagarika,* in the enactment of the social transformation of Anita in *Suryotoron,* and also in terms of the ethical choices that *Saptapadi*'s Krishnendu and Rina make to realise their subjectivities and love. These varied negotiations all voice their challenges to tradition and the enactment of modernity, not so much as a rejection of either, but as necessary adjustments at the individual level that would enable the lovers to realise the romantic utopia central to their self-fashioning.

1950s Media Reception: Debates around *Sagarika* and the Love Films

The 1950s reception circuit of the romantic couple star text was imbricated within a hostile discursive regime very similar to the stardom discourses analysed by Majumdar (2009) and Wani (2016: 16–18) in the context of 1940s–50s Bombay cinema. Majumdar identifies a particular critique of the star's economic value as the 'stardom racket' (2009: 13). Stars became assured guarantees against investments—or at least they were perceived as such—and hence they commanded astronomical sums as fees; conversely, they came in for their share of proportional blame if the film fared poorly. They were thus not only typecast, but were also repeated in many films in order to cash in on their popularity. The predominant trope that defined stardom in this period was a discourse of 'excess and morality' (ibid.). The women stars were also at the receiving end of a stringent discourse of morality, which can be located within the template of the domesticated ideal of the nationalist imaginary pertaining to the 'new woman' (Chatterjee 1999). A similar discourse of critique and moralistic value judgement is visible against the star pair in Bengal.

As discussed earlier, the *Rupmancha*[45] editor Kaalish Mukherjee, bemoaning the dearth of good stars to replace the Suchitra–Uttam duo, had called for concerted attempts to train and manufacture newer stars to break the monotony.[46] It needs to be reiterated that during 1954–56, the pair had appeared in thirteen films, and by 1959 in twenty-two films. These love films, designated as *pranaydharmi chobis* (loosely translated as 'romantic films'),[47] were at the receiving end of consistent critical assessment, as stated in the Introduction. Some of the responses expressed serious misgivings about the nature of 'unprincipled modernity' that these films were articulating, visible in newspapers such as *Jugantor* and *Anandbazaar*. Despite the overwhelming audience acceptance of the two stars, the films were panned and criticised for their unrealistic plots and storylines. It is important to highlight this hostile contemporary reception in the context of any 'recovery' of the love films in the present (Chatterjee 2010: 70).

The scathing criticism levelled against *Sagarika* focused on the blatant display of suggestive and titillating, lustful expressions, which were considered 'immoral'. This 'depiction of depraved lust' could be harmful for young audiences, who could lapse into 'erotic follies'.[48] The filmmakers were accused of following a '*videshi*' or 'foreign' love story style by the reviewer of *Desh* (presumably this was a reference to Hollywood love story conventions).[49] The reviewer claimed that in the case of these two stars—both of whom were married—the rampant display of on-screen lust was inflaming audience passion, evidenced by catcalls and suggestive gestures. This was deemed disreputable and harmful for the entire film industry. Predictably, Kaalish Mukherjee was at the forefront of the critical backlash. He launched a tirade against the use of Suchitra's real name in the publicity campaign, which would incite the audiences to see her as herself and not as Sagarika.[50] His response can be paraphrased thus: 'Srimati Suchitra giving new pleasures through herself, this is sexual pleasure, which will inflame the sexual appetite and satiate desires by filling all the veins and arteries of the audience'.[51] Kaalish Mukherjee continued to criticise the duo for displaying 'unseemly behaviour', which was repeated in their next release, *Ekti Raat*.

The readers took their cue from these reviews and flooded the magazine pages with objections, primarily centred on the woman star and her 'cheap commercial mentality', which was seen to be at odds with her social status as a married woman. Phrases such as 'cheap sex appeal' and 'sex-appealing capacity' were routinely used for her. Her on-screen characterisation, which deployed 'lustful behaviour' and her revealing attire of sheer chiffon and georgette sarees were deplored as cheap, commercial antics—not seemly for a *bhadramahila*![52] A reader blamed the producers for

> putting their money only to excite sexual appeal, *youna avedan*. In most films this sexual appeal is accompanied by revealing costumes which is not possible for any 'bhadramahila' to wear. With this there is shamelessness, with the facial expressions suggesting lust. This abundance of embracing and excessive physical closeness, it has reached endemic proportions. They are showing unseemly behaviour, pinching their cheeks. *Agnipariksha, Sobar Upare, Saap Mochon, Sagarika, Drishti*, not only embracing but actually pushing and shoving, *dhakkadhaki*. Publicity is like pimping, started with *Sagarika*, how far are you dragging us oh beautiful one? There is no sign of educated good taste, only obscene attitude. Amritabazzar ad says, Suchitra Sen means sensation when paired with Uttam, what does this mean? What is the meaning of such *Pranaya* [Romance]?[53]

In the 1950s, the Suchitra–Uttam pair and their romantic films thus came in for criticism as they were accused of objectionable acting with 'suggestive lustful facial expressions' and scenes featuring 'excessive physical closeness'. The 'unseemly behaviour' of 'pinching cheeks and excessive embracing' was deemed detrimental and would drag the entire 'Bengali community into the deep end'. These readers wanted the Bengal Film Journalists' Association (BFJA)[54] to intervene. In fact, the *Jugantor* Cinema page carried a news item which mentioned that the Bengal Cinema Chamber had taken up the issue of obscenity in the film publicity campaign, and its resolution condemned the 'low mentality that would be detrimental to Bengali culture and cinema'.[55]

This fraught and contentious backlash against the Suchitra–Uttam romantic films and their stardom continued throughout this phase. Assessments of their career in a magazine offer an illuminating insight into the critical template used to evaluate star value.[56] Discussing Uttam's career graph, the writer concluded that he had evolved as an actor and had justly acquired his unprecedented star status, not accorded to any other actor in the annals of Bengali cinema. The article on Suchitra's stardom accepted her box-office draw and analysed her star status with Uttam and other heroes. The writer commended Suchitra's good performances with all her male leads while acknowledging that the 'new, realistic modern romances' opposite Uttam had fantastic box-office appeal. Therefore, the 'excess of embracing and romance' was understandable as the producers needed to recover their costs and generate profit. Hence, the 'titillating publicity campaigns' were deemed necessary too. It is interesting that the article on Uttam does not mention the problematic publicity of their films and significant that the publicity language, visual stills, and readers' responses all come together to rest on the female star's body, underscoring the fact that stardom itself has been seen as feminine (Majumdar 2009; Morin 1961). So while *Sagarika* and other films have become important texts for the cinema studies canon as deploying the trope of female desire and articulating a certain kind of feminine subjectivity, contemporary responses expressed different kinds of anxieties resulting from the excesses of the female star, both on- and off-screen.

It is evident from these two articles that box-office successes did not translate into an easy acceptance of their star value as economic capital, although Suchitra seems to be at the receiving end of both moral and critical censure. It was felt that her responsibility to her spectators was conditional to her accepting that she had to behave in a decorous manner as well as temper her commercial instincts. Kaalish Mukherjee, though, put the blame squarely on Suchitra. He wrote that Suchitra was paid handsomely for all the excessive, erotic on-screen display and could not be absolved of her moral responsibility. Her producers wanted adequate returns; she dictated the terms of her remuneration, which was reportedly 4,000–5,000 Indian rupees at a time when the cost of production was approximately Rs 100,000. By the end of 1959, she was reportedly getting about Rs 10,000; moreover, she had demanded and received Rs 100,000 for *Saptapadi* (Chattopadhyaya 2005: 24).[57]

Perhaps this antipathy for commercial instincts can be explained through what Gooptu has termed as a peculiar discourse of 'film as art', which projected 'film as non commerce'. This particular discourse was, of course, central to the *bhadralok* self-imaginary and seems to be the context in which the entire commercial enterprise of cinema is held as culpable for displaying the worst possible consequences of this drive. Even the sphere of work governed by money and commerce had to temper its economic imperatives within the codes of respectability and decorum. She explains this antipathy to commercial interests as a peculiar manifestation related to the 'Bengali ideal of the ethical as rooted in the non commercial... money, or rather too much of it, was supposed to be a disruptive force, which violated the ideal of humanism and an ethical life' (Gooptu 2010: 93). Since Suchitra was delivering box-office hits, she was held culpable for not tempering her commercial interests, given her status as a married *bhadramahila* belonging to an elite family. This critical clamour indicates the contentious manner in which star texts were imbricated in contested meanings over labour, as I discussed in the Introduction, drawing upon Clark (1995). Clearly, her economic capital was not enough to endow her with cultural or symbolic capital in this constitutive moment. Her travels to Bombay were equally subjected to criticism. This fragment of negative evaluation needs to be contextualised within the larger historical matrix of Bengali industry at this time, as it perceived Bombay as a threat to its status.

This threat stemmed from the loss of the all-India market that Bengali cinema of the 1930–40s had been able to command. This could not continue in the late 1940s due to many factors. The war-time economy, the partition of Bengal in 1947, and Bombay's ability to sustain and augment its status via the star system and finances, as well as better infrastructural support, were responsible for Kolkata losing its position of eminence in the all-India market. However, in the 1950s, the movement of technicians, film personnel, and actors to Bombay was a given fact (Gooptu 2010: 115–49). Regardless of actual conditions, there seems to be a preference for unadulterated 'Bengaliness' that was evoked to differentiate Bengali cinema from Bombay cinema. Two readers' letters from *Rupmancha* that I quote below illustrate the general anxiety that contemporary Bengali cinema, in its aping of Bombay cinema, seemed to generate. Mr B, from Balaram Ghosh Street, Kolkata wrote: 'Bengali cinema has always shown the reality of its society, but now the audiences are "developing juicy tastes"! The Bengali audiences are in danger of losing their uniqueness. They are being seduced by visions of "taxi drivers" and their naked dances with sensuous women.'[58]

In the same issue, one Mr C writes,

> Bombay copies western films, but these can never be the idols made in Kumartuli, they are mere replicas of earthen images to be bought cheaply from the Chetala *haat*, in western films they show legs, here the camera shows waist. There the heroes kiss, here in the name of love they do something that cannot even be mentioned.[59]

Not only films, but the movement of people, especially stars, to Bombay was criticised. What is of particular interest is the deployment of a language predicated along gender. Besides the usual snide remarks at actors, actresses who were lured to Bombay by the charm and glamour of money and fame were commented upon for their lack of pride in their Bengali identity. To cite one example, this caption under the photo of composer Robin Majumdar, who had just returned from Bombay, said,

> ...this propensity to go to Bombay is the allure of the common prostitute. Bengali resembles the 'grihavadhu' [the domesticated wife], her beauty is sublime [*rup lavanya*, calm beauty], whereas Bombay's glamour is like that of the common public woman, all glitz and show. Only those artists, who can be satisfied with serving the softer beauty of Bengal and not be swayed by the glamour of the public woman, can achieve true success.[60]

In the 1950s, Suchitra began her Bombay travels as well.[61] Her first film *Devdas* (1955), opposite Dilip Kumar, was a big hit. But her casting in the Bombay-style musical *Champakali* (1957) opposite Bharat Bhushan and Shubha Khote did not garner appreciation from either the press or spectators in Kolkata.[62] Given the antipathy Bombay cinema seemed to be generating in the 1950s, it would not be far-fetched to suggest that along with her other 'excesses', this too gave rise to a display of sarcasm and snide asides at her commercial instincts that were luring her away. Not only was she behaving in an unseemly fashion through her display of 'cheap sex-appeal', but she was guilty of trying to make a career in Bombay, too.

It is evident that the region did not accept the tremendously successful romantic pair unconditionally, nor did it endow the female star with any cultural capital in this decade. It is worth recalling Michael Herzfeld's formulation of 'cultural intimacy' (2005 [1997]) to understand this antipathy against the pair and the woman star in particular. Cultural intimacy is an important construct that allows modern subjects to imagine their hold and power over cultural identities. He defines this as a 'recognition of those aspects of cultural identity that are considered to be a source of external embarrassment abroad but nevertheless provide insiders with the assurance of their common sociality…' (ibid.: 3). The pair's romantic aura and screen iconicity created a template of embarrassment in the reception circuits as the films and the stars were seen to ape non-Bengali cultural tropes to denote love on screen. Despite idealised ethical characterisations, the visual articulations of romance were deemed objectionable. Star monopoly and maximisation of star presence and value were not enough to accrue cultural capital. Additionally, for the woman star, her onscreen excesses, her career choices, and her professional status were all scrutinised incessantly and were used to create a stardom that fostered a negative image.

Her public appearances gave rise to anxieties regarding her *bhadramahila* status as well.[63] Suchitra's star text needs to be therefore slotted differently. This epitome of an elite *bhadramahila*, the daughter-in-law of a reputed south Kolkata family, inhabited a different terrain of public censure in this phase of her career. Her sexualised, erotic image, which enabled her box-office successes and helped her to negotiate better remuneration, was not a compulsion born from a deprived economic situation or familial impoverishment. Such narratives of poverty and belonging to a non-Bengali origin were very often invoked to justify the life stories of film actresses who came from 'questionable' backgrounds.[64] Her reputable spatial and familial location was comparable to that of Arundhuti Debi, who had a Master's degree; however, Debi had begun her career as a staff on the payroll of New Theatres. Suchitra was an independent actor who, as discussed earlier, was severely criticised for her commercial mentality. As I analyse in Chapter Five, her insistence on using her name before Uttam for the credit sequences of their romantic couple films is worth noting. She certainly played out all the polyphonic constituents of Dyer's formulation of the star persona, framed along the axis of a deeply gendered terrain. Did the popular then create a map of selfhood that enacted a particular form of gendered modernity? Was Suchitra the site/sight of the unease of an anxiety-ridden modernity that played itself out on her body?

In comparison, Uttam was a middle-class person who was located in Bhowanipur, while Suchitra was always located in a posh south Kolkata neighbourhood. He transformed his 'ordinariness' to become an 'extraordinary' superstar whose 'tragic' personal life did not detract from his audience base or symbolic and cultural capital. His long live-in relationship with divorced fellow actor Supriya Debi (1935–2018) was not seen as problematic since he continued to support his family in Bhowanipur, as I discuss in Chapter Four. If anything, this aspect seems to have added to his romantic appeal and he was allowed certain liberties that were denied to 'mere' humans. Suchitra, though, seems to occupy a socially and culturally liminal space that could only be overturned much later in her career, as I show in Chapter Three.

Notes

1. *Sagarika* was directed by Agragaami, a new collective that broke away from Agradoot. Agradoot, the first collective in the industry, was formed in 1946 (Bibhuti Laha, Camera; Jatin Das, Sound; Sailen Ghosh, Laboratory specialist; Netai Bhattacharya, Scenarist; Bimal Ghosh, Production). Agragaami, the second collective, had worked with Agradoot before breaking away from them. Saroj Dey, Nishith Bandopadhyaya, Parbati Sankar, and Jayanto Bhattacharya started their careers with *Sagarika*. They were young and able to challenge the accepted notions of love and romance. Despite its similarities with other films of the cluster, *Sagarika* was pathbreaking in many ways and more daring in its plotting of the screen romance.

2. Directed by Agradoot, *Suryotoron* released in 1958. The story credit did not cite the Ayn Rand novel *Fountainhead*, on which it was based. It was credited to Gouri Prassana Majumdar, the noted scriptwriter and lyricist.

3. *Saptapadi* was directed by Ajay Kar, the ace-cameraman-turned-director, and based on a novella by the noted writer Tarashankar Bandopadhyaya (1898–1971). The shoot was stalled twice due to differences between the

two stars. Suchitra had stipulated that while she was shooting, the producer would not be allowed on the floor. It was Uttam's home production. She reportedly also asked for Rs 100,000 as remuneration. In those days, this sum was unheard of in the Bengali industry. It took around two years to film (Chattopadhyaya 2005; Chaudhari 1995; Mukhopadhyaya 2000).

4. Love and romance became significant tropes that defined the new citizen in the 1950s. Scholars have drawn attention to the centrality of love and its enactment in 1950s Bombay cinema (Sangari 2011; Wani 2016). Sangari calls the 1950s Bombay cinema the 'episteme of love and romance' that became 'a sign of the national-secular' (2011: 267). After independence, the liberating exuberance of freedom became most apparent in the imaginary of love, as it 'could become a synonym for many freedoms including the freedom from religious ascription' since the citizens could 'envision themselves as secular citizens rather than members of a caste or religious community' (ibid: 268).

5. In the context of the Bengali modern, the journey of the modern self is tied to the *bhadralok* investment in the journey to the city, which enables this group to acquire the gloss of education, culture, and opportunities for employment. 'This move to the city involved much more than acquiring a degree. It was a lesson in urban life, in new notions, experiences and habits' (Bhattacharya 2005: 6). This particular trajectory of the Bengali middle class has been the subject of scholarly work (Bhattacharya 2005; Sarkar 1997).

6. The appeal of Uttam Kumar's filmic characters for middle-class audiences has been analysed by Someshewar Bhowmick, Iraban Bosu Roy, and others. See the special *Chitrabhash* issue on Uttam Kumar, Vol. 36, January–December 2001. Sharmishtha Gooptu (2010) too uses the *bhadralok* paradigm to explain his popularity. However, we need more archival research into this aspect of star appeal. Even a cursory reading of readers' letters in film magazines of the period give us enough indication that the spectators were fully aware of the performative codes of both the cinema and stardom, such as plot twists, the operation of chance as a narrative staple, the made-up and fashionable star appearances, and were not fooled by narrative slippages. I am referring to readers' letters from popular film magazines *Rupmancha*, *Deepali*, etc. The editorials and other features in these magazines repeatedly alerted spectators to these discrepancies, which were regarded as a peculiar problem associated with the melodramatic form. In the absence of reception studies, it would be more productive to engage with the spectatorial positioning and address mounted in the films as I attempt.

7. In the context of Hollywood, Virginia Wright Wexman (1993) has investigated the creation of the romantic couple.

8. It is common practice to use the term 'Uttam–Suchitra' in general. However, the term's inversion has been explained in the Introduction of this book.

9. Saratchandra (1896–1937) provided the star pair with four narratives, *Chandranath*, *Gribodaho*, *Kamallata*, and *Rajlaxmi O Srikanto*, which had extremely successful filmic adaptations and added to their box-office draw and filmic self-fashioning.

10. Other writers whose stories and novels were used for films discussed in this book as relevant are footnoted in the individual chapters.

11. Biswas reads *Agniparikhsha's* performance as a battle in the heroine which is absent from the hero's character. Therefore the moral discourse belongs to him. This moral discourse would act through the heroine in terms of a modern patriarchy. Hence, the heroine would be defined as 'modern=traditional' just as Bankim Chandra imagined her in his text, 'Prachina O Nobina': 'the new woman as the new old woman' (Biswas 2002: 109).

According to Gooptu (2010), this performance opens up an entire field of feminine subjectivity which cannot be accommodated within the film's overtly patriarchal locus (ibid.: 167). Sarkar suggests that this film 'echoes the curious vacillations of its female protagonist: it wants to be a reformist film with a feminine perspective but remains very much the product of a heteropatriarchal culture industry' (2009: 151).

12. *Lagnabhrashtha* implies 'a failure to commence one's work within the astrologically appointed hours'. This is related to the Hindu marriage ritual where the rites have to be performed within a specific time limit decided by the priest. If, for some reason, that time lapses and the marriage cannot be solemnised, then the bride is condemned as *lagnabhrashtha*, that is, one who has missed the opportune moment.

13. I discuss this aspect of Uttam's physicality in Chapter Four.

14. Uttam appears aggressive in very few films of their romantic cluster. In *Suryotoron*, Somnath is shown as a threatening male figure in a scene where he hints at harming Anita's reputation by spreading rumours of sexual intimacy. In a later film, *Alo Amar Alo*, he stages a kidnapping and keeps Suchitra imprisoned. I shall discuss the contours of Uttam's masculinity in greater detail in Chapter Four.

15. For a discussion of the colonial politics of masculinity outside Bengal, see Pandian (1996).

16. For an interesting discussion of androgyny in cultural traditions in India, see O'Flaherty, *Sexual Metaphors and Animal Symbols in Indian Mythology* (1980).

17. Gooptu (2010) does admit that commercial interest was important for the industry, but does not follow it through. Chatterjee (2007) does not engage with the commercial product differentiation and locates the romantic affect in the narrative and formal aspects of the films. But one cannot lose sight of the fact that these films were being made with specific commercial considerations, and therefore it is important to consider the box-office draw as a serious factor. Additionally, one needs to unravel the specific objections against star value and critical discourse that was a significant part of the discursive regime in which these romantic films circulated in the 1950s and 1960s.

18. It is important to remember Gledhill's observation that we encounter stars through their bodies (1991: 210). Therefore, the star body and its accoutrements are important for the relationship of the image and the spectator. The cinematic apparatus's objectification of the female star body has been extensively worked out in Laura Mulvey's work (1996). The spectacle of the female star body is both seductive and alluring, yet it conceals the marks of labour that have gone into producing that spectacular image. Mulvey draws upon Marxist and Freudian insights to decode this construction.

19. We know from star studies that the star is created when the 'private' and public images coalesce. In Indian star discourses, the private was very often elided or appeared in different guises. This aspect of the star text that used innuendo to cite gossip and rumour about star affairs is similar to what Neepa Majumdar (2009) has identified in the context of Bombay cinema and film journalism and film publicity. In the Indian context, the use of 'private lives' of stars was displaced in circuits of gossip that used the trope of innuendo and the literary wink, and not direct reportage, the 'official discourse' of Hollywood. She suggests that in Bombay film, the gossip about star love affairs is brought back to the surface of the screen in the absence of legitimised official discourse. Wani (2016) uses this suggestion to read the trope of romance in 1950s Bombay cinema and discusses the real and screen romances of famous star pairs such as Raj Kapoor–Nargis, Guru Dutt–Waheeda Rehman, Dilip Kumar–Meena Kumari, etc.

20. In effect, this particular fragment of the star couples' romance has travelled from the constitutive moment and survives in different sites in the contemporary as well. Bruno's (2002) intervention of the 'travel of emotions' that I have referred to in my Introduction is particularly useful for understanding this fragment. I excavate the reinvention of the Suchitra–Uttam romance in Chapter Five.

21. I am indebted to Subhajit Chatterjee, Film Studies, Jadavpur University, for drawing my attention to the film publicity mounted for *Sagarika* and allowing access to his unpublished PhD dissertation.

22. *Sagarika* publicity advertisement, *Jugantor*, 5 February 1956.

23. Subhajit Chatterjee (2007) surmises that this could be tied to the institutional changes affecting the industry in the wake of the 1951 Central Board of Film Censors report. This report made it possible to market films with generic categories. I think what he means is that the industry was responding to the categorisation and product differentiation that the introduction of the censorship categories would allow. The issue of U or A certification would allow directors and producers to create products that would have more 'adult themes' in the films. I feel that notwithstanding this surmise, the industry would still have preferred to have their films certified as U, and market the Suchitra–Uttam films to a universal audience, rather than limit their audience base. He too accepts that it is a tentative formulation and needs more rigorous archival work.

24. *Rupmancha* (July–August 1956: 83–84).

25. In contrast, Uttam's affair and live-in relationship with Supriya was well-known and featured regularly in film magazines. His fellow actor Sabitri Chatterjee has also stated that they had an affair and Uttam wanted to marry her. It is only his supposed relationship with Suchitra that remains cloaked in silence, albeit making appearances in fictional novellas and tele-serials. I discuss these re-imaginings in the last chapter, 'Afterlives'.

26. Uttam had confessed to Robi Bosu that he had platonic love for Suchitra and did not know if she understood his love for her (*Saat Rongo* Vol. 1: 400).

27. *Agnipariksha* occupies a prominent status in the Suchitra–Uttam canon as it is their first big hit and shows the cluster of concerns that was consolidated as part of their romantic status (Chatterjee 2007; Gooptu 2010; Mitra 2009; Nag 1998; Sarkar 2010).

28. Chatterjee (2007) regards this advertisement as one strategy that signalled the exotic nature of this romance. It is true that the quality of the dream-like picture does evoke the exotic, but more importantly, it was used in the narrative itself to create the unique nature of the overwhelming physical love that Sagarika experiences with Arun.

29. *Chandranath* (1957) was the first Bengali film released in Metro Cinema Hall in Kolkata. This particular theatre was owned by MGM in the colonial period and only screened English films at the time (Chattopadhyaya 2008: 24). However, I have been unable to corroborate this detail as the

Bengali Film Directory does not mention this. It only provides the release date. It ran for thirteen weeks at a stretch. The first week's collection was pegged at a stupendous amount in the 1950s, at 2,30,138 Indian rupees (Gupto 2003: 31). The post-publicity advertisements for this hit film showed serpentine queues of spectators surrounding the portico of the hall. The building was seen tilting at an angle as if unable to withstand the weight of the spectators. The rest of the advertisement featured a signed telegram sent by the Metro Company expressing delight at the huge success: 'heartiest congratulations. Never have we seen such huge rush at the box office' (*Jugantor*, 29 November 1957).

The huge public acceptance of the star pair circulated via these media sites as well. This seems to be a conscious attempt at deflecting the criticism against the display of excessive sensuality that had become a part of their screen text. *Chandranath* too came in for harsh criticism due to the enactment of erotic love between Chandranath/Uttam and Saryu/Suchitra. The criticism explicitly compared the film to the Saratchandra text and commented on why the producer and director would choose to show the principal characters in such an erotic manner. Saryu's characterisation was also criticised for resorting to specific framings that displayed Suchitra's body, and her manicured nails were particularly criticised (*Rupmancha*, November–December 1957). Post *Sagarika*, this trope of the erotic and sensuous display of love as well as the foregrounding of Suchitra's glamour came to define the Suchitra–Uttam star text, and became part of the discourse within which their stardom was imbricated. However, the framing of her sensuous glamour seems to have started around 1955 with *Sobar Upare*, as I have discovered readers' letters commenting on her sexualised framings in that film.

30. Film review, *Jugantor* (21 November 1957).

31. Edgar Morin has drawn our attention to the necessity of physical beauty in stars, which transforms them into superstars and creates a mythology around them. 'Beauty is one of the sources of "star quality,"' he asserted. 'The mythology of the romantic stars associates moral beauty with physical beauty. The star's ideal body reveals an ideal soul' (1961: 42, 47).

32. Biswas argues that there is an 'aspect of guiltlessness in the predominantly urban persona that Sen had, playing roles of highly educated professional women. It marks out this phase from earlier and later ones in the popular film where the modern woman is essentially a guilty construction' (2002: 122). This depiction of the modern woman as a guilty construction is narratively foregrounded in *Grihodaho*, which I discuss in the next chapter.

33. It is this particular form of melodramatic excess associated with the star persona that Gledhill (1991) has posited, and I extend her insight to

read the self-fashioning related to Suchitra's star text. I have discussed this relationship between the star figure and melodramatic form in the Introduction.

34. Suchitra's sexualised erotic image was contained somewhat with her essaying strong author-backed roles in the 1960s. However, her public appearances continued to be critiqued. I shall discuss this aspect in Chapter Three. This eroticised image finally gets reconfigured in biographies such as *Suchitrar Katha* and *Onno ek Suchitra*, which foregrounded her *sadhika* image post-retirement. I shall discuss in Chapter Five.

35. The lotus has symbolic resonances for Indian audiences as it is a common flower, while the rose is quite alien as a symbol of love and romance. Especially in Bengal, lotus has a ubiquitous everyday presence, used for religious and decorative purposes.

36. It is interesting to note that usually, this kind of trick photography is used in mythological films to show divine events, for instance Prabhat Film Company's *Sant Tukaram* (1936). For instance, this technique is used to depict Tuka's ascent to heaven, or in Phalke's *Kaliya Mardan* (1919), when the divine boy Krishna appears to slay the demon Putana. In contrast, in this Bengali romantic film, a similar camera technique is employed to show modern love in the mid-1950s.

37. A review in *Jugantor*, dated 28 November 1958, says that *Suryotoron* sees the trio of Agradoot and Uttam–Suchitra come together with a similar yet dissimilar story of love that the *rasiks*, that is, connoisseurs, would expect from them. Of course, the sarcastic tone of the reviewer is targeting the romantic thrills that this film would deliver to its audiences.

38. It needs to be noted that there was an unofficial ban on showing the kiss on screen by the 1950s. This ban was put in place after the 1951 Film Enquiry Committee report. Scholars have drawn our attention to the intense debates on the kiss in the 1960s (Mazumdar 2011) as well as the reasons for the ban, which was occasioned by the demands for a sanitised version of nationalist culture (Prasad 1998). Wani discusses the Bombay industry responses to these prohibitions and concludes that the 1950s moment was witness to intense debates on censorship that underscored the puritanical impulse of the nationalist state and the film industry and spectators (Wani 2016: 19–20). However, as is evident, the industry found ways of staging romance and love that were quite suggestive in their evocation, and not necessarily of coy dissolves of birds and flowers.

39. Saroj Dey (Agragaami collective) had described the last scene as very bold for its time, and this passionate embrace became an important

constituent of the screen iconicity of the star pair (quoted in Mukhopadhyaya 2000: 37).

40. This middle class-centric urban thematic drive is also seen in 1950s Bombay cinema. Vasudevan says, 'The city, urban space takes on an increasingly important function in setting a new generic dynamic in motion. 1950s negotiation of urban space will become central to the fashioning of new melodramatic narrative strategies' (2010: 68). This newfound romance of the self with the city is not the traumatic journey of self as Ashis Nandy (2001) has argued. Rather, the Andersonian idea of this journey of the modern individual as a 'secular pilgrimage' (Anderson 1991) perhaps describes this trajectory better. In the Hindi films of the 1950s and 1960s, a similar drive is seen in some films, such as *CID, Shri 420, and Taxi Driver* (Kaviraj 2004; Mazumdar 2009).

41. Wani has analysed this relationship in the context of 1950s Bombay cinema. See her discussion in 'City of Love' (2016).

42. It is interesting to note that the design of Suryotoron is influenced by the Bauhaus style of modernist design. This particular architectural style was known for its rejection of other modern styles and imagined buildings as vertical; it was seen as a socialist spatial architectural style. The first of these buildings in Kolkata was the New Secretariat building designed by the MIT-trained H. Rahman, who was well-known for this particular design. This building was constructed between 1952 and 1954. With its fourteen stories, grids, and square windows, this seems remarkably similar to what Somnath designs for Anita.

43. Krishnendu and Rina's love blossoms as they perform Desdemona's death scene from the Shakespearean tragedy. In the scene, we see the would-be lovers enacting Othello and Desdemona, using intimate gestures of touch and caress just before Othello smothers a sleeping Desdemona. After the end of the scene, we see Rina touch her cheek and throat where Krishnendu had caressed her. The novella does not have a happy ending. In the literary text, Rina disappears after their reunion. She has become an alcoholic and a dissipated woman, with multiple partners. Krishnendu dedicates his life to leprosy patients and by the end of the novella, he too contracts the disease. The text ends with a suggestion of his impending death. The film review in *Anandbazaar* on 28 October 1961 criticises the departure from the literary text. But the advertisement signed by the author Tarashankar endorses the change (13 October 1961).

44. I found Tarashankar's signed statement in newspaper advertisements endorsing the changes in *Bicharak* (1959), starring Uttam and Arundhuti Debi, as well as Prabahvati Devi Saraswati's statement that she liked and

approved of the filmic adaptation, *Sanjher Pradeep* (1955), starring Suchitra and Uttam, which was based on her book.

45. Suchitra had a disagreement with the *Rupmancha* editor Kaalish Mukherjee towards the start of her career, and for some time *Rupmancha* had boycotted her publicity advertisements (Gupto 2003: 65–66; Mitra 2009).

46. *Rupmancha* (February–March 1956: 58).

47. This phrase, *pranaydharmi chobi*, seems to have been a coinage of newspaper critics. The industry did not market these romances as such. They would actually demarcate them as films with the two stars. It was an acceptable marketing practice. In the case of the two stars, however, by 1955 the credit sequence or advertisement would use Suchitra's name before Uttam's or place it in the same font and line. This practice began with *Saanjher Pradeep*. I shall engage with this practice in my discussion of Suchitra's professional status in Chapter Five.

48. All the English phrases that describe the criticisms or reader's responses in the book, song lyrics, and dialogues have been translated by me from the original Bengali.

49. *Desh* (11 February 1956).

50. *Rupmancha* (May–June 1956: 113).

51. This particular objection was responding to a series of newspaper advertisements that I have referred to earlier in the chapter. For instance, the 5 February 1956 ad referred to the 'terrible winter being warmed up by the aggressive flow of love'. Another series referred to the new depiction of 'Suchitra–Uttam leela'. 'Leela' is a word that carries connotations of sexual peccadilloes, very often used for the Radha-Krishna sexual games.

52. I have to admit that my archive is incomplete as I could only locate selected copies of this magazine and the responses quoted above seemed to come from men. I do not know if women would have expressed a different reaction as they too might have been governed by their middle-class location.

53. *Rupmancha* (July–August 1956: 89).

54. This has since been renamed as the West Bengal Film Journalists' Association (WBFJA).

55. *Jugantor* (12 February 1956).

56. *Sharadiya Chitrabani* (October 1956).

57. As mentioned earlier, this film had a chequered journey and was produced by Uttam Kumar.

58. *Rupmancha* (May–June 1954).

59. The responses are marked by class anxieties, as is obvious. The locales need some explanation. The reference to Kumartuli is to the place in the city where the artists make idols of the goddess Durga for the annual Durga Puja

festival. Chetala is the local bazaar, where cheap goods are available. The comparison is to artistic creation and value as opposed to sleazy replicas.

60. *Rupmancha* (July–August 1956: 99).

61. Uttam's Bombay sojourn began only in 1967 with the Hindi remake of *Agnipariksha, Chhoti si Mulaquat.*

62. Suchitra also starred in *Musafir* (1957), *Bumbai ka Babu* and *Sarhad* (1960), *Mamata* (1966), and *Aandhi* (1974). The last two films enabled her to garner critical acceptance and she was awarded for both. I shall discuss this aspect in Chapter Three.

63. I shall discuss this aspect of her star text in Chapter Five.

64. For instance, Kanan Devi, the big star of the studio period, came from a socially castigated background as her mother belonged to the singing profession and her father was unknown. Her mother was an abandoned woman. Kanan Devi had to strive very hard to achieve a respectable status within the film industry, and it was her second marriage to Haridas Bhattacharya that greatly facilitated an improvement in her social status. In her autobiography, she describes the terrible economic condition and social marginalisation that necessitated her joining the film industry (*Sobare Aami Nomi* 1971). Sabitri Chatterjee came from a poor *bhadra* family and had to join the industry due to her impoverished family situation (*Chena Mukh* 1980).

2

The New Woman

Marital Sagas

Introduction

In Chapter One, I examined the iconicity of the Suchitra–Uttam pairing as the 'ultimate romantic couple' through their on-screen love stories, which were such a rage in the 1950s and 1960s and came to define, for many, the idea of romance itself. In this chapter I shall look at three films, *Indrani* (1958), *Grihodaho* (1967), and *Nabaraag* (1971), which articulate the cinematic experience of the post-marriage phase of the romantic couple. I focus on the marital relationship here as an important transaction that, apart from defining the individual self, also acts as a map that enables entry into the social via the personal. 'Love marriage' as a social category was an important construct of the modern Indian self. Like 'romance and love', marriage too was not only a matter of individuation, but also a transaction that participated in varied negotiations of the colonial (and post-independence) modern in Bengal (Orsini 2007). A marital partner chosen of one's individual volition was a significant step towards articulating individual choice and freedom. Marriages made on the basis of mutual love and attraction challenged the acceptable modes of behaviour for both men and women. Given the structure of the *ekannavarty paribaar* (joint family/single kitchen), choosing one's marriage partner oneself was considered a threat to the prevalent power structures in the family. Marriage is a significant experience that defines the self in its relation to the social and the familial. It is important as a normative paradigm in patriarchal society as it ensures the continuation of the family lineage. Hence, the choice of a marriage partner acquires tremendous significance.

Moreover, traditional Bengali society was governed by the idea of *kulinism*, where the clan and community lineages were extremely important. Marriages could only be contracted between acceptable partners selected on the basis of their affiliation to the *kul* or *jaat*, loosely translated as clan/caste. It was considered a sin to marry outside of these *kul* or *jaat* affiliations, as that would result in crossing rigid caste boundaries (Ray 1995).

Given these social mandates, the romantic ideal of 'love marriage' was a deeply threatening and contested one, and the marriage that realised this ideal framed significant questions about the self-fashioning of the modern individual in colonial and post-independence Bengal. The questions that I address in this chapter through the films I have identified include: What contours of modern love marriages get enacted in these three films? Does the formation of the nuclear couple, which became a significant social institution in the post-independence period, appear as an uncontested domain of compatibility and togetherness, or do the films stage marriages as discordant? How does the new woman, the *bhadramahila*, transact the married state, and how is she placed in relation to her marital home? How does the star text intersect with this cinematic conjugal map? Before turning my lens on the cinematic articulations of these issues, I will map the issue of conjugality as it emerges in the text of this ultimate romantic screen couple.

SUCHITRA–UTTAM: 'MADE FOR EACH OTHER', BUT NOT FOR MARRIAGE?

Of the thirty films that they acted in together, Suchitra and Uttam appear as a married pair in six films. These films are *Agnipariksha* (1954), *Chandranath* (1957), *Harano Sur* (1957), *Indrani* (1958), *Grihodaho* (1967), and *Nabaraag* (1971). Why do narratives of 'married love' form a negligible part of their couple corpus? Their iconicity as the ultimate screen couple participated in and relied on their romantic desirability, and perhaps enacting the married couple was not considered a safe box-office bet.

It should also be noted that in their canon as a married couple, marriage as a structure of affect is a deeply contested and fraught transaction. Is on-screen marital conflict merely the function of the melodramatic form, in order to stage the crisis of self that domestic melodramas are meant to enact, or is it also the unravelling of their 'private' selves into the diegetic? Suchitra was separated from her husband, Dibanath, and had moved out of her Ballygunj Place house to her own home in the same area sometime in 1963. They had reportedly had a tumultuous married life as Dibanath was predictably jealous of his successful and working wife (cited in Chattopadhyaya 2005: 57; Gupto 2003, as Dhiren Deb's reminiscence). Uttam never formally divorced his wife, Gauri Devi. He moved in with Supriya Debi around 1963 and lived with her for seventeen years, but maintained his marital household as well. However, in her autobiography, Supriya claims that as soon as her divorce came through, her father took them to Kalighat to be married. There is a photograph of them as a married couple in *Amar Jibon Amar Uttam*, her memoirs. Despite living with her, Uttam reportedly went every morning to his house in Bhowanipur before going to work, and touched his mother's feet as a mark of respect. He was known as the good son, and also a responsible father who worried about his son's future and did his duty and married him off. He was equally seen as the responsible partner who participated wholeheartedly in the wedding of Soma, Supriya's daughter. Predictably, his troubled relationship with Soma does not appear in most narratives that speak of his other life. It is only in the issue of *Anandalok* magazine published after his death in 1980 that Soma's version of the 'one sided attraction' that 'she felt for this handsome man who lived with her mother' appeared. Their troubled personal lives, marital estrangements, and Uttam's long live-in relationship with Supriya Debi was also perhaps one of the axes that reshaped this particular fragment of their star text as the married couple. In their individual careers, both of them appeared as married couples with other actors.[1] Uttam's pairing with Sabitri Chatterjee or Madhabi Mukherjee in *Mouchak* or *Chadmabeshi* successfully deployed the playful generic components of romantic comedy, which are not present in his on-screen marital coupling with Suchitra. I now turn to a brief exposition of the filmic marriages of the star couple.

Agnipariksha stages the conflictual pulls of modernity and tradition experienced by the woman protagonist Taposhi/ Suchitra, who chooses her lover Kiriti/Uttam but discovers that she had already been married as a child. She has to choose between her lover and the man who is her husband. The plot resolves her dilemma by making the lover and the husband the same person. *Harano Sur* is about lost memory and the recovery of that memory, and is not strictly about enacting a discordant marriage. Roma/ Suchitra and Aloke/Uttam marry when he is under her care and treatment for loss of memory. After regaining his lost memory, he returns to his family but has no recollection of his life with Roma. She comes in search of him and impersonates his niece's governess in an attempt to win his trust and love. So in effect, marriage itself is not the focus of these two films, which are really about the staging of love and the formation of the couple. Besides these two films, the two Saratchandra adaptations, *Chandranath*[2] and *Grihodaho*, and two others, *Indrani* and *Nabaraag*, narrate interpersonal marital conflicts. All three films that I discuss delineate the spatial negotiations of the subjectivities that are related to the domestic realm. The idea of the *domus* (Walsh 1995) became a significant trope for the conjugal self-imaginary of the colonial Bengali modern. This discourse of domesticity was articulated through the figure of the new woman and her location in her domestic realm, as well as her negotiation of the outside world.

What I find significant is that in all three films, the intimate relationship of conjugality that defines these negotiations of selfhoods is predicated along an arc of discord. My analysis will map varied forms in which the issues of domestic space, the marital home, and discord unfold as the social intrudes into the personal. Different psychological states of near breakdown and disconnect are experienced by the couple as a whole, but especially by the new woman or the married *bhadramahila* as she negotiates her conjugal relationship. Before I turn to the analysis, I provide a brief plot summary of the three films below.

Indrani, based on a story by Achintya Kumar Sengupto,[3] narrates the problems encountered by Indrani, a working woman who is educated, a professional, married, and belongs to the Brahmin caste. She dreams of being the ideal companion for her non-working husband, Sudarshan/Uttam, who does not belong to her caste. The married couple encounter familial disapproval resulting from the inter-caste/inter-religious marital union that the lovers desire. They are able to marry despite this obstacle due to the new forms of marital transactions validated by modern law.[4] However, their married life runs into rough weather because of the joint family structure, and they move out of Sudarshan's ancestral home to make their nuclear home. Soon, the social intrudes into the insular space of the home that the couple creates beyond the familial. This conflict arises from the changing gender roles brought about by the professional working woman stepping out into the world in the 1950s. The couple drifts apart as both partners seem unable to adapt to the role reversals brought on by the working woman, her inability to 'balance' her home and the professional space, and the husband's inability to adjust to this new configuration in which he is the non-working spouse. The question that the film asks is: Are romantic love and the nuclear home enough to sustain and maintain the marital bond? The imaginary of an exclusive space for the couple does not become the utopia they desire as the romance cannot withstand the personal and social pressures that they encounter. The stay-at-home spouse of the successful working wife becomes a wasted, distraught figure.

At this point, the plot ensures that Sudarshan leaves their home in Dinajpur. He travels to Kolkata and chances upon an old man, a *mastermoshai* or teacher, who has dreams of creating a commune of homeless, hungry people who will live in an *ashram* retreat of peace and harmony. This encounter enables Sudarshan to refashion his self. Sudarshan's success in this experiment of community living is reported in the news and resolves the plot insofar as it enables Indrani to locate him. The sequences after she reads about him are instructive. She is advised by her coterie to not rush to her husband, as the newspaper reports of his tremendous success may not be true. But she staunchly defends him and firmly declares her intentions of going to him. This altercation underscores her appreciation of her husband's success. In this sequence, we see Indrani dressed in the traditional saree with vermilion on her forehead, signifying her married status. In most of the film, we see her wearing the saree in the modern manner.[5] It is after her marriage that she is shown wearing the saree in these two alternating modes of the traditional and the modern, depending on her location. Outside her home, she is shown wearing the modern saree, signalling her space outside. Inside, she wears it in the traditional manner. I suggest that her decision to seek him out is undertaken as his wife, who can now claim her place beside him after he succeeds in overcoming his shortcomings. In fact, after Sudarshan leaves her, we see her repeatedly wearing her saree in the traditional manner, and I suggest that this visual image signals her changing perception of her married status in the absence of any indication of a psychological transformation. This change involves the synthesis of the modern with the traditional image of the married woman. It is his disappearance that makes Indrani realise his importance for her, as well as the lack in her as the married woman. She too had abandoned all her 'normative wifely' attributes while pursuing her space outside the home.

In *Grihodaho*,[6] we see the upheavals unleashed on the couple Achala/Suchitra and Mahim/Uttam as their love marriage has to confront social ostracism occasioned by Achala's religious identity: she belongs to the Brahmo community, while Mahim is a high-caste Brahmin. Their marriage is further troubled by Achala's inability to adjust to village life as she is a city woman. The plot gets complicated as she becomes the object of lustful attraction for Suresh/Pradeep Kumar, Mahim's close friend. Suresh inveigles himself into the family's good books by taking advantage of Mahim's absence. He manages to persuade Achala's father, Kedar Babu/Pahari Sanyal, that Mahim is impoverished and hence not a good match for his daughter. He pays off Kedar Babu's loan and is all set to marry Achala in the full knowledge that she will never love him, and will probably just endure him as her husband. Mahim returns to find that Suresh has become a part of Achala's family. She herself is undergoing a terrible emotional strain as she cannot bring herself to go against her father's wishes. Yet, in a highly charged state, we see her put her ring on Mahim's finger, signalling her desire. The lovers get married.

When Achala moves to her marital home, she meets Mrinal/ Sabitri Chatterjee, Mahim's childhood companion, whose existence was not earlier known to her. Achala feels excluded from their friendship. Achala and Mahim remain trapped in their personal, self-inflicted pride, which drives them apart. The widening gap is further exacerbated by the arrival of Suresh. After an accidental fire in her marital home, she is forced to move back to her father's house, while Mahim stays back in the village. The couple has a brief reunion when Mahim falls ill and Achala nurses him back to health. They decide to travel to Jabalpur for Mahim's convalescence, but during this journey, Suresh engineers Achala's abduction. They take refuge in a Bengali gentleman's house and pretend to be married to avoid a scandal. During their stay, Suresh forces himself on her. In another twist, Mahim comes to visit the same gentleman, who happens to be his relative. Achala becomes a recluse; Suresh flees to a nearby village that has been struck by plague and soon succumbs to the disease. Achala is forced to confess to the old gentleman that she is not Suresh's wife, and therefore has no right to light his pyre. She is condemned and left with Mahim, who had visited Suresh on his deathbed.

Achala is completely devastated and does not know what to do. She seeks Mahim's help, but he refuses to make any decision on her behalf. In the last scene, we see Achala being left at an ashram for women while Mahim walks away. However, suddenly Mahim stops, and then the last shot features the customary embrace of the star couple. The film's end differs from that of the novel. In the novel, Achala is left alone at her father's house while Mrinal asks Mahim to inform her about the home for women, which she wants to go to. In the film, however, the last scene is of Mahim helping Achala to stand, and then they embrace.

Nabaraag[7] unravels the love marriage of Reena/Suchitra and Vipulananda/Uttam across ideological fissures under the fraught political/social conditions of 1970s Kolkata.[8] Their marriage seems to be disintegrating in the face of emotional and social pressures.

Reena feels trapped in her role as the trophy wife whose husband is unable to provide her with the sensitive companionship she craves. This marital world is divided along the ideological polarities of the law of the father and the space of the mother. Vipulananda is a ruthless industrialist who does not care for his labourers. His arrogance and selfishness are being transferred to his son, and the mother remains a mute spectator and outsider to this father-son relationship. The mother also experiences an emotional disconnect from her son. In this film, we do not see the mother as the primary care-giver of her child as it is the father's care and ideology that nurtures the son. This difference and disconnect between the couple is enacted via the trope of parenting, and plays with the notion of 'mothering'. In an interesting conflation, this mother is also imagined as the 'mother' of the dismissed factory workers and is made to fulfil her role as nurturer, similar to the notion of the bountiful *Annapurna*[9] figure. Reena stands in for the values of naturalness, compassion, trust, and honesty that the husband dismisses as inconsequential and harmful for his business. He is driven by his pursuit of material riches and social status, and does not allow humane values to interfere with his rise to greater wealth. In the process, he is immune to the other necessary requisites of sensitivity and grace.

The marital and maternal disconnection that the woman experiences is staged via the use of two Tagore (1861–1941) songs in the sequences that emphasise her loneliness, shut in her bedroom, or in sequences where her disconnect with her son is staged. The crisis reaches its breaking point when the father has to deal with the nightmarish disappearance of his son, which has actually been engineered by his wife. She stages his disappearance and sends him away to an *ashram*, a commune, which will make him a better human being who will be more responsible towards his paternal wealth and inheritance. This extreme situation enables the woman to claim the right of 'mothering' that had so far been denied to her. Her individual subjectivity rests not only on her wifely position but also on her maternal space and role, which she does not give up. The film ends with Vipulananda finally acknowledging Reena's position as his wife and his child's mother, signified by the couple's embrace.

My primary concern is twofold: to demonstrate how these films stage the dissonances and discord of conjugality, especially through the use of songs; and how they locate the disjunctions experienced by the new woman as she inhabits the roles of an ideal companion, as the *grihalaxmi* or *sugrihini*, the ideal homemaker, the *adarsh mata* or ideal mother, and the economic provider. These concerns foreground the contested space that the *bhadramahila* had to negotiate as she emerged into colonial and post-independence modernity in Bengal. As I have remarked in the Introduction, I consider the use of songs very useful in decoding the specificity of the melodramatic enunciation in popular films. Bhaskar's (2012) intervention in this regard informs my engagement. I examine two songs each from *Indrani* and *Nabaraag*, as these provide cues for the unfolding discord in the marital relationship, as well as express the deeply felt emotive charges experienced by the characters, experiences that cannot be articulated in everyday language.

Songs of Discord: Marital Disconnect

In *Indrani*, the first song is placed in the honeymoon sequence. Two panning shots allow us entry into the space of the married couple; we know from the previous scene that the couple had eloped to Ranchi to get married. After the camera pans over the landscape, we move from the daytime shot into a moonlit night shot. As the camera moves back, we see Indrani and Sudarshan on a verandah in the corner of the frame, looking out on the full moon night. They are dressed in wedding finery, the garlands around their necks a testament to the fact that they are now married. The camera pans to the figure of a mandolin player singing a love song, '*Sab kuch lutakar*'.[10] In Subhajit Chatterjee's (2007) reading, this song is part of a set of formal narrative strategies that this cycle of romances deployed to create the insular spaces that were outside the familial, where the couple could come into being, and helped create the aura of the couple (ibid.: 77). While I do not disagree with his general idea of the enchantment of space and song, I would argue that both this song and another duet sung later in the film need some explanation. As is the norm in the *pranaydharmi chobis*[11] starring Suchitra and Uttam, the enactment of the marriage ceremony is absent. Chatterjee reads this absent ritual as one more enunciation of the romantic space, which does not require the sanction of the legitimating figure of authority. Hence, he argues that the melodramatic displacement of framing and ellipsis in terms of the absent ritual is significant. He further argues that the absence of scenes showing the marriage as being solemnised is a deliberate strategy that adds to the romantic charge of the sequence. But we know that familial sanction has not been forthcoming. It is my argument here that Chatterjee's reading of a fragment out of the text as evidence is not completely tenable in this particular case. In doing so, I foreground the various displacements that this song stages, which help us to reorient our reading of this union and what is to follow in the personal space of the couple.

The lyrics of the song are

> *Sab kuch lutakar, hue hum tumhare; ke hai jeet uski jo dil aaj hare*
> *Yeh khoya sa chanda, yeh bahke sitare; to phir kyon na machle arman hamare...*

That is,

> I gave up everything to become yours,
> The one who will lose his heart will be the winner
> The lost moon, the dark stars are astray
> Then why wouldn't my desires throb?

The song is, of course, articulating the fruition of their romance into marriage, and the lovers' desire for each other, but also, importantly, it is about a significant loss. The first line reminds us of the loss of their individual families that has made this union possible, and that the marriage took place despite familial disapproval. The opening line underscores the loss of the familial in the creation of the couple. As the song progresses, we see Indrani turning to Sudarshan to ask if he understands what the man is singing. Visually, the camera constantly alternates between close-ups of the couple as Sudarshan explains the song to Indrani, and reverse long shots in almost deep space composition where we see the mandolin player in the frame. Sudarshan translates the lyrics for her. It should be noted that we are meant to realise that this is their wedding night. On this night, instead of a more conventional love duet, we see the staging of a romantic song sung by a wandering minstrel in an alien language incomprehensible to the woman. Is the song then merely adding to the romantic charge, or is it reminding us and underscoring the dissonance that has already been felt earlier in the form of parental opposition, while also prefiguring the other dissonances that become apparent in the future?

The evocation of the charged romantic aura via the haunting love song is, to my mind, displaced by the Hindi lyrics. Like her incomprehension of the romantic lyrics, will Indrani be unable to understand what her spouse requires? I cite this song and others as an important melodramatic marker of the Indian popular, where the songs are used to articulate either the inexpressible or the siphoning off of the ineffable into the *mise en scène* resounding with the implications of the song. I agree with Bhaskar's (2012) reading that argues for the centrality of the song as an important narrative and emotive element that signifies and intensifies affective states, as well as works to stage what the narrative will unfold as part of the plot. This charged song functions not only to evoke a zone of enchantment, as Chatterjee argues, but also functions across the textual field to open up the narrative conduits of incomprehension, dissonance, and discord that will govern the marital relationship.

The varied disjunctions that the first song signalled are repeated in the second. This is staged as a duet in Indrani's quarters in Dinajpur, where her job has required the couple to move. I shall analyse this figuration of the working woman later in the chapter. Before the song begins, we see Indrani at home, dressed in a Bengali-style saree denoting her marital homely state, moving around the room putting flowers on the mantelpiece and table. Sudarshan is standing next to the open window. As she moves across the home she has set up, she tells Sudarshan that this home is too small for him. We know that the reference is not only to the inadequate space, but also to the fact that his ancestral house—which they have left behind—is a mansion, and she acknowledges that she can only provide him with a small home. Her remark is layered with the opening lyrics of the song, '*neer chhoto, khoti nei...*' [even if the home is small], and from a close-up of her, we move to her stepping towards Sudarshan, who is singing the opening lines. The couple is framed with their backs to the camera, looking at each other and then turning to look out of the open window. The male voice sings,

> *Neer chhoto, khoti nei, akaash toh boro*
> *Hey mon balaka mor, ojanar ahobaney*
> *Chanchal pakha meley dhoro*
>
> [Even if the home is small, it does not matter as the sky is big,
> My heart spreads its wings like a crane to fly into the unknown]

FIGURE 2.1: *Neer chhoto; Indrani*

The camera zooms out to the open skies and the outside, reiterating the reassurance that the male is providing for his wife. The next shot moves to a night scene in a different location in the house. We see them sitting on the verandah stairs:

> The moonlight writes its poem on the night sky,
> The thirsty feather sways with desire....

As we see them on the steps, Indrani is in right profile with her face lit, and her profile and the flowers in her hair illuminated by the backlight, while Sudarshan sits with his face in shadow, barely lit. We are able to see her expressions clearly, while the male remains shrouded. The female voice joins in the refrain, and it is at this point that we see Indrani singing, 'the home is small, it does not matter' with a little smile and reassuring nod of her head. Perhaps this gesture and her illuminated profile reiterate that her contribution has enabled the creation of this space for her mate. This sequence is not merely evoking the cinematic aura of romance; it is symbolically staging the woman's place in the marital relationship. She is the dominant partner and provider in this abode of love. The next lines seem out of place in this song, '*megh rod sob badha paar hoye jag, tobo oui duti bhiru chokhe*' ('cross all hurdles of clouds and sun, conquer the world with your timid eyes and make yourself beautiful'). The ensuing shot in daylight frames Sudarshan continuing the song. He is standing on the portico and we can see the landscape outside; Indrani, though, is placed inside the threshold, looking off-camera with her back resting against the doorframe. Significantly, as he sings, the camera moves to a close-up of Indrani's pensive expression, and as his voice continues, the camera moves back to her again, as she repeats the opening lines and Sudarshan joins in. At this point, she sighs as he is singing.

How are these gestures and the lyrics of the last lines to be read? Initially, the song speaks of the new abode of the couple, but suddenly we see Indrani's reassuring nod. It is as if she is underscoring her ability to provide her husband with shelter, however inadequate the 'home' might be. The male voice asks his wife to cross all hurdles and achieve her beautiful self with 'timid' eyes. Is this his imaginary of his perfect woman/mate? Does the song prefigure the clash and the mismatch between the dream and the reality of the home that we will see shortly? Is he sanctioning her stepping out, while still expecting her to retain her womanly timidity? What is the model of the modern professional working woman that is being imagined here by her partner?

The Indrani that the film has presented before us is hardly timid. The independent, proactive, and romantic woman whom we encountered in Chapter 1 morphs into a domineering wife in this film. Is the new space going to be one of idealised companionship and emotional bonding that will be adequate for the couple? Indrani feels confident of her ability to provide what her partner needs to realise his potential and complete his work. Will he really be able to find himself and give his talent the space it needs, or will he remain under her shadow?

It would be pertinent to remember the shot of the near kiss that I had discussed in Chapter One as an instance of creating the romantic charge of the love films. Does the covering of Sudarshan's face by her head, which subsumes the entire frame, denote the engulfing nature of her persona that will increasingly stifle Sudarshan? Is her spouse capable of being her partner? The sigh in the second song probably makes her conscious of the enormity of the burden of stepping out into the world, as well as prefigures Sudarshan's fears. Is it alerting us to the conflicts that the narrative is yet to reveal?

I have already mentioned Bhaskar's (2012) formulation concerning the centrality of songs for reading the specific local registers of meanings in Indian melodrama. It is obvious that both this song and the one that preceded it compress the entire range of dissonances via the aural register and work as cues for the narrative to unfold. Let me now turn to the songs in *Nabaraag*, which alert us to similar dissonances in Reena's marital life and her maternal disconnect with her son Raju.

In *Nabaraag*, the first song starts as the credit sequence ends. The camera frames a lit chandelier, with the crane shot moving down as we see Reena laughing and the song refrain begins:[12]

> Whom have you left behind, O my heart?
> Your life spent, you did not find peace, O my heart
> Now you have forgotten the path that you came by
> Now you have forgotten the path that you came by
> How will you return to him, O my heart?
> Who have you left behind, O my heart?
> The ears listen to the water flowing
> The soul shivers with the sound of rustling leaves
> The soul shivers with the sound of rustling leaves,
> I feel I'll find it if I can understand the language of the flowers,
> The path that has gone with the evening star, O my heart....

While the song plays, the camera moves from the long shot to a close-up of Reena's sombre expression and grief-stricken eyes. In a series of shots, the camera keeps framing Reena and the singer. The intercutting frames Vipulananda standing apart with a drink in a different corner, deeply immersed in conversation. As the song nears its end, we see Reena standing, almost mimicking a bejewelled portrait, the frame intersected almost three-fourths by the open lid of the piano. It's as if this woman is placed next to it like a still photograph, beautiful to look at and admire, yet her limpid, liquid eyes are brimming with unshed tears, and the slow track to her close-up almost freezes her face in repose. An almost deep space top angle shot sees Vipulananda move closer to Reena, who is still standing near the piano in mid-frame. As the camera tracks back, we stay with the woman placed amidst the throng of people. This longing for the path that she has travelled clearly refers to the past that she has left behind. Her point of view shot, cueing to the close-up of her husband standing apart, seems to imply her separation from him. Her ill-spent life, which has not allowed her solace, is perhaps indicating the deep unhappiness she experiences in her disconnected marital relationship. The longing to comprehend the language of flowers implies her separation from her natural natal village space and her transformation as Reena in the artificial world of her husband. The deep sense of despair embodied in her stricken close-ups denotes inarticulate feelings that Reena cannot express in her everyday language, and which can only be signalled via the song, again underscoring the centrality of this form. These inarticulate longings are again brought forth in the next couple of scenes, as we see Reena remain withdrawn and quiet.

The second song stages the deep despair Reena experiences after a few disturbing confrontations with her son, Raju. All her son can talk about are shootings, police, and killing people if they do not complete their work on time. This second song articulates her desolation more forcefully. She sings despairingly of the poison she has willingly drunk:[13]

> I have drunk poison knowingly
> I have given up all hope of life, I have surrendered myself,
> I see him and I burn
> I suffer my burning in silence
> I still cannot be afar, I still remain
> I suffer the lighted arrows
> The smile scorches, inflames my thirst for love
> Even as I desire the nectar of love
> It only becomes a thunderbolt

The performance of her distress at her son's imbibing his father's masculine aggression cannot be more explicit. This song has been preceded by sequences showing Raju being taught how to shoot and playing at being the ruthless business tycoon, supervised by his father. In the song, she is dressed in her finery and has been complimented on her ravishing appearance; yet, she sings this deeply disturbing song which acts as an expressive register for the feelings she is unable to articulate. Over the course of the song, we see her almost laying herself on the piano, seemingly in the grip of intense despair. This startling image and its effect on the onlooker is shown through Vipulananda's gaze, and his concern and distress at his wife's inability to control her drinking, which leads to this 'unseemly' behaviour. Her display of her emotional turmoil goes against the code expected of her respectable *bhadramahila* status.

FASHIONING THE NEW WOMAN AND COMPANIONATE MARRIAGES

The four songs from the two films alert us to the dissonances that define Indrani and Reena's married lives. What do these disjunctions signify in terms of the fashioning of the new woman, which rested on her role as the ideal wife and mother in her domestic realm? Most accounts of the new woman and her imaginary as the ideal wife imagine her refashioning to suit her husband's work-related lifestyle. The setting up of the nuclear home had become an increasing reality in post-independence modern Bengal, brought on by the clashes that ensued when women began to refuse to make adjustments.[14] Changing circumstances of education and work resulted in many young men moving to the city to take examinations or to newer places to take up jobs. This led to a readjustment of the wife's responsibility and role in shaping the husband's career. Because of these economic changes, the ideal of an educated companionate wife became desirable (Chakrabarty 1995). The nationalist position on women's education and social upliftment is also a part of this shift, and reshaped the cartography of the Indian middle-class woman's self-fashioning as she stepped into modernity. The 'new woman', who was now to be a companion for the 'modern Indian man', had to be able to refashion herself using the tools of education and grooming in order to take her rightful place beside her husband and provide the necessary 'home' for his personal and professional advancement (Sarkar 2001). She also had to bear the responsibility of educating and grooming her children so they could become model citizens inhabiting the new world of opportunities, and not remain dependent on feudal structures of patronage and advancement. The position of women was always tied to their varied roles as wives, mothers, companions; in effect, as an adjunct to some social relation or other. Very rarely did ideas about women's education and social position have to do with them as individuals, with their own personal needs and desires.[15]

In *Indrani*, we encounter the figuration of the new woman as not only educated and independent, but also proactive and capable of taking charge of her life and destiny and becoming the primary economic provider for her stay-at-home spouse. This film lets us enter the debate from the woman's domain. The moving away, the break from the *ekannavarty paribaar* to the constitution of the nuclear family is imagined differently in this film, insofar as it is initiated by the working woman. This is in contrast to a normative heterosexual union where the man would be the provider and make the couple's home. *Indrani* stages the consequences of this reversal in the role of the idealised companionate wife in startling terms. It is the woman's education and her economic independence that enables the couple to set up their separate nuclear unit; however, this exacerbates personal conflict instead of providing the married couple with the necessary space and place in which to realise their subjectivities.

As the opening out of the narrative space via the songs demonstrates, the marriage becomes a battleground for Indrani and Sudarshan. Even if the ideal of the 'modern wife' differed from the traditional hierarchical conjugal relationship, as Chakrabarty (1995) argues, it was rarely a relation of 'reciprocity'. The 'reality' for 'real' women did not involve transactions of gender roles with both men and women as equal partners. In their incisive introduction, Powell and Lambert Hurley (2006) remark on the 'rhetoric' and 'reality' of gender experience in South Asia. Even a professional woman doctor such as Haimavati Sen[16] testifies to the contradictory role that she had to negotiate with her husband, who happened to be a Brahmo (Forbes 2006). Examples of writings by other educated women also bear testimony to women's fraught lived experiences of inequality as they negotiated newer forms of selfhoods via education and work (Dutta Gupta 2010).

This dichotomy was not peculiar to Bengal. Writings from other parts of India also indicate the personal and social churning that women and men experienced as they tried to inhabit modernity, not as equals but as contestants, with the women being denied a level playing field. Indrani's economic independence does not ensure her acceptance as an equal partner. She flowers in the life and work outside her home.

FIGURE 2.2: Working Woman, *Indrani*

Sudarshan, on the other hand, feels increasingly isolated and alienated. He cannot accept a life of idleness and feels threatened by his wife's rising professional and social popularity. He is unable to accept that his wife has a social standing and a world that does not include him. His diffidence and reticent nature make him sensitive to the realities of having an independent working wife who goes out to earn her living. The earlier romantic imaginary of their life together in a small house under the big sky cannot sustain itself in the face of the harsh reality of everyday slights, real and imagined, that Sudarshan feels he is being subjected to.

The insular world of love and togetherness unravels in the face of social intrusion and the taunts of people who designate him an 'honorary husband', and an appendage of the working woman.[17] The 'reality' of the educated and working professional woman scars the non-working spouse, who seems uneasy in accepting this non-normative social and economic status.

The idea of the modern marriage perhaps enabled a relationship of intimacy and an exclusive bond between the couple, but it did not automatically alter the subtexts of power in the conjugal bond. Feminist historians have usually cited economic disparity as the primary reason for unequal gender transactions between working men and their non-working wives. *Nabaraag* makes the case that it is also significantly tied to the gendered ideas of self-fashioning available to the new woman, whose role was linked to her husband's class and status. The prescribed code of socialising expected of her depended on the requirements determined by the husband's social position. Narayani's transformation and re-fashioning into an idealised, fashionable trophy wife involves layers of hard work and erasures, which are compressed mostly in flashback sequences.[18] These erasures are geographical and linguistic, where even her traditional name, Narayani, is modernised into the more cosmopolitan Reena. It is only in the last sequence that Vipulananda addresses her by her given name; in the rest of the film, he addresses her simply as 'Darling'. She is his Reena, refashioned in the image that he wants to project for the world. Her journey to Kolkata and her marriage, as well as her new avatar of the polished wife, underscores the many ellipses that have rendered her past obsolete.

Narayani belonged to East Pakistan and had been sent to Kolkata after the beginnings of communal tension in her village. This past resurfaces in the interstices of her self, mostly brought out in the first song sequence, her insomnia, and her drinking.

It impacts her present in ways that prove to be deeply traumatic for her. The historical catastrophes and losses that have impacted Narayani's life include the impossibility of her return to her village, because the new boundaries created by Partition meant that her home was now part of a new nation, one she was barred from, the loss of her native dialect, and her name.

Thus, all markers that denoted Narayani's selfhood have been systematically wiped out, and sometimes forcibly altered. The sequences of her dancing lessons show the 'labour and work' that she had to perform to become the desirable, polished wife. The allure and attraction of the natural rural woman has to be excised with precision and replaced with the finesse expected in the elite world of her husband. Modern love is not enough; it seems, for Vipulananda's social position, that his wife has to be moulded in his image. She has to learn to express even her spontaneous reactions in the English language, which will denote her elegance and status. The space/place of this 'new woman' was thus deeply tied to both class and gender. This refashioning, however, does not translate into personal happiness for Reena. The sequence where she breaks down in a drunken, depressive fit and tells her husband that while everybody feels she is the queen, nobody realises the torture that this sobriquet makes her undergo is poignant in its evocation of the hidden trauma experienced by women's torturous negotiations to fashion their subjectivities, not as individuals but as ideal mates for their husbands. The artificiality of the *domus*, her domestic space, where she feels stifled is suggested in many sequences in *Nabaraag*, especially through the credit sequence, the two songs I have discussed, and the shower scenes discussed later in this chapter. Is Narayani's cry also that of the successful top woman star who possibly felt trapped in the make-believe world of cinema?

We may wonder if the star herself experienced such traumatic upheavals due to her professional and troubled personal life. All the erasures that I have referred to above actually transpired in Suchitra's personal life as well. Suchitra had moved to Kolkata after her marriage to Dibanath in 1947. She had faced a linguistic hurdle towards the beginning of her career. She found it difficult to speak without the twang of the *Bangal* dialect, the Bengali language spoken in East Bengal, her birthplace (now present-day Bangladesh).[19] Her name, Roma, was changed to Suchitra when she joined the film industry. In her case, it was not a Muslim identity that had to be erased, as was the case of many actors of the Hindi film industry (such as Meena Kumari or Dilip Kumar, for instance); it was felt that this new name would add to her glamour (Uttam had also to change his name from Arun, as he was unable to deliver hits under his own name). Suchitra had to erase the East Bengal dialect from her diction as it was not considered acceptable for a heroine in the industry. Her star text was not allowed to be formed on the script of her native land, unlike the comedian Bhanu Bandopadhyaya, who built his career out of his Bangal language (Gooptu 2010). It is also pertinent that in her filmic career she plays a Partition victim from Punjab in *Bipasha* (1962), and only in this film, towards the end of her career, is she specifically located in her natal space. In *Alo Amar Alo* (1972), she plays a refugee woman living in the refugee colony. Clearly her star text was constructed across layers of erasures and ellipses.

The enabling and affirming tropes of education and work that fashioned the new woman in the romance cluster become sites for contestation in the married *bhadramahila*'s life. Imbricated in this terrain was the contested space of the educated woman and her domestic household (Forbes 1996; Sarkar 2001; Walsh 1995), as well as notions of social change occasioned by love marriages. According to Orsini,

> Two... conditions for an actual social change in the institution of marriage—consensual marriage and economic independence before marriage—though at times vociferously demanded, were much resisted and came to form the stuff of many fictional narratives of this period...although romantic love...or its Indian equivalent 'prem', became an established ideal by the beginning of the twentieth century, the patriarchal system made few allowances for it and for the emergence of the modern couple.... community concerns vociferously claimed precedence over individual choice.... These tensions [were] usually narrativised as a clash between love and family, between romantic aspirations and the duty of loyalty to the kin.... (2007: 33)

In *Indrani*, we encounter both consensual marriage and the economic independence of the wife, yet the conflict becomes unavoidable as the couple remains caught in 'normative' gender roles. In a charged confrontation after Indrani accuses Sudarshan of taking up a low-paying private teaching job that threatens her social standing, he suddenly turns to stare at her. She pauses and asks him what he is looking at. He says slowly that he is looking at the new Indrani who stands before him and remembering the earlier one who has gone away. The camera zooms into a shot of the same window that we had seen as the *mise en scène* for the *neer chhoto* (the house is small) song, now dark and static, an empty space signifying the demise of the couple's dream and replacing it with this dark open abyss. The woman seems to have become almost a parody of the arrogant working woman who cannot, and will not, define herself in terms of the *domus*, the demands of domesticity. If Sudarshan seems a victim of his personal insecurities, then Indrani too seems to have been trapped in the role of the 'man' of the house. Indrani's public persona of a crusader for women's education and rights challenges the limits of dwelling inside the domestic sphere and underscores the woman's right to refashion herself in the *bahir*, the external.

This dichotomy of the *andar*, inside, and *bahir*, the outside, had been central to the imaginary of spaces that defined the new woman's negotiation of her selfhood in the colonial period. Access to education and public spaces were imbricated in the discourse of 'respectable feminine deportment' and also resided in notions of how the *bhadramahila* had to define herself in relation to the outside (Chattopadhyaya 2005). Indrani's self-fashioning challenges this spatial configuration. In effect, after the song celebrating their move, '*neer chhoto*', we hardly see her inside the home. She is continuously on the move, going out to work and juggling her busy professional commitments, while her husband withdraws into his shell. The remarkable spatial mobility of the new woman whom we encountered in Chapter One does not seem to have the same affirmative charge of freedom with regard to the married *bhadramahila*.[20] However, Indrani's desire to be 'outside' is left unresolved as the film, at this narrative juncture, is unable to provide her an adequate space to house herself in her romantic idea of 'home' while simultaneously interacting with and having a position in the world outside.

The resolution of the plot is staged in Indrani's decision to join Sudrashan in setting up the commune for homeless people and be his mate and partner; she declares, 'I tried to create a home without you and failed, you tried to make a house without me and it got burned, we both need each other to create a home'. Indrani's willingness to give up her job signifies her eagerness to participate in the 'work' of nation-building as an important track on which this couple can refashion its conjugal bond. I think it is this imaginary of the conjugal union, where the couple comes together to give up their self-centred pursuit of personal and professional advancement, replacing it with a markedly different work, that differentiates Indrani from the other two working women figures that are a part of the normative discourse of 1960s Bengali cinema: Ritwik Ghatak's *Meghe Dhaka Tara* (1960) and Satyajit Ray's *Mahanagar* (1963). Aarti in *Mahanagar* is content to discover herself through her job and add to the family's economic stability. Neeta is forced to sacrifice her life in the process of providing sustenance to her refugee family in *Meghe Dhaka Tara*.

Indrani, on the other hand, chooses to partner her mate in an endeavour that places the couple at the centre of an ethical enterprise that signals the utopian vision necessary for forming the new couple in the exuberant, yet troubled, social circumstances of the 1950s–60s. I have explained in the Introduction that the 1950s was both marked by the joyful exuberance of independence and scarred by the trauma of Partition. Her commitment to this new communitarian project is similar to the manner in which *Suryotoron* imagines the couple formation within the new space of governance, as discussed in Chapter One. The romantic couple needs to be located within the ambit of a new vision of social responsibility, which will not only articulate the affective bond in the personal domain but will also speak to the social. The film's end signposts the necessary renegotiations of selves that need to be enacted before the couple can be reunited. How is the ending to be read? Is the woman giving up her independence when she rushes to the rural commune where her husband finally finds personal and social recognition?

Definitions of selfhood not anchored in productive social roles seem incapable of flourishing in this romantic utopia. The film is not only about Indrani but is also about Sudarshan finding himself, taking responsibility for his productive role as a modern citizen. Both their subjectivities are tied to a sense of 'work' that is central to how they choose to create/refashion themselves. The married couple can only be united if both realise their potential as romantic lovers and socially productive beings.

In *Grihodaho,* we see the reverse journey of the new urban woman who has to move to the village. The usual motif of the romance that we encountered in the post-independence narratives discussed in Chapter One is overturned in this film. Instead of the urban woman who remains in her stable city space, this film shows her in a space in which she becomes the outsider. She is the 'other' on account of her religion and her urban roots. Mahim, on the other hand, is able to negotiate both spaces with equal ease.[21] Achala, as the city woman, is completely out of her element, especially in comparison with Mrinal, Mahim's childhood friend, who is the model of the traditional woman. Achala is dressed in flowing chiffons; drinks tea delicately from her cup; and is more concerned with her appearance than with the hard labour involved in housework. Even when she nurses her husband back to health, she looks tired and burns his soup.

This staging of the Westernised model of the educated urban woman, located in the formative period of the colonial modern, is different from the figurations of the 'new woman' that we encounter via Suchitra in the post-independence period. One of the anxieties that the new woman unleashed was the imaginary of the modern woman becoming Westernised due to her education. Both Indrani and Achala are subjected to this anxiety; their poise and education denote negative accomplishments. They are snidely called *pater bibi,* a sarcastic term often used for a 'modern educated' married woman living an indolent, luxurious life of leisure, who looks down on housework. Achala is unable to adjust to the rigours of rural domestic life. Her narrative articulates the fissures and gaps between the romantic premise of the ideal companionate wife that was so central to the fashioning of the new married woman as the 'goddess of the house', the 'ideal domestic woman', the *grihalaxmi* and the *sugrihini* (Walsh 1995), and its negotiations by this urban woman who is placed in an alien space. Unlike Achala, Indrani and Narayani seem more proactive in dealing with their domestic and other issues. Achala's location in the emergent moment of colonial modernity makes her unable to step out of her historical location.

Commenting on the nineteenth-century imaginary of the new woman as the new bride, Swapna Banerjee (2006) writes that ideas about the new woman not only revolved around her position as the ideal woman who would take her rightful place in the new nation, but also addressed the new bride who had to mould herself to the demands of her married status and her husband's home. '(The) New woman addressed was actually the new bride...she became the crucial mobiliser on whose performance and capacity of being a *sugrihini* or good housewife, the success of family and nation rested' (ibid.: 19–20).[22]

The married *bhadramahila*, then, had to become the ideal wife and her performance of that particular role ensured the well-being of her home. Achala is far removed from the *sugrihini* ideal, the imagined ideal of the new woman. She is not slighted due to her inability to contribute to her domestic role as the homemaker, but is definitely shown to be out of her comfort zone in this alien space. The film seems to contest what Orsini suggests in terms of the Brahmo imaginary of the ideal of women's education and companionate marriages:

> The Bengali reformist religious group Brahmo Samaj, though a tiny minority in absolute numbers, came nonetheless to exert a disproportionate influence as a model of absorbed Westernization, and Brahmos not only spearheaded women's education but also were the first to introduce the new notion of companionate marriage. (2007: 31)

The imaginary of the new woman as envisaged by the model of social reform spearheaded by the Brahmos seems hopelessly inadequate in the face of 'real' situations of marital adjustments, as well as the societal prejudices that this new Brahmo woman had to encounter.

Clearly, the Westernised urban woman is not accepted as the desirable model within the entrenched, prejudiced social milieu that she finds herself in, as she discovers when she moves to Mahim's village. The villagers stop visiting Mahim and do not send their children to the school he has started for them. The village elders also couch the accidental burning of his house as an act of divine retribution, brought on by Mahim's 'sin' of keeping the Brahmo woman inside his home.

Mahim is asked to abandon her and do penance for his sins.[23] He, of course, is 'modern' enough to not concur with their outdated views; however, his modernity is unable to prevent the marriage from disintegrating in the face of both personal and social pressures.

Nabaraag stages Reena's marriage as one divided along ideological lines, where she is a stay-at-home wife and a mother. This conception of the ideal mother, referred to as the *adarsha mata*, enlisted scientific and modern child-rearing practices for the purposes of creating an ideal value-based atmosphere in the home, so that the child would grow up to be a responsible citizen of the new nation. I have referred to this ideal, as Banerjee (2006) explains it, in my discussion of Achala as the model of the educated liberal woman who does not become the *sugrihini*. Banerjee's work analyses various nineteenth-century advice manuals, which were primarily didactic literature, such as *Lalana Suhrid* (*Child Rearing*) and *Santaan Charitra Gathan* (*Building Child's Character*), which advised the new mother on appropriate child-rearing practices that would supposedly build the character of her children. *Nabaraag*, on the other hand, explores the gap between this imagined ideal prescribed for the new woman and the reality of experience as it unravels for Narayani. She is not 'allowed' to be either the companionate wife or the ideal mother.

DISSONANT *BHADRAMAHILA*, CONFLICTING FASHIONINGS

In *Nabaraag*, we encounter the conflictual relationship of the married couple, with the 'idealised refashioned trophy wife' located in a domestic world created by her husband in which she remains peripheral. This inner psychological world of the stay-at-home domesticated wife will let us enter the debates about marital companionship, which imagined the companionate, idealised, and equal relationship that I have referred to above (Chakrabarti 1995). The imaginary of the new woman as the ideal *grihalaxmi* (Walsh 1995), her location in her home, her *domus*, is also unravelled in the context of the personal and the deeply troubling social problems of the crippling strikes and labour unrest in Reena's husband's factory. The Kolkata of the 1970s witnessed these eruptions on a regular basis. Reena is only expected to remain a fashionable trophy wife. Her husband is solicitous of her well-being, but she seems in the grip of some charged, inexpressible despair that makes her appear distraught. In most close-ups we see her with a still expression, as if she is frozen in these spaces. She laughs and socialises, but her stillness makes it obvious that in this luxurious space, she feels closed and hemmed in. The camera remains in the stationary 180 format; the dialogues signal the almost dysfunctional marriage.

Her marital disjunction, which the first song expresses, is underscored in the shots of her in her nightgown, walking to her dressing table, her image split in three as she sits, applying lotion on her face. The camera cuts to a long angular shot as we see her on the sofa, the song we heard at the party resonating almost like a disembodied voice. The high angle camera underscores the loneliness experienced by this solitary figure, who cannot forget the haunting lyrics. The ensuing top angle shot, this time of Vipulananda looking down at some plans spread on his table, is intercut with shots of burnt cigarette stubs strewn around on the table. The placement of the shots makes it clear that the couple inhabits different physical and emotional locations. This distancing is referenced in the scenes where we see the woman lying face down on her bed. Abruptly sitting up, she suddenly reaches out to light the bedside lamp. We see a shot of bathroom taps, and her hand, laden with gold bangles, reaching out to open them and then we see her as she steps under the shower. She keeps moving her hand over her face, signalling the state of her mind and body.

FIGURE 2.3: Reena's Distress, *Nabaraag*

This could signal either her sexual disconnect from the busy husband who works through the night, unable to satisfy her desires, or some other cleansing that she yearns for. What is being staged here?

In this film, the social pressures that impinge on Reena/Narayani's body are unravelled through the tropes of food and labour unrest, which were rending apart the social fabric of 1970s Kolkata. These tropes play on her mothering and her concern for the labourers' security. The film uses a montage, juxtaposing shots of Raju's birthday party with that of striking workers to stage Reena/Narayani's disturbed state. The sequence opens with a shot of posters of the labour movement with the labourers expressing their right to strike, contrasted with shots of big cars driving in, cut with shots of the locked factory, police, a group of workers sitting on *dharna* [demonstration and protest], and the cutting of the birthday cake. Soon, the boys start a food fight, and we see a close-up of Reena/Narayani, who freezes with a laden plate. The shot cuts to a mass of rice cooked with some lentils being ladled onto aluminum plates. The camera shifts to a group of boys sitting on the floor and eating in the same space. The sequence portrays the dichotomy between the striking workers, whose problems remain unresolved, and the life of the rich household, which continues, intercut with this sudden scene from Reena/Narayani's point of view. In the birthday party sequence, too, we see the table laden with various kinds of food. The film keeps intercutting shots of the birthday food well laid out, Reena/Narayani serving food, children eating, and their food fight. It would not be far-fetched to suggest that the film very consciously references the terrible food crisis and hunger marches that the city had witnessed in 1966. This was a result of the drought of 1965, the failure of the monsoon, and the rationing and cordoning that Kolkata had witnessed. The memory of that terrible time, though not referenced in concrete terms, seems to haunt Narayani. She cannot bring herself to forget that the workers were merely demanding a 15-paisa increase in their allowance so that they could eat one full meal.

In another sequence, the retrenched workers who appeal to her mount their argument not within the domain of law, but within the domain of the feminine nurturing of the 'mother'. We see her slowly descend the stairs, alone, upright, positioned against the motley, dirty group of workers bunched in a corner just below the staircase. She comes and sits on the sofa. She is dressed in a saree, but unlike the preceding sequence at the breakfast table with Raju, she has covered her head with the end of her saree. This clearly denotes her status as the lady of the house. But as the sequence progresses, we see the varied symbolic registers collapsed into this image. The workers inform her about their dismissal and acknowledge that the management is within legal rights to dismiss them as they only had temporary contracts. Their union cannot intercede on their behalf either, as they have no legal rights. She is not sure how she can be of help. The shot works with a medium framing: Reena sitting on the sofa, arms resting on the armrest, and the workers standing a little distance towards the back if she is in the foreground. As they implore her to intercede with her husband, they tell her, 'We have not come to you with the mandate of law. We are dependent on your benevolence, *daya*. After all, the hungry child will rush to his mother for food.' The camera suddenly cuts into a tracking shot, going forward to her, as she simultaneously seems to sit upright and move into the frame. This doubling reiterates not only what the workers imagine her to be, the bountiful mother, the Annapurna, but also plays with the latent symbolism of her earlier name

(Narayani, another name for Annapurna, Narayan's consort), which has been erased by her present avatar. She then has to be both, the mother who will fulfil the child's desire for food, and also use her status as Reena to bestow the grace of her material boon. Her moving into the camera equally underscores her own self-imaginary of her status as the maternal nurturer figure.

However, we know that within the diegetic world, this desire has also been thwarted. The predictable fallout of these developments is unleashed by Vipulananda, who is angry with her for interfering. In the charged confrontation between the two, we see Reena demanding to know what her rightful place is. Is it only limited to her social skills, partying, dancing, and drinking? She is also expected to perform 'social work' at her husband's command, yet she is dismissed as sentimental if she chooses to intercede on the workers' welfare demands. Her role is to be his mouthpiece and nothing else! He predictably refuses to be swayed by sentiments, but is willing to take the workers back since she has promised, and he will accommodate her wishes. Her reasons for interceding on their behalf are dismissed as sentimental nonsense, which have no place in the real world. She has to remain the trophy wife with no 'real' contribution in this conjugal space; her location seems similar to the 'honorary husband' tag that was foisted on Sudarshan in *Indrani*. Like him, Narayani too feels trapped in this opulent mansion, although the *Indrapuri* [Indra's abode; Indra is the god of affluence, lord of the universe in the Hindu pantheon][24] is far removed from the small, humble house that was home to Indrani and Sudarshan.

These states of near-breakdown and hysteria keep spilling over as we repeatedly see Narayani in the grip of these intense emotional upheavals. The layering of her distress in the visual field deploys the trope of excess that is central to the melodramatic text. In the first, we see a low angle shot of a table with a glass of whisky, with an almost empty bottle dominating the frame. We see shots of her showering, deploying the same gestures that are a repetition of the first shower scene, creating a doubling and intensification of her emotional state which she is unable to articulate otherwise. The excess of her emotional condition is thus 'siphoned off into the *mise-en-scene* or into the music', to use a well-known intervention from a different context (Nowell-Smith 1987: 73). The question that this siphoning off raises is the following: Is her distress merely personal, or does it cite other repressed historical states and desires that seem to burst forth via these expressive means?

However, as the film progresses, it becomes clear that the two songs, the shower scenes, her drunken despair, and her disavowal by her son press forth meanings and significances that signpost other states of desolation and distress, not merely occasioned by her present. Rather, they seem to signify the most brutal dislocation that Narayani has experienced: her uprooting from her natal place due to the Partition. The first song clearly articulates her dislocation as it refers to the path that she has left behind, one that cannot be travelled on ever again. The second song, which refers to her drinking poison knowingly, clearly refers to her maternal disconnection. The consequences of her maternal disconnect are foregrounded in two sequences that stage her descent into a nightmarish drunken haze as she relentlessly remembers Raju's initiation into a masculine virility which sanctions the use of aggression and violence. As she stands up, we have inserts of Raju learning to shoot, framed with his father; the son yelling on the phone as he enacts the role of an industrialist angry at a production shortfall, threatening to shoot if the workers do not complete their targets, telling his father that he will surpass him in his stature as businessman. She goes to her son's room and stares at his sleeping form. But interestingly, as he mumbles in his sleep, the camera cuts to her close-up and then inserts the shot we had seen in the first scene when the couple had returned after the party of the credit sequence. We had seen the mother step up to touch his cheek. Raju had curtly shrugged her away and taken his father's hand to lead him to his room for a private conversation, which he does not want his mother to be present for. Raju will continue to seek his father's 'touch' while rejecting the mother's 'touch'. The camera stays on the empty hand in close-up as we see the son walking with the father while the mother is left standing. This is followed by a close-up of Reena's distraught expression. She again stands still and the camera cuts to the son walking with the father, briefly turning to wish his mother good night. The camera moves to another close-up as she whispers 'night', with just a soundless movement of her lips.

In fact, the film constantly stages this affinity between father and son from which the mother is excluded. We repeatedly see the polarisation of the parents' role in the upbringing of the child, with a foregrounding of the father's nurturing and the constant disavowal of the mother by the son. Private conversations, gestures, as well as formal compositions are mobilised with remarkable consistency to emphasise this disconnect. We see the mother placed at a distance, observing the father and son, looking on or being informed about their conversations. She becomes almost a voyeur, peeping from behind parted curtains, or removed from this exclusive domain of masculinity that privileges aggression and rationality. It is clear, then, that the state of desolation and despondency that she experiences at home are consequences of her marital and maternal disconnect. It is important to note that in the same period, Suchitra appears as the drunken professional cabaret dancer in *Fariyaad* (1971)[25] where, as a single mother, she tries to cope with her son becoming the neighbourhood *mastaan* [goon]. That film, too, stages the entropic, closed world of maternal and personal disintegration that the exploited cabaret dancer experiences. Both films articulate the terrible sense of dislocation experienced by the new woman as she negotiates the unravelling of her maternal self amidst the pressing social upheavals unleashed in the 1970s modern city.[26]

What do these drunken states signal? I argue that for Reena/ Narayani, the maternal disconnect is not merely evoking her personal role as the mother, but also points to a larger rejection of values that are thereby signified. Raju's disavowal of the mother's touch is not only undesirable but also dangerous, as he is then disregarding the affective and the emotional that Narayani connotes. If he has to inherit the father's mantle and take his rightful place in the social world, then he has to balance his masculine self with the values associated with the feminine being. In the disjointed and fraught world of labour unrest, lockouts, and strikes, he cannot become a ruthless tyrant. His ideal inheritance would mean being a benevolent human being who can carry the responsibilities of being connected and grounded. It is for this reason that the film marks the woman's space as an essential, if neglected, locus on which the social can call for restitution and compassion. Just as she cannot disengage from her son's welfare, she cannot disengage herself from the social. And because she cannot disengage, she pretends, even though these pretensions create further marital disharmony. Unlike Achala, she refuses to stay within the set parameters of her married status. She is really the embodiment of the new *bhadramahila* who does not remain trapped in this enforced role-play that has been imposed on her by her gender and personal status. Using the excuse of a visit to Delhi, she plans Raju's removal to Nondo's ashram. Vipulananda ultimately manages to find his 'lost' son with the help of the police. He returns and is furious with his wife. She tells him that she is willing to accept whatever punishment he deems necessary, but she was driven by her sense of responsibility as a mother; a space that we know has been systematically wrested from her. Her exclusion may not have been intentional, but it did consign her to the periphery in her domestic space.

We also need to keep in mind that the domestic is the only available legitimate space that she can lay claim to. She does not have economic independence; in any case, as Forbes mentions, independence and modernity did not automatically translate into personal freedom of decision-making for Indian women after independence (1996: 237). Even Manisha Ray's (1993) anthropological accounts of women from 'respectable *bhadralok*' families of Kolkata between 1951–59 and 1965–69 demonstrate the uneasy negotiations that even single working women had to undertake in their families regarding their rights over their incomes and decision-making.

Unlike Indrani or Narayani and their strong individuated subjectivities, Achala seems to be caught in the trap of a victim. In the film, we continuously see Achala either on the floor or fainting or crying, with the two men, Mahim and Suresh, positioned over her. The unequal gender positions are continuously underscored via the cinematic framing of the woman. Achala symbolises the modern woman, but social conditions do not provide her with the necessary liberatory frame. Deeply entrenched gender roles and the norms governing her social status as the married woman make it impossible for her to define herself in terms other than her marital self, which is tied to that of her husband. Additionally, the schism between her religion as Brahmo and her husband's Brahminical religion also add to the problems encountered by this new woman in the colonial period. Both Achala and Mahim are unable to transcend their social and historical locations, despite their modern education. Social and historical circumstances retain their grip on the subjectivities, especially that of the woman, who cannot enact radical choices. The film imagines her construction as an educated modern woman who embodies the inherent contradictions experienced by the new woman. This woman is completely circumscribed within her personal, social, and historical location. She ultimately has no agency and is continuously being acted upon, even remaining dependent on the men who let her down. She is not the traditional woman, she is 'different'; however, her difference does not enable her, but takes a disastrous form.

Bhaskar (2012) identifies these features as inherent to certain aporias of the modern, where the historical conditions that can give voice to individual desires for selfhood cannot be realised within the available historical mandates. Achala is caught in her historical location, which makes it impossible for her to break out of her sanctioned zone of action determined by her married status. Her education or urban lifestyle cannot allow her to transcend her historical location, as is possible for Indrani. She is also trapped in her own socialised construct, where she herself accepts her culpability in her ambivalent desire for the other man, and wants to be punished for her sins. She has stepped out and hence will be made to suffer. She seems to accept her role in making Suresh lose his perspective. The enactment of Suresh's lust as he forces himself on her reiterates Achala's inability to speak for herself or stand up for her rights.

The narrative foregrounds the splitting of male desire for this woman by positioning the husband and the lustful lover as the two axes that will determine and redefine this woman. Elsaesser's argument regarding such splitting in the context of domestic melodrama in Hollywood is significant for this film as well. This melodramatic splitting functions 'in an enclosed field of pressure, [which] opens a highly dynamic yet discontinuous cycle of non fulfillment' (Elsaesser 1987: 183). This enclosed field will erupt finally through the illicit attraction of the other man; meanwhile, the husband will find it impossible to bridge the widening chasm with his wife. The combined force of illicit desire and aborted desire maps itself out on this woman's body in the form of abandonment by the husband, and abduction and molestation enacted by the other man. She is cast in the mould of a victim who remains trapped in her gendered subjectivity as the traditional woman who will suffer all the injustices visited upon her. She can be described as the modern woman who is imagined as a 'guilty construction', who herself considers her own presence as the cause of disturbance and disaster (Biswas 2002: 122).[27]

Conflictual Negotiations

The individual desires for emotional plenitude that drive the protagonists in these films do not validate radical individualistic choices. They signpost the conflictual terrain that the couple has to negotiate as married lovers in *Indrani* and *Grihodaho*, and as parents in *Nabaraag*, in their search for affective fulfillment as a couple. The melodramatic finale, insofar as it deploys chance and coincidence as a trope for plot resolution, imagines the union as a complementary relationship rather than as deeply individualistic or antagonistic. The affective, effective, and normative marital unit cannot be formed by the ascendency of one over the other. It has to include them both.

In conclusion, I would like to point out that these three films from three different historical locations signpost the varied nature of the marital discord that seems to haunt the iconic star pair. As romantic lovers, they manage to create their affective unit. However, the enactment of individual choice in marital transactions does not enable any seeming conjugal bliss. All three films stage the new woman in her varied manifestations, negotiating circumstances that challenge her in the continuous fashioning and refashioning of available positions, or those that she needs to map out for herself.

The desired romantic/feminist utopia cannot function outside the personal, social, and the familial. These are political transactions that each self has to negotiate, and they are firmly located in the interstices of the contingent positions that become available within particular social formations. In the words of Rajeshwari Sunder Rajan, the processes of feminist and political appropriation 'must provide the (different) grounds of gendered subjectivities that will enact more contingent, varied and flexible modes of resistance' (1993: 11). As I have demonstrated, all three films embody varied forms of self-fashioning that are contingent upon the different experiences and modes of self-expression that might be traditional, yet carry the marks of their historical and social locations as well as the different ways in which individuals negotiate modernity.

These narrative and cinematic resolutions cannot be confined to a symptomatic ideological reading insofar as they reinforce status-quoist gendered endings; the popular and commercial success the individual films enjoyed needs to also be factored in. The endings staged via the star pair's embrace remain constant in all three films; the logic of this coming together of the couple is dictated by the star draw and romantic desirability signified by the two stars, despite the narrative staging of discordant marriages and fraught gender negotiations. *Indrani* ran for nine weeks at a stretch and was declared a moderate hit by the star pair's standards. Both *Grihodaho* and *Nabaraag*, advertised as comeback films for the celebrated star duo, ran for fifteen and thirteen weeks, respectively. Their box-office success can be explained by sheer commonsense: audience expectations and the power of star draw. What might get occluded in this explanation is the fact that *Grihodaho's* commercial draw enabled Uttam to recoup some of the losses he had suffered due to the box-office debacle of *Chhoti si Mulaquat*. These commercial aspects need further research, but can signpost the tremendous spectator charge that the films carried. As I have shown by positioning the diegetic and narrative within the star text and its self-fashioning germane to each film, the contours of cinema's involvement in fleshing out these issues of the new woman and her modernity via marriage, as well as its intersections with the individual star biography, can alert us to the myriad ways in which cinema allows entry into fraught gender negotiations. These negotiations are performed under specific social conditions, and enable audiences to either accept or reject these cinematic renditions enacted through star self-fashioning. The delineations of the new woman, feminine identity, sexuality, and rethinking gender identities and dynamics contribute to the embodied desire for modern selfhoods and their enactments. The agency that Indrani and Narayani demonstrate in choosing to shape themselves seems unavailable to Achala.

However, how does one factor in the tremendous box-office success enjoyed by *Grihodaho*? Is it the allure of the sexually transgressive woman who suffers, or the figuration of her as the victim of fate and circumstances beyond her control that can explain the popular reception of the film? Is Achala then the embodiment of a feminine self that Bhaskar refers to, citing Williams, to denote the particular charge of melodrama that 'moves us to pathos for protagonists beset by forces more powerful than they and who are perceived as victims?' (Bhaskar 2012: 162). As I have mentioned above, out of the three films, this one had the single longest run of fifteen weeks. I am interested in what it is that this and the other Saratchandra film—*Chandranath*, which broke several records—signify for the fragment of the conjugal map that I have sketched in this chapter. Unhappy marriages by themselves were perhaps not the draw; the star pair's iconicity as the married couple was also being mapped along their off-filmic private selves, and was one likely axis of this fragment. The other, more potent reason seems to be the embodiment of victimhood that the woman/star carried. I suggest that the terrifying predicament of Saryu and Achala unleashed a vicarious release of emotions that the spectators found irresistible. This particular aspect of spectator charge that unleashes emotions in audiences has been regarded as the most significant reason for the power of melodrama (Williams 1998: 42, cited in Bhaskar 2012: 162). I further suggest that the fact that it was Suchitra, the most glamorous and independent of the female stars, the proud Mrs Sen of Ballygunj, who communicated these narratives of victimhood that carried such a tremendous fascination for the suffering displayed by both Saryu and Achala.

Moreover, the gap between the actual self of the woman star and this figuration of victimhood and suffering that validated her star text functions as the most potent symbol of feminine selfhood. The deeply ambivalent anxieties that the contrary pull of the 'Janus faced modernity', identified by Gyan Prakash and exemplified in the new modern woman as analysed in these three films, are also perhaps the reason for the popular appeal of these melodramas. Even the literary text set in the colonial period but adapted in the mid-1960s drew a huge audience response. It is with the examination of these representations that I turn to other figurations of suffering and loneliness that reconfigured Suchitra's star text in the 1960s in Chapter Three.

In the following two chapters, I move away from the star pair to map the selves that emerged during the 1960s and 1970s. Chapter Three will unravel Suchitra's star text in the 1960s and 1970s, when she is not paired with Uttam. Chapter Four will focus on Uttam through the lens of the troubled 1960s and 1970s where he does not star opposite Suchitra. It is not as if the iconic romantic pair does not appear on screen later; however, the heyday of the romantic coupling was effectively over in the 1960s.

NOTES

1. Suchitra appears as an urban married woman in *Saajghar* (1955), *Bhalobasha* (1955), *Mejo Bou* (1955), *Amar Bou* (1956), *Sandhya Deeper Shikha* (1964), etc., all opposite Bikash Ray; as well as in *Saat Paake Bandha* (1963), *Fariyaad* (1970), etc. In a filmography of fifty-eight films, she appears as a married woman in thirteen films. Some notable films in which Uttam acted in marital narratives include *Kaamna* (1949), *Kankabatir Ghat* (1955), *Bidhilipi* (1955), *Shyamoli* (1956), *Bicharak* (1959), *Jotugriho* (1964), *Shankhabela* (1966), *Suksaari* (1969), *Bilambita Laya* (1970), *Nishipadma* (1970), *Andha Atit* (1972), and *Bagbondir Khela* (1975). Other films which saw him as a married man were romantic comedies, such as *Shudhu Ekti Bochor* (1966), *Chadmabeshi* (1971), and *Mouchak* (1975).

2. *Chandranath* stages the abandonment of Saryu/Suchitra by her husband Chandranath/Uttam after it is discovered that her mother was *kulbrashtha*, that is, she had run away with another man. Saryu leaves her marital home

as a pregnant woman and cannot bring herself to commit suicide as she is expecting a child. Chandranath feels that he cannot accept his wife, yet fears to turn her out as her beauty would make her easy prey to other men. He expects her to kill herself, but does not want the blame. He demands that she poison herself in his absence. After Saryu leaves, she delivers a son and finds refuge in an ashram. Years later, Chandranath chances upon her and his son and takes them back. This underscores my point that both acted in films that narrated the tensions and fissures in the marital relationship. Despite my best efforts, I could not locate a copy of this film. As per my research, this film has still not been released in digital format. I have only been able to locate a publicity booklet and a newspaper advertisement.

3. Achintya Kumar Sengupto (1903–76) was a well-known and established modern Bengali writer and part of the Kallol group, which was active during 1922–29. This group of writers moved away from the Tagore style of writing to focus on everyday life and foregrounded the experiences of urban living and its attendant issues. Their language differed from Tagore's 'poetic language', and their insistence on using even slang as a manner of expression marked their writings as contemporary. They were also influenced by European writers and Freud.

4. The discourse of law in the colonial period and controversies regarding the Age of Consent Bill, Widow Remarriage, and Abolishment of Sati framed and re-framed the domain of marital transactions. In the post-independence period, the laws amending the Special Marriages Act of 1872, legalising registered marriages between consenting adults in 1954, and ultimately the Hindu Marriage Act (1955) created possibilities for newer forms of marital transactions that could be negotiated by citizens. Many memoirs of mixed caste and inter-religious marriages in Bengal provide us with varied accounts of the problems faced by couples in convincing their families to agree to their marriage. This law came as a boon, as they could retain their religious affiliations (Chaudhuri and Ray 2005).

5. The traditional Bengali style of wearing the saree involves draping it in a circular way, without the front pleats in the modern style that has an eight-fold drape. In the 1870s, Jnanadanandini Devi, Satyendranath Tagore's wife (she was Rabindranath Tagore's older sister-in law), started the modern way of saree draping by modifying the Parsee saree style with a petticoat and blouse as she had to accompany her husband, an Indian civil servant, to his official functions.

6. *Grihodaho* was written by Saratchandra (1896–1937) and is set in the 1920s.

7. *Nabaraag* was based on Ashutosh Mukherjee's (1920–89) novella, *Notun Tuli* (*The New Brush*). The film's name means 'new *raga*', or new attachment. It was advertised as the comeback film of the couple. After *Kamallata* (1969), they reappeared with *Nabaraag*.

8. In the 1970s, Kolkata was engulfed by the Naxalite movement and the state violence unleashed on the Naxalite youth. Politically, economically, and socially, the city and the state of West Bengal were in a state of turmoil. I shall elaborate on this fraught condition in Chapter Four.

9. Annapurna, the goddess of bountiful produce and food, one of the manifestations of Goddess Laxmi, Vishnu's consort.

10. Hemanta uses Mohammed Rafi's voice and Shailendra's lyrics. This was one of the rare Bengali films that had a Hindi song. It went with the apparent realism of these melodramas as the newlywed couple is in Ranchi and the wandering singer would obviously sing in Hindi. However, an *Anand Bazaar* review (17 October 1958) finds the use of a Hindi song incomprehensible and jarring. According to this review, most songs are unnecessary; the reviewer is clearly using the realist film lens to critique the songs. However, as I show from my reading, both songs stage certain specific emotive states and are not using realistic narrative codes to do so.

11. Romantic films.

12. The film uses two Tagore songs, '*tui phele eschechis kaare o mon re amar*', and '*aami jene shune beesh korechi paan*'. The first is picturised on Kanika Majumdar and the second is sung by Narayani/Reena herself. Both songs articulate and press forth the turmoil that the woman is experiencing at those specific moments.

13. As I have mentioned above, this song is sung by Narayani herself. In the film review in *Jugantor*, this song's picturisation was referred to as superfluous, merely used to 'show' that the heroine could sing! However, using the melodramatic critical lens instead of the realist one that the review uses is more productive, and can open up the interpretive possibility of reading Narayani's inability to articulate her distress in everyday language.

14. In films such as *Punarmilan* (1957), Uttam is the elder son and wants to move away to a flat in Kolkata as his wife refuses to live in the ancestral house and wants a carefree life in her own home.

15. However, women expressed themselves as fraught beings, which testifies to the contested territory of subjectivities available to them despite changing social circumstances. The dissatisfaction of even educated women from illustrious families, such as the Tagore family, is testimony to how these accomplished women suffered as they were unable to claim uncontested spaces to be themselves (Ghosh 2000).

16. Dr Haimavati Sen (1866–1932) was India's first foreign-trained woman doctor. She was a child widow (Forbes 1996: 6, 157).

17. This was one of the reasons cited for the breakdown of Suchitra's marriage to Dibanath. During the mid-1950s when her career took off, he reportedly remained at home and the household was run on her income. He was also jealous of her rumoured involvement with Uttam and other men (Chatopadhyaya 2005). In her autobiography, *Sobare Ami Nomi* (1973), Kanan Devi too mentions the frequent fights between Suchitra and her husband.

18. Narayani has to learn modern dance, speak in English, and acquire a sophisticated etiquette as demanded by her husband's social status.

19. Suchitra was targeted and lampooned for her dialect and nasal twang. See the discussion on her star career in Chapter Five.

20. In Chapter Three, I discuss another figuration of the divorced woman in *Saat Paake Bandha*. There, Archana chooses to wait for her husband despite her legal separation from him. I analyse the significance of this waiting and the lifetime of solitude that she chooses for herself.

21. This was an important component of Uttam's star text, his ability to belong both to the rural and the urban (Biswas 2002). Suchitra, on the other hand, was deeply urban, and this film stages her discomfort in a manner that underscores not only the diegetic but also the casting choice, which was perfect. Suchitra was able to bring into sharp relief the visual incongruity of placing the highly glamorous chiffon-clad woman in heels, who carries her parasol and handbag as she follows her husband on a tour of the village. She had enacted very few roles which saw her as the rural woman.

22. Tanika Sarkar (2002) has rightly pointed out that the concerns of nationalism were not merely political, but involved all aspects of the material, domestic, and spiritual life of the citizens. And the figure of the woman was at the centre of these negotiations. See also Dipesh Chakravarty's (1993) analysis of the *grihalaxmi* and the discourses on the new woman in the colonial period.

23. Achala's Brahmo religion makes her impure, especially as her presence has contaminated the Brahmin home.

24. Nondo uses this phrase to describe Vipulananda's house. He, of course, does so to denote the elite status that this marriage has bestowed on Narayani. Suchitra's marriage to Dibanath Sen, the scion of an elite south Kolkata family, was also predicated along this track, which denoted her elite marital status. However, her marriage too was an unhappy one and ultimately did not provide her with a lifetime of marital bliss. This particular trope of

material wealth as signifying the married woman's social elevation is again repeated in *Saat Paake Bandha*, which I discuss in Chapter Three.

25. *Fariyaad* released after *Nabaraag*. Suchitra enacted a cabaret dancer who is sexually exploited by the night club owner, Baren Mullick. This is also a maternal melodrama as the narrative explores her nightmarish world of suffering along with her conflicts with her son.

26. I shall explore the troubled and violent social and political turmoil that Kolkata witnessed in the 1970s in some detail in Chapter Four, where I discuss some films from this decade. Briefly, this period saw the city subjected to strikes, lockouts, and urban violence occasioned by Naxalism, police crackdown, etc.

27. Biswas (2002) argues that most of the characters essayed by Suchitra in the love films—or otherwise—can be described as strong independent urban women who did not acquiesce to the 'guilty construction' of womanhood, which was another variation of the new woman. This construction of the woman as guilty made the woman regard her own actions as sinful, and hence punishable. Biswas contrasts Suchitra's characters with the figuration of Sandhya Rani in *Bratacharini*, with the latter appearing as the epitome of the woman as a trangressive subject who imagined that the mere touch of her husband's friend had made her impure, and is hence willing to be punished. In this film, Achala's figuration contradicts the usual strong characters that Suchitra was known for.

3

The Female Star / The Lonely *Bhadramahila*

I now turn my lens on Suchitra, the woman star who remains the single most important female superstar that popular Bengali cinema has seen in the post-independence period. Moving away from her romantic image, this chapter places her star text in the 1960s in order to examine its fashioning after the 1950s, in films that created box-office records; in films that could be described as her star vehicles; and in films where Uttam is not her lead actor. All through the 1950s, she had starred in many films with Bikash Ray and other heroes that saw her essaying strong woman-centred roles.[1] Her 1952 film *Bhagwan Sri Chaitanya,* directed by Debaki Bose, was a super hit. It was the veteran director's showcasing of Suchitra's photogenic beauty in her role as Vishnupriya, Chaitanya's wife, that started the trend of using close-ups and backlighting to highlight her glamorous presence, and was later mobilised in her couple films with Uttam with such spectacular effect. Her successful Bombay sojourns, which I have discussed in Chapter One, added to her status and stature as a successful star.[2]

From 1959, there was a hiatus in her romantic pairing with Uttam, fuelling rumours about their break-up. Routinely cited reasons included rumours about her secret illness, her demands for better remuneration, her marital problems, the rumoured love affair[3] between them (which had created trouble in Uttam's marriage), as well as Suchitra's apparent inclination towards religion, which led to her becoming extremely devout (Mukhopadhyaya 2000: 53). It can be surmised that the big gap in the 1960s, that is, the five years from 1962–67 when the iconic pair did not appear on-screen, was also due to Supriya's centrality in Uttam's star text. Their affair, which possibly began during the filming of *Suno Baranari* (1960), culminated in their becoming live-in partners from 1963. In effect, whatever may be the 'real' reason, Suchitra chose to script her individual star text to fashion her status as the *mahanayika*.

SUCHITRA'S FILMIC BIOGRAPHY: 1960–70S

Suchitra's star text displays the crucial features that have been identified in Majumdar's reading of female stardom in the Indian context (Majumdar 2009). According to her, female stars have limited options in terms of the roles they are given: the romantic lover, the wife, and the mother (ibid.: 144). Suchitra's star text with Uttam too was fashioned along the axes of all these screen roles, fixing her romantic iconicity, as I discussed in Chapters One and Two. In this chapter, I analyse characters essayed by Suchitra to link them to her individual star text[4] that fixed her image as the iconic woman superstar, underscoring a particular property of the star text, which is in itself a melodramatic text.[5] As Majumdar has remarked, the 'narrative of the star text or the melodramatic text tends towards the iconic in the form of familiar and relatively fixed character types and scenarios' (ibid.: 145). Further, she notes that this iconicity gets linked to and accentuated by the deployment of star charisma and authenticity (ibid.: 146).

Suchitra's double roles in *Smriti Tuku Thak* (1960) and *Uttar Phalguni* (1963), her International Film Award in 1963 for *Saat Paake Bandha*,[6] her Filmfare award for Best Actress in *Mamata* (1966), the Hindi remake of *Uttar Phalguni*, and her strong author-backed performances were instrumental in providing her with a firmer foothold as the woman superstar or *mahanayika*. Both Uttam and Suchitra had won the BFJA awards for *Saptapadi* in the Best Actor and Actress categories. Suchitra received her Padma Shri in 1972. After her retirement in 1978, she refused even the Dada Saheb Phalke award in 2005 as she was unwilling to step out from self-imposed seclusion to receive this highest film honour in India in person. Her Banga Bibhushan award in 2012 was handed over to her daughter and granddaughter. The only missing fragment in her career map was the opportunity to have been cast by the auteur Satyajit Ray. Uttam managed that coup as he was cast in *Nayak* (1966) and *Chiriakhana* (1967). This is despite the fact that Ray had reportedly expressed an interest in casting Suchitra in the mid-1950s in *Ghare Baire*, and later in *Devi Chaudhurani*.[7] Had this collaboration materialised, then perhaps her star text would be written and coded differently from the way it is usually done. She is not accepted as an accomplished actor; on the contrary, her popular appeal and charisma is accorded negative valuation. Despite her resounding box-office draw and her popularity, she remains present mainly in the popular circuit, inhabiting numerous unauthorised biographies and speculative discourses. Her refusal to appear in public or give interviews and her complete withdrawal from public life had accorded her an exotic, iconic status that remained impregnable. The most-cited refashioning of the glamorous woman star who dared to pose for a semi-nude picture with a 'no kiss' sign on her cheek[8] is that into the *sadhika*, the woman ascetic who devoted her life to Ramakrishna.[9] This trajectory of her star text in the oral circuits of memory, gossip, and biographies is in sharp contrast to the hagiography accorded to Uttam, which I shall discuss in Chapter Five.

Do her filmic narratives of loneliness that emerge in this decade prefigure, accentuate, and give voice to the reclusive retirement into which Suchitra receded? And yet, her confinement gave her a most potent and charged presence, residing in the interstices of memory that refuse to disappear. This self-imposed text of loneliness is perhaps a result of—and tied to—the break-up of her iconic screen love with Uttam, as I have mentioned above. However, as I discuss below, despite the on-screen break-up and gap, the two stars kept up their collaborations through other circuits. Uttam's presence and absence both haunt Suchitra's filmic selves, either as an imaginary voice, as an idea embedded within the loneliness engulfing this woman's star text, or in concrete, material terms as the producer of her hugely successful *Uttar Phalguni*. If she could not be his romantic lover, she still retained the space that no other heroine who acted opposite him was accorded. The 'filmic romance' discussed in Chapter One gets its last airing in another story that I shall narrate in Chapter Five.

What happens to the utopian possibilities of self-fashioning, both feminine and masculine, if we take away either of the partners who constituted the iconic romantic couple of the 1950s–1970s—Suchitra and Uttam? Was the utopia of love in the popular Bengali imagination contingent on them? This is the primary question that I seek to answer in this chapter and the next. If, as a romantic couple, they could intervene in and create cartographies of subjectivities that spoke to and participated in the exuberant freedoms of the 1950s, and which later voiced the fraught 1960s and 1970s, then what cinematic configuration did the individual star text of the woman take in the 1960s?

The entire decade of the 1960s was witness to a deepening sense of disquiet as contemporary political and social events made the euphoria of independence seem like a distant dream. As Rochona Majumdar remarks:

> The Nehruvian promise of modernising India with a strong, socialistic public sector, where government took responsibility for generating wealth and jobs through its control of public works as well as railways, banks, mining and other industries, had begun to falter from the late 1950s. The declaration of the first National Emergency in 1959 in Kerala where the Communist Party had been elected to power in 1957 marked a break in the longstanding pattern of a single party hegemony in Indian politics. External issues such as border wars with China and Pakistan (in 1962 and 1965 respectively) and internally the huge rise in unemployment, food shortages, and labor problems led to strikes and lockouts in different parts of the country. Together, these events made the period from the mid 1960s onwards a time of acute political instability in India. (2011: 24)

If the new woman of the nationalist imaginary became the body that embodied the ideal of the nation and carried forward all that its inner core stood for, then what figurations did her varied selves take in the 1960s, the decade that witnessed a growing dismay at the fast deterioration of the dreams of Nehruvian modernity, saw two wars, rising inflation, decaying civic structures, and, especially in Bengal, strikes, lockouts, and the crumbling of dreams (Chatterjee 1990: 29–31)?

I seek to answer the questions posed above by examining the cinematic circulation of a certain 'text of loneliness'[10] that gives voice to the disjointed times where historical conditions are no longer conducive to the imaginary of romantic utopia. In her analysis of the 1940s–50s Bombay films, Bhaskar (2012) argues that the exploration of melodrama as a genre and issues of gender can also be mapped through certain tragic narratives where the enactment of limit situations[11] articulate the impossibility of achieving emotional plenitude. These impossibilities indicate the conjunction of history and modernity that these films narrate. Not all depictions of cinematic modernity remain playful and exuberant or stage the utopian possibilities of love and desire. Her reading challenges those offered by Vasudevan (2000) and Biswas (2000, 2002) on the 1950s melodramas, which articulated the affirmative possibilities of the new nation.[12] I use Bhaskar's intervention to argue that in the 1960s films starring Suchitra that I focus on, this formulation can be an enabling entry into the 'text of loneliness' that I analyse. Do these situations of suffering and anguish then stand for the loneliness of the times, the playing out of all the negations particular to their historical location?

I am particularly interested in the use of the cinematic melodramatic convention where the genre pushes gestural or performative articulations to stage the conflict between this woman's desire for her love and the constricting professional, familial, or social norms. She is the 'modern new woman', not perhaps a radical feminist, but one who still displays a strong sense of self-worth and pride. She is not comparable, for instance, to Lora's ambitious trajectory which goes against the 'natural maternal instinct' seen in Annie, her maid, in Sirk's *Imitation of Life* (1959). These cinematic trajectories also map the betrayals that she encounters from men who are unable to protect her, or those who function as her true companions but end up betraying her, similar to the woman characters analysed by Bhaskar (2012), who are betrayed by their ineffectual lovers. They push her to extreme conditions of psychotic breakdown, suffering, death, pathos, and in one case, lead her to commit murder and face retribution. There seems to be a clear and deliberate attempt at breaking away from the romantic persona without eschewing her sensuous screen image as the object of 'erotic desire' that had been the driving force of her characterisation and screen realisation in the 1950s, as discussed in Chapter One.

FIGURE 3.1: The Woman Alone: Radha in *Dweep Jele Jai*; Archana in *Saat Paake Bandha*, opening shots

The three films *Dweep Jele Jai* (1959), *Saat Paake Bandha* (1963), and *Uttar Phalguni* (1963)[13] are interesting as the narratives foreground the crucial choices that the middle-class woman, the *bhadramahila*, makes with regard to love and marriage, her work, and motherhood. It can be argued that the three iconic films were citing her private life on-screen. Suchitra's personal life as a woman superstar was difficult and tumultuous. She had a troubled married life; she had separated from her husband, Dibanath Sen, during the 1960s and was effectively a single parent to her daughter, Moonmoon. A look at Suchitra's filmography in this decade throws up these characterisations of the 'woman alone' (Byars 1991) quite consistently: *Smriti Tuku Thak*, all the three films discussed in this chapter, *Sandhya Deeper Shikha*, *Fariyaad*, and *Megh Kaalo* are some of the notable hits of the 1960s and early 1970s, where she is left alone at the end. Let me turn to a plot summary of the films before I explicate my argument.

The demands of her professional role as nurse in a psychiatric clinic in *Dweep Jele Jai* forbid Radha from experiencing true love; nevertheless, love unhinges her mental balance. She falls in love with her patient Debashish, who is cured and returns to his fiancé. Her other patient, Tapas, falls in love with her but she does not reciprocate his feelings. She performs the role of lover to cure psychotic men jilted by their beloveds, but this performance of the 'love cure' makes her lose her own mental balance, and by the end of the film she becomes a lunatic, screaming and raving against the emotional sacrifices demanded of women in their roles as nurturers and givers of love and affection. *Dweep Jele Jai* thus offers a critique of this trope of gender socialisation that women become a victim of. It lays bare the premises of our expectations and prejudices by turning the trope of romantic love on its head and staging the consequences of performing love on the psyche of the woman.

Saat Paake Bandha depicts the love marriage and eventual divorce of Archana, who marries a low-paid college professor, Sukhendu/Soumitra Chatterjee. She marries below her social status and her mother, Chhaya Debi, is unhappy at the social demotion this marriage signifies for her family status. Archana tries hard to adjust to her husband's household, which is quite different in terms of its material and social status. However, she is caught between her mother's attempts to create a comfortable married home for her daughter and Sukhendu's male ego, which is unwilling to acquiesce to this 'interference' that poses a challenge to his position within the household, which was made precarious due to his lower economic status. This film articulates the problems faced by the modern, educated woman who marries out of choice, but cannot attain happiness in her marriage due to familial interference. She divorces Sukhendu and moves back with her family, finding work in a small town girl's school. Eventually she decides to put her ego aside and rushes back to her husband, only to find that he has left the country. She chooses to wait for him, and this state of loneliness is as binding for her as her wedding rites: '*saat paaker bandhan er cheye ei pratikhar bandhan kom kise*' ('this waiting is as binding as the binding vows of the seven steps').[14]

Uttar Phalguni narrates the story of a *baiji*, a courtesan, Debjani/Panna Bai, who is forced into an exploitative marriage to pay off her father's debt and is rescued by a *kotha* (salon) owner. It renders the experience of the woman's work through a profession that bestows a marginal social status on the *baiji*.[15] She is forced to send her daughter Suparna away to boarding school to prevent the drunkard father from consigning the daughter to a similar fate. Years later, the drunkard husband rediscovers his wife and daughter, the latter having been adopted by the mother's ex-lover, who was unable to marry her as his family did not agree to the love match. This lover, a well-known barrister, has raised Debjani's daughter as his own. Debjani is forced by circumstances to murder her husband. Her England-educated lawyer daughter defends the mother in court, and the film ends with Debjani's death in court. The sacrificing mother gets her moment of recognition in her daughter's arms.

Despite the differences in narrative employment, all the films mentioned above display features of what can be productively termed as the 'woman's film', to borrow Doane's term, with a caveat (see Doane 1987).[16] My work draws on her insights, especially her analysis of the medical discourse, but I do not limit myself to the tools of psychoanalysis to frame the discussion of the broader figurations of the woman in these Bengali films. It is also important to note that unlike the Hollywood genre of women's films, which were 'directed towards a female audience', these films did not address only female viewers.[17] They do depict compelling scenarios of the doomed woman in love, the divorced woman, the abandoned single mother, enacting 'mythemes of femininity (which) trade on their very familiarity and recognisability' (ibid.: 3). In this sense, then, they present us with certain familiar articulations of femininity, which, despite their particular historical location, can speak powerfully (ibid.). Furthermore, I explore the cinematic articulation of the figure of the 'woman alone', to borrow Byars' use of the term, for the genre of women's melodrama from 1950s Hollywood (1991: 77).[18]

All three films deploy feminine subjectivity as a structural principle in that the opening and ending are framed with the woman's location in the spaces that define her. Like the particular relationship between space and gender that the 'Love Films' articulated, these 'Woman Alone' films also place the woman in spaces that are significant to her fashioning. In the opening of *Dweep Jele Jai*, Radha's spatial location in the psychiatric centre, followed by her close-up demonstrates this logic powerfully, while in *Saat Paake Bandha*, the framing of the first shot of the bare, denuded tree branch and the rain-soaked platform on which Archana alights, and where we get her first close-up, connote the loneliness of her life, which has been shaped by her choices. In *Uttar Phalguni*, the first shot of Debjani's performance of the *hori*[19] as the *baiji* Panna Bai in the *kotha* is an example, like the others, of the consistent deployment of a particular narrative strategy that aligns the star text with the melodramatic text, as I have argued in the Introduction, drawing on Gledhill (1991) and Majumdar (2009). These narrative strategies and rhetorical modes that are significant for defining melodrama and the star text include typecasting, excess, and hyperbole (Gledhill 1991; Majumdar 2009).

Figure 3.2: Maximising Star Value: Iconic Framings

These hyperbolic framing strategies include using close-ups of Suchitra in profile, with the same shot split into two faces, where one is located in the present, and the other, with her reflection, evoking memories of the past that are being narrated as voiceover. The double role works as another instance of star presence and its intensified usage in *Uttar Phalguni*. Other such consistent alignments are the stylised poses of the lonely woman in the end shots and the female protagonist's voiceover, both in the opening and end credits—what Silverman has described as the embodied voice, mostly used for film noir, but also for the woman in classical cinema (Silverman 1988: 43–71).[20] These voiceovers signal situations of pain, suffering, and the past that haunts this woman's present.

What is the significance of the melodramatic address in mapping the limitations of the social and the ideological by foregrounding these conflicting psychic drives in the woman? Here, I am influenced by Gledhill's argument that

> If melodrama can only end in the place where it began, not having a programmatic analysis for the future, its possibilities lie in this double acknowledgement of how things are in a given historical conjuncture, and of the primary desires and resistances contained within it. (Gledhill 1987b: 38)

Therefore, it is important to delineate how the melodramatic mode circulates in these narratives. Does it effectively operate only to articulate the figure of this oppressed woman who is a victim of patriarchy? Or do we see her negotiating her choice and agency in the films that nevertheless seem to perpetuate the status quo in the end? Do the closures denote her failure to achieve 'plenitude of meaning' (Brooks 1984)? Do these articulations of her 'gender performance'[21] as a woman alone create tensions within the conventional narrative structure, posing a challenge to the status quoist ending? These are some questions that I address in this chapter.

Love as Performance: *Dweep Jele Jai* (1959)

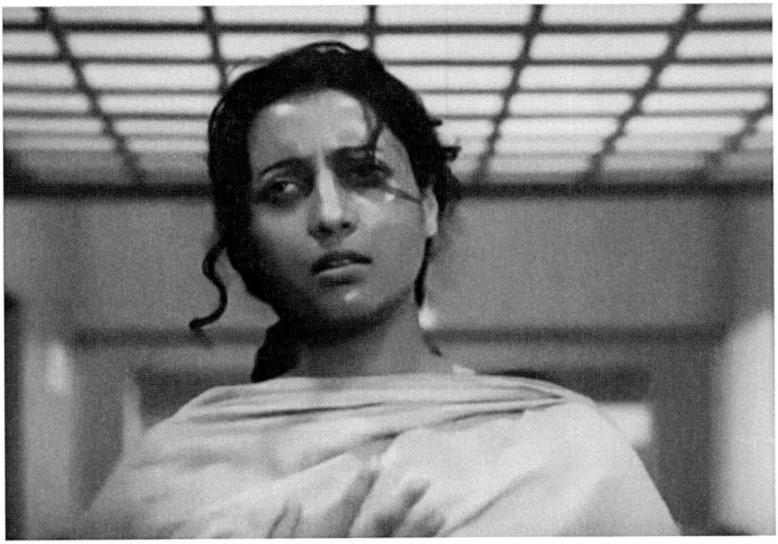

Figure 3.3: Radha, the Mad Woman in *Dweep Jele Jai*

Dweep Jele Jai stages an inversion of the woman's film discussed by Doane in her chapter on 'The Medical Discourse'. Instead of the narrative of the 'diseased woman' who is cured via her doctor's intervention with the help of various psychoanalytical tools, or the male doctor performing a 'love cure' (Doane 1987: 46),[22] here the nurse (doctor)/patient relationship is staged as the female/male dyad.[23] Radha's caring ministrations to her male patients are medically successful, and her performing the 'love cure' is part of the treatment. Radha is not emotionally numb; her unrequited love for her patient/beloved and the excruciating pressures of her 'love work' unhinge her mental balance. In fact, I would suggest that this 'madness' is deeply tied to the display of affect/nurture that she is made to perform. In Chapter One, one of the subjectivities that articulated the modern new woman was that of the idealised nurturing lover who cared for her impaired beloved and restored him to health and sight, as seen in *Sobar Upare*, *Sagarika*, and

Harano Sur, with some variations. This display of the lover's touch and intimacy also deployed the woman as an eroticised love object. In this film, too, we see the display of nurturing and caring that this woman is made to perform, and how this 'acting' out the idealised lover creates emotional pressures on her and the terrifying consequences of that 'role playing' for the new modern *bhadramahila.* Both her love work and her relation to her workplace are central to her self-fashioning as the modern professional woman, yet both ultimately end up overwhelming her, negating the affirmative possibilities of both work and the professional space.

Radha's performing love as work as a nurse does not give her any emotional sustenance, that is, it does not translate into her first patient, Debashish, reciprocating her love. This unrequited love, which haunts Radha, is continuously pressed forth in the narrative via flashbacks and the use of music, especially the whistling tune which works as a leitmotif.

Most of these flashbacks do not contain dialogue; they are purely gestural and performative, staging the *mise en scène* of repressed desires that are important in portraying the impossibility of Radha's situation. In one sequence, as we see Radha in the hospital corridor, we hear the male voice hum the tune, while the female voice narrates the lyrics. She then comes into the room (where Debashish had stayed as a patient) and sits on the bed as we hear her say, *this night, let this night spread.* She is then seen on the bed, placing her head on the pillow, caressing it as if she were caressing someone's head on that pillow; we then see her slowly rest her head on the same spot. As she lies on the bed, she says, 'this song will take my life away'; the camera zooms on her face, the male humming now louder. With a zoom into her eyes, lips, and nose, the entire frame is filled with her face, while the charged song of intimate desire is repeated in the woman's voiceover. The camera stays on the same frame till we see a lone tear in the corner of her eye. It stays gleaming like a little pearl against her face, intensifying her anguished inner self as well as star presence. This mobilisation of her spatial location, her voiceover, point of view, the whistling which she hears and which haunts her and the aural register, the space of the room—number 24, which she will occupy towards the end—the empty chair, and the use of flashbacks creates her '*mise-en-scene* of memory' (Doane 1987: 47). It alerts us to her emotive mentalscape, which is tied to her work and professional life but hints at some poignant lack that she is unable to voice.

The demanding emotional intensity of her work and its cruel aftermath makes Radha initially decline taking on Tapas, a new patient. The clinic-in-charge, the colonel, cannot understand why she is shirking her work, at which she excels. This scene is a classic example of the Brooksian idea of melodrama as the text of muteness, where the form resorts to a complete breakdown of the linguistic register as the characters seem to be in the grip of extreme emotional states (Brooks 1984: 56–80). The accumulation of her distress, which she has been unable to articulate, is siphoned off onto the musical register (Nowell-Smith 1987: 73). As she moves, we stay with her in a low-angle medium shot, almost in a classical Hollywood-like composition where the ceiling is visible, making her dominate the space. The intensity of her emotional state is thus magnified in the shot composition by using the low-angle camera, which makes her appear to almost touch the ceiling. The shot dissolves to her sitting at her worktable reading an open diary, the music audible. As she turns the pages, the shot cuts to a close-up of her diary entry, which refers to Debashish leaving. We remember the opening shot; we are now allowed to read what she had said in her voiceover.

> Debashish left today. Before leaving he told me I was his greatest friend. He would never forget me. But no one realised that today I was really able to act. I sent him off with a smile... I am a nurse; it's my job to light the flames in the lamps that get extinguished in people's lives....

The multiplicity of feminine subjectivities involved in this affective role-play, predicated along an excess of affect and nurture, ultimately lead to her breakdown as she is unable to experience the lover's touch of intimacy and togetherness. This is because her first patient, Debashish, returns to the woman who had jilted him, while the new patient Tapas falls in love with her. However, Radha cannot bring herself to love him. So while she performs exemplary work by becoming the caring, nurturing woman he wants, she is unable to experience the emotive, caring touch as she actually does not love Tapas. The pathos of her situation is pressed forth cinematically when we see Tapas caressing Radha while her off-camera look and voiceover constantly speak to Debashish. Her inability to enunciate the excruciating pain and suffering that the love cure has caused is displaced onto the song, whose haunting tune she (and we) have been hearing as an articulation of her innerscape. The song is saturated with the lover's desire for togetherness and the promise of an exclusive lover's night. But we know from previous scenes that Radha knows she will be unable to gift a book of poems she had brought for her beloved as he will leave the clinic to get married. The dissonance created by visually placing the beautiful woman sensuously dressed for a lovers tryst, juxtaposed with the song lyrics and what they actually signify in terms of her thwarted love cannot be more forceful.

The staging of this song that seems to haunt her memory and her mental space is a cinematic delight, mobilising an expressionistic staging of her aborted desire. As explained above, Suchitra's star value was accentuated through this kind of song picturisation, which added to her star status. This accretion was dependent on using the melodramatic mode of shot composition, framing, charged song lyrics, and her performance style. It also underscores the centrality of the song to the form of Indian melodrama that Bhaskar (2012) has argued for, and as I have demonstrated in my analysis in Chapter Two.

Towards the beginning of this song, we see Radha dressed in black chiffon and with open hair, standing outside Room 24, its iron grill door in a diamond pattern communicating the sense of a cage. The male voice hums the opening bars of the song; the ceiling is suffused with squares of light. As the humming becomes louder, she moves in and opens the wired door. We see her in mid-shot looking ethereal, the wind blowing through her open tresses, but her saddened expression undercuts the joyful anticipation that she had envisaged towards the beginning of the sequence. As the song starts, we see her look at the book in her hands,

> This night is yours and mine, Let it be yours and mine,
> Just the two of us, let my song beautify this night for us

> Let this night go forth and create an epic,
> You and I are on two shores
> I want to reach out to you
> Just the two of us alone
> This night is yours and mine
> Let it become yours and mine
> Just the two of us.

Through a series of tracking shots and close-ups, we move back and forth to Radha standing still in the room with the book, her present for Debashish, clutched to her bosom. All through the song, the man standing against the window does not look at Radha: there is no exchange of looks, and he is in fact unaware of her presence in the room. As he finishes singing, he moves away from the chair we had seen in the credit sequence, and once again the empty chair fills the frame. As the song ends, Radha turns and walks away, and the shot cuts to her back on the staircase in a deep space composition, her solitary figure clutching the book and standing on the landing, head bowed as the closing bars of the music waft across the frame. She turns and looks up, as if to cast one last look at what she has left behind, and the scene dissolves to a shot of the book in frame while the same music heard earlier layers the aural track.

What is interesting about this song is not only its signifying location within the diegesis, but also how it draws upon a cluster of ideas that are part of the romantic iconography of the love corpus associated with the Suchitra–Uttam film. In terms of lyrics, this song has a similar repertoire of images of night, which were exclusive for the two lovers, and the intensity of romantic possibilities that can envelop them within its fold are limitless as well. The memory of Suchitra singing longingly of her love for a blind Uttam in *Sagarika* (1956) is not very far removed from the affective intimacy that this song imagines. That song spoke lyrically of 'the honeyed night, which was only the lover's night'. Both films had the same lyricist, Gouriprassana Majumdar. The use of Hemanta's voice for this song in *Dweep Jele Jai* would also remind the audience of Uttam, as he provided the superstar with most of his playback vocals in the Suchitra–Uttam love films. So even if Uttam is not her romantic lead in this film, his absent presence seems to haunt this woman star's cinematic map. I borrow the germ of this idea from Mukherjee (2010), who argues that the 1960s Suchitra text is created and sustained by Uttam's appearances in different guises. He mounts a general argument but provides no corroboration in terms of film analysis.

Diegetically, the entire song sequence works at various levels. It serves to signpost the love that Radha imagined would translate into a union with her lover; the present that she clutches to her bosom is the empty signifier of her thwarted love; and while the erotic and emotion-laden song encapsulates the intensity of the love that the male is singing about, clearly Radha is not the intended object of his desire. The first case in which Radha successfully enacted the love cure was not staged in the present of the diegesis. We have only been provided access to that performance through Radha's memories, evoked through the song and voiceover. In the present case, the film 'shows' Radha enacting/performing this loving role-play, but also foregrounds the disjunction and unravelling that this leads to for her subjectivity. This is staged visually by placing her with her new patient, Tapas, while we continue to hear her remembered conversations with Debashish, predicated along a notion of femininity where she perceives herself also as an erotic love object.

It is worth recalling Doane's argument in this context. According to her, the doctor/patient relationship in a woman's film, set within the terms of medical discourse, 'insure(s) the compatibility of rationality and desire... and this relation is eroticised in many of these films' (1987: 61). Citing Foucault, she rightly points to the intensification of the medical figure in modernity as diseases become more psychologised: 'As Foucault stresses, the doctor and the patient form a "couple" in complicity against disease and madness' (ibid.: 63). She links this particular cinematic drive to the classical film text centred on the formation of the heterosexual couple, where 'the language of medicine and the love film become interchangeable' (ibid.). In this film too the nurse/patient relationship is highly eroticised. We see the display of sexual attraction and passion that Tapas experiences as he falls in love with Radha. These sequences with Tapas work at different levels;

they eroticise their relationship while at the same time staging the disjunctions that the woman experiences as she is haunted by her memory of her first patient.

In one sequence we see Tapas on his bed with Radha sitting next to him. He holds her and in the visual field her face is placed leaning over his, a classic shot composition denoting two lovers, as she helps him get ready for the night, recalling the iconic romantic couple shots seen in the Suchitra–Uttam love films. While she looks after Tapas, she is continuously thinking of and remembering Debashish. In this shot, her memory of Debashish is portrayed via a fade to her smiling profile. In the visual field we have two close-ups of her face, one in the present, and the other of her remembered self in the past with her lover. The ensuing dialogue is spoken in a soft, tender timbre as she puts Debashish to bed.

In the majority of scenes, Radha is dressed in a white nurse's saree, with a wristwatch, stethoscope, and white coat, but no jewellery, and sometimes with her vanity bag, denoting her busy professional status as well as the fashionable star look which was often criticised in the reception circuit as it went against cinematic realism. In this '*mise en scene of memory*', however, she is dressed in a flowing, dark zari-bordered chiffon saree and earrings. We see her cradling Debashish's face, caressing his cheeks as his face rests on her throat. She moves her hand over his hidden face, trying to soothe and calm him, but the tight close-up and the gestures denote the lover's touch rather than purely professional medical attention. In any case, her look is in complete contrast to her 'professional' nurse's look. We see her murmur Debashish's name lovingly and a fade to the present brings us back, as we see Radha with her eyes closed, murmuring soothing words, her face now resting on Tapas's arm. She is still calling 'Debashish', but suddenly her eyes open and we see them widen in fear as she realises how her mind has wandered. She moves back; two swift cuts portray Tapas in deep sleep and Radha with a shocked expression. *Dweep Jele Jai* is a mirror image of the most iconic of the love films, but with the disastrous consequences that performing love can have for the new woman as she descends into madness as a result of this gender performance.

The impending breakdown is signalled visually through Radha's tired, slow walk, halting speech, and the dark circles under her eyes, accentuated with 'naturalistic nude make-up' and minimal eye liner.[24] We also see her displaying her aversion to Tapas and his insistent physical demonstration of his feelings. She eventually asks to be excused from meeting Tapas as he is about to be discharged. He refuses to accept the Colonel's explanations about Radha's pretence of love and rushes to her room, banging on the door while she sits inside on a chair in the middle of the room. The cut to the inside of Radha's room frames her still pose as we hear his imploring voice. He keeps repeating that he will never leave her; he wants to see her just once. His words remind us of Debashish's promise that we had heard earlier. He is dragged away, and we move back to Radha, now seen in a high-angle shot, sitting still on the chair. The three windows at the back create three spools of light on the floor and reflect the window bars. The camera zooms in to a close-up, the blowing wind and music intensifying the eeriness of her still pose.

This particular last shot of Suchitra sitting alone, framed in a solitary state, is repeated in *Saat Paake Bandha* and *Megh Kaalo*. It became part of a repertoire of shots that formed an integral element of her 'woman alone' films that accentuated the intensity of her star text and fixed her iconic framing, which I have argued is central to both the star and melodrama as a genre.

In the last sequence, we see her as patient No. 24, being led through the hospital corridor, her erstwhile workspace. Her pealing and echoing laughter, her sobbing, uncoordinated movements, and her dishevelled hair and crumpled saree mark the madness that has engulfed her (see Figure 3.3). As she is being led to her room, she sees the colonel, her former boss. Upon seeing him, she quickly turns away, eyes wary, and we see her standing with her back to the wall as if trying to protect herself. She keeps telling him that she did not act and collapses at his feet. He calls her name, the aural track begins playing the tune of the song, and there is a flicker of recognition in her eyes at hearing her name. She raises her face and repeats her own name, smiles, keeps calling out her name, and walks with a vacant look as the tune continues, until she is behind the caged door touching the wires and the shot fades into the end title.

Radha's madness is caused by her ability to feel deeply; by not drawing the line between the professional requirements of a display of pretended emotion and the intensity of emotion that she feels for her patient, and by the betrayal of her feelings by the man she loves. Her inability to contain her emotions eventually manifests itself as a nervous disorder, a psychical disturbance, which is marked on her body, which was also the site of her eroticised romantic self. However, it can also be argued that this insanity that has confined her has done so into the 'space of her love', the same room where we had witnessed the performance of a love that was taboo for Radha. In the end, her insanity has freed her from all social prohibitions; it now sanctions her 'living and imagining' her union with her lover. Her calling out to herself as 'Radha' when she enters the room is perhaps an echo of her soul—she can now call herself the woman who loved Krishna but could not achieve the desired physical union with him as he was Rukmini's husband. It is only in the state of complete breakdown that Radha can achieve her affective bonding with her absent lover, depicted again through the deployment of the haunting whistling we had heard in the opening credits. We need to remember that the Radha–Krishna love story is not only a mythic love of the devotee and her lord, but also deploys the physical and sensuous bond of love. It is imagined as a love that can never be actualised, since Krishna leaves Vrindavan to be crowned the King of Dwarka and then marries Rukmini. As I have shown in my analysis, Radha keeps hearing the whistling, and though she sees Debashish, we do not. It is the haunting absence of her lover's flute/whistle that drives her to fulfil her desire through the mode of insanity, which allows her to imagine a union with him.

In a similar manner, we see Suchitra stage another nervous breakdown in *Sandhya Deeper Shikha*. Jayanti becomes a street-walking alcoholic, roams New Delhi at night, goes to bars, and picks up strangers who ply her with drinks in an attempt to forget her loneliness occasioned by her husband's death in the 1962 war with China. Her inability to accept his death ends in her suicidal death trek to the snow-clad mountains where her husband had died. In both films, the experience of intense emotional trauma and scenarios of breakdown are tied to psychic desires which cannot be accommodated within 'normal' states. In this decade, Suchitra's star text seems to be haunted by tragic narratives of aborted scenarios of failed love. Perhaps her private self, her troubled marital life,[25] and the onscreen break-up of her iconic pairing with Uttam spilled over into these narratives, staging a descent into insanity and psychotic breakdown. From this first cinematic exploration of the 'text of loneliness' I now move to a discussion of the second film, where this lonely *bhadramahila* appears as a divorced woman.

THE DIVORCED WOMAN: *SAAT PAAKE BANDHA* (1963)

Saat Paake Bandha remains an extremely significant film in Suchitra's career, not only because it fetched her her first ever international award, but also because it has acquired an iconic status due to its apparent similarity to her private life and experience of marital estrangement. Like *Dweep Jele Jai,* this film cinematically presses forth her star presence from the opening credits, as I have mentioned above.[26] The use of her close-ups and her voiceover, as well as her fashionable raincoat-clad appearance[27] (see Figure 3.1), marks out her narrative, expressing her past disappointments, the dreams of married life, and love for Sukhendu that she wanted and could not realise, and her present, in which she has to don a mask behind which she can hide.

The crux of the marital discord is located in the tensions and conflicts caused by differences in social status and an interfering mother-in-law. Instead of marrying above, Archana has married below her class.[28] Archana's mother remains caught up in maintaining appearances with her upwardly mobile relatives and social acquaintances. Sukhendu is *sadharan madhyabittya* (Sarkar 1997: 169), 'ordinary middle class', not the elite upper class within the *bhadralok*. The difference in the two families is staged as we see Archana doing all the household chores.

Since this film was also Suchitra's star vehicle, these scenes continuously position her in the visual field, highlighting an accumulation of details of her married life, her *domus,* with all its cumulative associations of domesticity that add to her screen presence. In fact, Suchitra's star text was also created via her personal location as a married *bhadramahila* who was seen to be presiding over her own household. I have seen film magazine pictures showing her cutting vegetables for her home's *Laxmi puja*, foregrounding the fact that despite her star status, she was a happy domestic woman too.

In a typically populist manner, the film masks her labour; she seems apparently content to preside over her married household.[29] The model of this domesticated new wife has been described as *sugrihini* (Banerjee 2006). I have discussed this aspect of the married woman's status in my discussion of *Indrani, Grihodaho,* and *Nabaraag* in Chapter Two. Here we see the modern woman trying to be a part of her husband's household, which is lower in the economic scale from her natal family.[30] The domestic sphere, the *grihasthali* (the household), is the crucial space that defines the married woman. It also locates her within the imaginary of the *gribalaxmi*, the goddess of material wealth and status; the married woman is supposed to bring in the blessings of the goddess into her new home. But what it involves is her complete containment within this domain, and even her natal family is outside this threshold. We see Archana trying to refashion herself as she is expected to completely mould herself according to her husband's expectations and social status, similar to Narayani's refashioning in *Nabaraag*. The schism within her is occasioned by the realisation that her husband's disapproval of the influence/interference of her family implies a disavowal of her natal family and their claim on her. In a charged sequence depicting a marital fight, Archana demands to know what she is supposed to do with her family—are they not his family too? But clearly, within the normative patriarchal set-up, she has moved into the husband's house, and hence is bound by its threshold.

The disjunction that Archana experiences between the demands of her status as the married woman and her mother's interference is articulated through two confrontations between the couple. In the first short but evocative sequence while she is away at her parents' home for a function, her husband attempts to decorate their bedroom and marital bed in an effort to make up with his wife. From the preceding scene, we know that Archana had gone alone to a family function at her parents' home as Sukhendu had not returned home on time. Archana comes back to discover the well-decorated room and a smiling Sukhendu waiting for her. The significance of the flowers and incense and the play of light and shadow in the bedroom denote Sukhendu's expectations of the night to come. Archana's stern and impassive expression signals the anger, hurt, and disappointment she is experiencing, occasioned by Sukhendu's absence from the function as well as her family's comments on her husband's unstable and lower economic position. As Archana stands at the bedroom door, the rising smoke from the burning incense is visible, covering her angry profile that underscores her raging emotions. This close-up of Suchitra resembles a *Saptapadi* sequence which showed an angry Rina shooting at Christ's picture in Krishnendu's hut. Even in that shot, Ajay Kar had deployed a similar shot composition, with Rina's face leaning over the flickering shattered lamp and then, as her breath blows the flame out, the smoke rises over her face. The circulation of these shot compositions across filmic texts is significant in adding to the iconicity of the star. This iconicity is not limited to one text but, as I have remarked in the Introduction, is available for use across texts. The closing shot, framing the empty marital bed and torn flowers, signifies the dissonance of the marriage. It can also be argued that if Uttam's absent presence haunts her star text and her marriage to Dibanath plays itself out via this filmic rendition, then this marriage cannot have a happy end; it will have to stage its end in separation and the woman's single status.

The second confrontation is staged after the couple's estrangement when Archana moves back to her natal home. She learns of Sukhendu's aunt, that is, his Pishima's departure to Kashi, and rushes to confront Sukhendu, who is seen sitting and writing in his study. His calm demeanour aggravates Archana's anger. She speaks of her effort to continuously preserve his dignity, but feels saddened by his inability to stand by her, his refusal to help her adjust to the new surroundings. And then she asks him why she is burdened with balancing the marital relationship. The couple trade insults, both feeling hurt and disappointed in each other. Archana is anguished to hear that he blames her for his aunt's moving out. She demands to know why he thinks that she has driven Pishima away. His reply—that it is all immaterial, she may not be involved but her mother is definitely culpable—angers her. She swiftly moves to stand in front of him and grabs his left arm to ask, 'All the same? It's all immaterial?' In her hurt and rage she grabs his collar and tells him that everything she imagined was a lie. And as she says this, suddenly in a sweeping motion we see her tearing his *kurta* apart.

This scene has acquired mythical status and is narrated in all her biographies. The circulation of this narrative is used to foreground her professional commitment to better her performance, for which she drew on her personal trauma of marital estrangement and fights. Suchitra had apparently suggested this scene to Kar on the morning of the shoot. She claimed in a 1993 interview published in the film magazine *Television* that this incident and fight had happened the night before with her husband (February 1993: 32).

The intensity of the woman's feelings of betrayal, hurt, and anger is underscored by the man's still posture. Even when she tears his shirtfront, we only see his jaw muscles twitch. They are both in the grip of the emotional moment, and Archana's unshed tears and Sukhendu's stillness complement each other well. He asks if she has anything more to say; she answers in the negative. With a last look at Archana, he slowly walks out of the room. The camera tracks to a close-up of her, stays on her, and then the shot dissolves to a long shot of her standing with her back to the window looking out, alone, with the empty bed in the foreground. The next morning, Sukhendu comes into the room to dress for work. Archana is still standing at the window and as he moves around the room, she suddenly tells him that instead of pretending to be husband and wife, they should separate legally. The close-up of his reaction, with the hardening of his facial muscles, stages his shock, as he cannot fathom what she is saying. But he remains mute and says nothing, and the next reaction shot of Archana's parents makes it obvious that she has moved back to her natal home. Both the sequences described above articulate the anger, hurt, and anguish in an expressive register, where the woman's point of view dominates the navigation of the visual and narrative strategies. In effect, Sukhendu disappears completely after this scene, and we see Archana sign the divorce papers at the behest of her mother and older brother.

It is on the occasion of her sister Baruna's marriage that Archana experiences the enormity of her decision and remembers her own wedding. Unlike the absent or glossed-over marriage ritual in the Suchitra–Uttam love films,[31] in this film, the ritual itself is staged elaborately to signify the woman's inability to accept the legal dissolution of her marriage, which the law sanctions but which is at odds with her deepest desires, as the ritual foregrounding the conjoining of two souls, united in front of the holy fire, is supposed to be a lifetime bond. This sequence, cued via her voiceover, uses a series of close-ups of Archana and Sukhendu dressed in the traditional attire of a Bengali bride and groom, layered over with the chants[32] describing the seven vows speaking of two hearts becoming one, of each accepting the other as an equal partner for life, echoing in the soundtrack.[33] However, the shot composition foregrounds the couple and their exchange of looks, excluding any shot of her family. This exclusion underscores the individuality of the decision that Archana has taken: we know that this marriage was not acceptable to her mother and older brother.

Her divorce is a loss that is brought forth through her sister's marriage sequence that takes place just after she has signed the divorce papers. In a series of shots we see her participating in all the pre-wedding rituals, and the entire sequence is mobilised to stage the lack in her life. We see her sitting alone in a room laden with wedding gifts, with the traditional headgear that the groom wears displayed for us, and the camera track emphasises her point of view. The tracking shot positioned over her shoulder focuses on an inscribed woven mat that reads, 'the night is woven in the seven steps, and the whole life will be wrapped in a hundred weaves', signifying the wedding ritual that is imagined as a lifelong bond. We learn that Archana has fasted throughout the day.[34] It is unclear whether she is fasting in memory of this significant ritual, which was central to her subjectivity as a married woman, and is now a form of penance that she undertakes for having broken that sacred vow.

Unlike Archana's marriage, Baruna's marriage is framed with a crowd of people witnessing the event. We see Archana standing alone, placed a little apart from the milling crowd. She seems engrossed; as the camera zooms to her close-up, her eyes are looking down, off-screen, the angle of her gaze clearly on the wedding ritual of the two hands wrapped in a garland of white flowers. The camera now moves back to Archana, her expression sombre as the same vows reverberate over the aural register. As the chants continue, the shot moves to a tighter close-up from the earlier medium close-up. She suddenly turns slightly to her left and looks off-screen. Now the shot splits into two, with her face filling the left frame while on the right we have a shot of her own wedding with the priest in between the couple, who have their hands placed palm up over each other's. This framing of her close-up signifies, of course, the intense emotional charge of the ritual that Archana is witnessing, as well as intensifying Suchitra's star presence. In my discussion of *Dweep Jele Jai* I foregrounded the use of this particular framing, which is a melodramatic use of the rhetoric of externalising emotions and fixing the iconic star image, as well as staging the '*mise en scene* of memory' (Doane 1987) and the heroine's repressed desires. In the next film, the device of a double role intensifies the star text, as I discuss later.

Archana's memory of her wedding continues, with the priest wrapping the garland over the couple's hands. After a few shots, she looks off-screen and walks past the guests in a daze, the aural register still reverberating with the seven vows that the couple is articulating. The shot dissolves to her slowly walking down a staircase, still in a dazed state. The half-lit staircase creates an eerie atmosphere, as if suggesting to us the separation that will follow. The next dissolve portrays her running on the street. The blurred street, with her running foregrounded, follows the logic of her flight. She seems to be panting with the exertion of her run, and the camera follows her through the busy street with two cuts of her in different locations on the roads. As the second shot concludes, we move back to the studio set: we see Archana laying her head against the closed door of her marital home, and then she starts banging on it. The next few shots build up the suspense, with light falling on her face, and the cut to a married woman standing at the open door shocks her and the spectators. After a few shots both realise that Sukhendu has gone abroad, leaving the house to his friend and his wife. Sukhendu's friend is angry with Archana and accuses her of selfishly destroying her husband's life. As he continues, we see Archana's tear-filled eyes darting around the house for one last time, and she slowly turns to leave. As she is on the threshold he asks her one last time, 'Was there any good reason why Sukhendu's life had to fall apart?' We see her crying as the angry man informs her in no uncertain terms that all of Sukhendu's acquaintances hold her responsible. She then walks out into the empty street; the next dissolve envelops her in a tearful haze as she remembers the accusation. We see her walk through smoke and the shot fades to a smoke-filled screen, fading again to her sitting still on her chair, taking us back to the present when she had started narrating her story.

We hear her voiceover: 'Everyone is against me, but I have no grudges against anybody. I did rush to him. I sacrificed my ego, I could not find him.' From a darker shadowed effect, her face is suddenly suffused with a focus light as the camera starts tracking back the light spilling in from the open door at her back. She speaks of an entire lifetime of solitude that she has experienced. The camera now tracks back to a crane shot as we see her sitting in a stylised composition with her arms on the armrest and her *saree pallu* flowing down. As it tracks back further, we see a single bed, and two chairs placed opposite with Archana positioned in the middle. The shot stays still and the end title appears on frame right.

Her sitting posture almost creates a doubling effect, as we had seen Radha sitting in her room when Tapas had wanted to see her. Here there is no one; she is left holding on to a commitment made by her soul and heart that has been torn apart by her family and the law. But she herself refuses to bow to social dictates and chooses to remain true to her emotional selfhood, waiting for her lover/ husband who may never return. Suchitra had divorced Dibanath sometime after 1963 (Chaudhuri 1993). This fact is only corroborated in her remark in the interview cited in *Television* magazine. But despite her estrangement, she reportedly wanted

Dibanath's body to be flown back after his death so her daughter could perform the last rites for her father (ibid.: 32; Chaudhuri 1995: 39). Despite marital tension and separation, she chose to remain Mrs Sen and, according to Kanan Devi, she never forgot her first youthful love for her husband (Chattopadhyaya 2005: 40). Like Archana, we see Nirmalya in *Megh Kaalo* choosing to stay single, denied the possibility of being a wife and mother by her lover's inability to stand by her. For these lonely selves, the woman's still pose carries the marks of her silence, but the framing of the stylised posture makes the silence eloquent. This silence is not the inability to speak, but the determination to remain mute, to withdraw into the inner recesses of the self which provides a sanctuary from social and familial constrictions.

The Maternal Melodrama: *Uttar Phalguni* (1963)

Uttar Phalguni[35] (1963), produced by Uttam, saw the two stars collaborate despite not acting opposite each other; their names both appear, albeit as the producer and the leading star. Uttam managed to place his name before hers, as he was the producer, thus inverting the credit sequence order that she had dictated since 1955 with *Saanjher Pradeep*, and which was followed subsequently for the films in which they starred together. This film saw Suchitra in the double role of a mother and daughter, consolidating her star status further. (She had earlier played a double role in *Smriti Tuku Thak* [1960].) Majumdar (2009) has noted that one of the important ways in which star value could be capitalised on was by getting that star to perform a double role. Along with this doubling, this film also enabled the splitting of the woman into the older mother and the modern, foreign-educated daughter. The splitting of femininity enacts two of the most significant selves that women are expected to embody in patriarchy, the sacrificing mother and her noble daughter. Yet, by intensifying the star presence, this stereotypical embodiment vis-à-vis the maternal melodrama articulates an excess that emphasises the emotive bond of the mother and daughter. *Uttar Phalguni* brings together two genres—the imaginaries of a contemporary courtesan film and the maternal melodrama (Bhaskar and Allen 2009; Doane 1987; Byars 1991)—on the same plane in the Bengali popular. Female stars across film cultures mapped their stardom through maternal melodrama;[36] one of the most iconic performances in post-independence Indian cinema is Nargis's enactment of the mother in *Mother India* (1957), although that film foregrounds the mother-son bond. In Bombay cinema, the courtesan genre also provided female stars with a performative space that was quite spectacular.[37]

FIGURE 3.4: Suchitra/Panna Bai, *Uttar Phalguni*

As noted earlier, the film opens with shots of a sensuously dressed Panna Bai singing a '*hori*' *thumri*, '*kon tarah se tum khelath hori*' in a *mehfil*, surrounded by her male audience.[38] The entire performance of this bejewelled, beautiful courtesan draws on the tradition discussed in Bhaskar and Allen (2009).[39] The space and work of the woman performer, the *baiji*, evokes a highly stylised and cultured imaginary, although that space is marginalised as it is the obverse of the respectable home. Yet, this film makes an unusual statement about the value of this space and the work performed for the subjectivity of the performer, which is not given its due in the courtesan film. The importance of work and the spatial relationship that I have argued is central to middle-class self-fashioning is not limited in a narrow restrictive sense to only the 'respectable' *bhadramahila*. Panna Bai/Debjani occupies these related but different working and spatial coordinates. This conversation about the value and pleasure of the performer's work takes place early in the film when Debjani is being trained.

Chhaya Debi says to Debjani, showing her the space where the *mujra* is performed in the *Kotha* located in Lucknow,[40]

> ...*yehi woh jagah hai jahan suron ki jhankar mein mujhe har roz ek nai zindagi milti hai, log gaana sunke chale jaate hain, par unki taarifen mujhe har roz jeene ki ek nai raah deti hain, maana ki log is jagah ko achcha nahin maante.* [This space enables me to recreate a new and fulfilling life every day, amidst the praise from those who value my musical talent. The people who come here will leave once my song is over, but their appreciation paves new pathways for me. Even if this is an accursed place, this gives me enough sustenance to live.]

This is a radical statement of intent/agency that critiques the popular prejudices reinforcing the marginalised space accorded to a courtesan in this filmic tradition. For the woman performer, this is her workspace, which, in the enactment of her artistic locus, imagines a particular form of polite conduct and appreciation from her male patrons. Here, the woman is making a valid point about work that gives pleasure to her male clients and also provides her with creative satisfaction at the same time. There is no attempt to invoke sympathy for what is regarded as a demeaning profession; instead, it is presented as one that she has learnt to remould to her advantage. This statement embodies a different view of this socially ostracised and marginalised group, articulating the pleasure that the woman performer achieves through her singing. It is this artistic accomplishment as a virtuoso that enables Debjani to provide her daughter with a good convent education.[41] The foregrounding of her sensuous photogenic close-ups, profile shots, and the display of *ada*, gestures, especially the delighted expressions denote her pleasure. If work and space define selves, then that self-fashioning also involves a sense of achievement in work done well. Both the woman performer and the star can then lay claim to that achievement, which is not only an economic imperative but is also crucial to the inner core of subjectivity, especially if we conflate the filmic and off-screen selves. It is central to our understanding of what this work—involving a display of the woman's virtuosity as a performer—means for the performer herself.

Uttar Phalguni uses the tradition of the courtesan film and also draws on certain tropes of the suffering/exploited wife and the maternal melodrama.[42] Panna's previous self, Debjani, was tied to an exploitative marriage, which she has run away from. Debjani's[43] husband Rakhal soon finds her and demands that his runaway working wife provide for the expenses incurred by his gambling and drinking. There is an interesting cinematic, reflexive, and ironic moment as the wastrel husband refers to their marriage as *saat paake bandha*,[44] the Vedic union of a man and woman in the Hindu marriage, even though we know that Rakhal's union with this woman was anything but ideal. It could signpost Suchitra's tumultuous married life to a scion of a *bonedi* family and her subsequent separation from her husband. Suchitra essayed the role of another betrayed wife in *Fariyaad* (1971).[45] In that film, Ratna is married to a cowardly man who is unable to protect her from the clutches of Baren Mullick/Utpal Dutt, owner of Hotel Merlin, where she is a cabaret performer.[46] Both her father and husband prove to be useless in safeguarding her. In fact, in most of these 1960s films, the characters essayed by Suchitra are let down by the men in their lives, giving form to the melodramatic trope of ineffectual male figures. They have neither the courage nor the dignity to stand by this strong, independent woman. She is either the abandoned wife or lover, or the exploited woman who has to cope with the vicissitudes of her gendered and familial locus, as is seen in all the three films discussed here and also in her characterisations in *Hospital* and *Megh Kaalo*.

Uttar Phalguni enacts the mother/child relationship as one of sacrifice and separation. Debjani is forced to send her daughter away to save her from her father's greedy demands. The scenes portraying Debjani playing with her child evoke sympathy and pathos, which are central to the topos of maternal melodrama. Doane describes the genre thus,

> Maternal melodramas are scenarios of separation, of separation and return, or of threatened separation—dramas which play out all the permutations of the mother/child relation. Because it foregrounds sacrifice and suffering, incarnating the 'weepie' aspect of the genre, the maternal melodrama is seen as a paradigmatic type of woman's film. (1987: 73)

The immanent separation lends a curious poignancy to the scene as we see Debjani clinging to and hugging the child, who does not understand what is to come.[47] Her decision to send her child to a convent school underscores her desire to ensure that the child is brought up outside of the social environment of her mother's context. However, Debjani's socially liminal status as Panna Bai results in the cancellation of her daughter's school application, a narrative also seen earlier in the decade through Suchitra/Sharbari's single parent travails in *Hospital* (1960). In a long emotive sequence, we see Debjani pleading to the Mother Superior of the convent, framed against a wall affixed with a statue of Christ on the cross. Panna demands to know why, when Jesus Himself had rescued a prostitute, her daughter is being discriminated against because of her mother's profession. Appealing to human compassion, she asks the Mother Superior to listen to her story and then take a decision. The framing now captures the mother and child against a portrait of Mother Mary with an infant Jesus in her arms. The ensuing flashback narrates her traumatic marriage, undertaken as an economic transaction by her father to stave off financial ruin in the face of crippling debt, and her journey to become a courtesan to provide for herself and her daughter. Her body therefore becomes a tradable commodity, and we know that in reality it becomes a living nightmare for her as she is forced to tolerate all the emotional and physical violence that Rakhal unleashes on her. This scene also provides us with clues to her past as we are told of her lover Manish, who is studying abroad, unaware of her traumatic marriage. Her voiceover tells us that she thought of fighting and resisting, yet could do nothing as she soon became pregnant. Debjani's story and her determination to win a better life for her daughter convince the

Mother Superior, who agrees to take in Suparna and give her the educational opportunity that would change her life.

In a plot twist, Debjani's lover Manish comes back into her life through a chance encounter. Pained by the sacrifices that she has had to make in trying to raise her child on her own, he now wants to accept Debjani despite what her social locus implies. She refuses and asks him to look after Suparna instead. He goes to Suparna's school, meets the child, and adopts her. It is interesting that the older pair sacrifice their love and desire so that Suparna can have a fulfilling life in the future. Like Debjani, Manish too is giving up his beloved to dedicate his life to raising her daughter as his own, with all the socially sanctioned benefits of class, status, and education that his *bhadralok* location will make available for Suparna. She grows up to be a promising young lawyer without any knowledge of her origins. This sequence of sacrifice enacted by the older lovers is staged via a well-known song by Tagore, which plays on the soundtrack: '*Aguner parashmoni chonwayo prane*'.[48] The lyrics emphasise the essential purity of fire as it touches the soul that bows in supplication to God. This act makes the soul pure and refined so that the mortal body/life also becomes perfect and achieves plenitude through sacrifice. The film makes the trope of Panna's/Debjani's purity and sacrifice very obvious. We see a shot of Manish in the car, dissolving into shots of a beautiful Suchitra with her hair blowing in the wind, standing against the open window, as the lyrics on the aural register (now in a female voice) are overlaid with a series of dissolves, the song staging how this woman is purifying her life by burning her body.

The female voice sings of lifting her body to light the lamp in the temple. The juxtaposition of a puja song with the courtesan's body is used to underscore the sharp polarity between the real life of this woman and the noble sacrifice she enacts by offering her musical art as a commodity, even as her vocation places her in a degraded social position. Yet that commodification does not degrade the body or soul; rather, it uplifts them to enable their use as an offering to the deity. Her purity is possible as the particular performative tradition of the good courtesan taps into this character trope. Even when she is hired to entertain her clients at night, she 'remains' untouched by any contamination. In contrast, Ratna, the cabaret performer in *Fariyaad,* is trapped in a claustrophobic and demeaning sexual relationship with Baren Mullick. In *Uttar Phalguni,* we do not see Panna Bai experiencing sexual exploitation except, ironically, as a married woman in her previous avatar as Debjani, where her husband had solicited a man for her and continues to exploit her economically. Frustrated by his blackmailing, she shoots him dead to ensure that he is unable to destroy Suparna's life.

In a dramatic scene of revelation, as Suparna confronts Manish, who has taken on Panna Bai's defence, she learns about the reality of her birth, her mother's story, and the sacrifices she made to keep her daughter safe from the clutches of the avaricious, exploitative blackmailer. A traumatised Suparna is comforted by her lover Indraneel/Dileep Chaudhuri, who also agrees that they need to support her mother against the injustice she has been subjected to in the name of a sham marriage. In the revelation scene, the film explores interesting questions of law and legality in terms of justice and morality. Manish asks Suparna to step outside the parameters of ethics and morality that are invoked against public women who commit violent crimes. He asks her to see if our responses are as objective as we think, or if the educated class is as prejudiced as the rest in condemning this woman—who has shot her husband not in a fit of marital rage, but as a desperate act of justice—as a petty criminal. How is the individual to be constituted before law? Is it possible to imagine subjectivity outside of the legal and juridical system? Foucauldian analyses would deny the possibility of justice and individual subjectivity being constituted outside of the judicial system. Foucault suggests that it is the modern juridical system that produces the subject and then represents the same in a court of law. However, if it is the same structure of power and institutionalised legal system that has produced the subject, then the legal system will not be available in any emancipatory/compassionate sense (Foucault 1980). Yet, the film provides a space of 'affect' within the melodramatic address where that moment of reconstitution is available, albeit fleetingly.

This film enacts the bonds and limits of maternal love and the daughter's refusal to accept societal restrictions on her love for her mother, as she becomes the figure through whom the marginalised *baiji* can return to the personal familial fold from which she had been excluded. The trial sequence opens to the two women meeting for the first time in court and stages the coming together of mother and daughter, as the young daughter confidently tells the court that the woman being tried for murder cannot be judged on circumstantial evidence as she committed the crime under extreme provocation. Unlike her mother, who lacked the confidence to publicly acknowledge her daughter, the young, professionally-educated woman has no qualms in accepting the 'fallen public woman' as her mother in front of the whole court, and her lover is equally supportive of this woman's decision to confront the social stigma head-on and question its deep-seated patriarchal prejudices.[49]

The entire sequence mobilises Suchitra's star presence spectacularly in the double role as the camera moves back and forth between Debjani/Panna and Suparna through their close-ups. The use of deep space composition and Suparna's voice echoing in the courtroom mirrors her mother's singing, with which the film had opened, while Suparna mounts a spirited defence of her mother, almost doubling the rhetorical appeal to sentiment and humane values that her mother had once used to admit her into school. In a series of profile shots, we see her telling the court of the terrible suffering this murderess had to experience, and then ask if her crime is bigger than the law of natural justice, which demands that this woman be judged as a mother and not condemned as a common prostitute. The use of Debjani's close-up signals her maternal locus, which is finally given its due recognition. Suparna's echoing voice refers to Debjani as a *Devi*, the eternal mother goddess, symbol of nurture, care, and plenitude, eschewing the language of law and legality to resort to the mythic structures of nature and organic life; while her performance, her rhetorical language, and the use of her echoing voice fills the entire court with her presence. The ending shows Debjani collapsing and dying in her daughter's arms as Suparna rushes to embrace her mother.

The final shot brings together the two women who could not be with each other throughout the narrative, but can now be recognised as mother and daughter, as Debjani's voiceover proclaims that Panna Bai's death would ensure Suparna's life. The camera pans back with a shot of the courtroom, freezing them together as the others look on. The film does not seem invested in reinstating the 'fallen public woman' into the social, but appears more keen to bring together affectively the mother and daughter who constitute a single family unit. The doubling of the star presence, which Majumdar has argued was an effective strategy to intensify star presence as a melodramatic text, is used differently in this film. She has suggested that the double role works as a moral index highlighting star charisma and authenticity; it celebrates performance and also articulates the inherent entertainment value of stardom (Majumdar 2009: 146, 165). In this film there is no splitting of the good and the bad: both Panna Bai and Suparna are good and noble; the intensification of emotive and sentimental affect is heightened through this splitting of the same star into two selves, signifying moral indexes, the sacrificing mother and the noble daughter.

What is significant in *Uttar Phalguni* and *Fariyaad* is the agency being transferred onto the children of the two protagonists. The sacrificing mothers in both films are rescued by their offspring, who take it upon themselves to provide what the father/husband could not do for them. In *Fariyaad*, the son, Prasanto, who is a neighbourhood *mastaan*,[50] stabs Mullick and sets his mother free, though his jail term leaves her forlorn, as she waits for her son to return to her. What both films demonstrate are the deeply contradictory impulses that these two mothers/performers experience in their negotiation of one of the most significant—as well as hegemonic—structures of patriarchy that are made available to women. Motherhood is not merely a site of 'comfort and nostalgic pleasure—a position to which a patriarchal culture ceaselessly and somewhat desperately attempts to confine it—it is a site of multiple contradictions' (Doane 1987: 81–82). Motherhood is a sacrifice and a struggle that Debjani experiences; it can also be a trap that the woman may find constricting and blame her child for, as we see with Ratna, who finds it impossible to 'love' her son. In the entire film, we do not see Ratna playing with or embracing

Prasanto. In fact, the mother-son relationship is staged as a distant one, and does not use the trope of the maternal as a caring nurturer. In this film, Ratna is unable to accept her child, since it is because of him that she was forced into accepting a degrading and exploitative sexual relationship with the club owner. He is also a constant and painful reminder of her weak and emasculated husband, who did not have the courage to protect his wife from the clutches of the lecherous club owner. In contrast, Debjani, who is portrayed as playing with her child, and Sarbari, the single mother in *Hospital*, do not feel trapped by their maternal responsibility. Yet both mothers are brought back into the familial and the personal by their offspring. It is the abiding, yet fraught bond that has been staged in the maternal melodrama of the woman performer.

These 'texts of loneliness' that I read as the defining trope of Suchitra's star text in this decade need to be positioned beside the question of the particular ideological enactment of modernity that these filmic subjectivities signify and embody. As I mentioned in the Introduction, the dyad of the traditional and the modern does not function as binaries of the self or the other; rather, the very imaginary of the new woman, as well as Indian modernity as it defined itself, rested on its ability to be 'Janus faced', to borrow Gyan Prakash's (1999) formulation. The varied modern selves of the urban *bhadramahila* as the professional nurse, the divorced woman, the sacrificing mother, and her noble daughter inhabit this double-faced modernity in all its complexities. The woman/star as the symbol of modernity performs the inherent contradictions of her gendered identity, embodying perhaps the varied anxieties that are played out through women and their negotiations of selfhoods. All three films articulate the emotive subjectivities of these modern women, and their self-fashioning demands a space that is denied to them. These negotiations of selves are fraught and conflictual, yet retain their hold on imaginaries precisely because they enact 'mythemes of femininity', to use Doane's phrase (1987: 3). The endings of the three films, which stage the woman left alone, cannot be read simplistically as just texts of loneliness, but are also texts that articulate the agency of the protagonists, painful and poignant as they may be.

The stereotypes of the sacrificing lover, divorced wife, and the sacrificing mother are not to be conflated with false consciousness or as untruth. The power of stereotypes lies in the very fact of their being both true and false. These are powerful discursive forms (Byars 1991: 72–73) that can signpost the unmasking of the very contradictions that they supposedly display. The feminine subjectivity that the three films use as a structural, cinematic, and affective principle, the mobilisation of the woman's voice, and her 'choosing' to be that which gives plenitude to her heart's desires has to be calibrated in our responses to the images and the endings. Radha, Archana, Debjani, and Suparna attain their selfhoods via scenarios that depict the limits of their selves. Yet the emotional charge and cinematic staging of these characters and their actions imbue these images with a power that goes beyond the limits of the endings, mobilised along the melodramatic staging and externalisation of repressed desires, the intensification of the three women's emotive selfhoods, as well as the iconic articulation of Suchitra's screen presence. This cinematic accretion of her screen presence did not eschew her glamour and erotic image. However, the particular, eroticised star presence in her 'woman alone' films seems to have been acceptable, given that her screen characterisations articulated tragic dénouements of madness, loneliness, and death, accentuating her 'text of loneliness' as opposed to her romantic, erotic, and risqué image in the previous decade.

Yet these very limit scenarios also give voice to the times, and the impossibility of realising dreams of fulfilling selfhood within the available material and historical structures of the 1960s. Her suffering and loneliness, her still posture and silence embody the crumbling dreams and desires that could not be actualised. The Romantic Utopia of the couple is no longer being staged here; perhaps that time is over. It is the lonely woman, and not the romantic lover, who chooses her loneliness above the social, the personal, and the familial to refashion herself. It is interesting to note that Suchitra had remarked that she might have chosen to be lonely post-retirement, but she was not alone, she had found her life in her devotion to Ramakrishna and God (Ray 1992: 129; Chaudhuri 1993: 26). I shall discuss this *sadhika* image in Chapter 5.

These enactments also brought Suchitra some measure of critical recognition. This fragment of her star text seems to underscore a certain 'economy of prestige' and 'branding' (Ponzanesi 2007) that allows for a reconfiguration of acceptance based on recognition abroad. Ponzanesi argues that Indian authors writing in English gain tremendous prestige and currency if they win international awards for their books. Similarly, actors too can be seen as gaining symbolic currency for international recognition through film awards. This particular insight allows me to understand how the template of critical discourse surrounding Suchitra changed shape in the 1960s and enabled an accretion of cultural capital that was denied to her text earlier. From the trope of 'cultural intimacy' (Herzfeld 2005 [1997]) that I have used to understand the backlash unleashed on her sexualised romantic image, her text in this decade, predicated along an arc of suffering and loneliness, while still glamourous, shifts shape from 'embarrassment' to being coded as '*biswa bandita*',[51] world renowned, in the words of Kaalish Mukherjee, the *Rupmancha* editor whose strident reviews and criticisms I have cited previously. It is in suffering and tragedy that the region willingly embraced the star value of this woman superstar who gave it its most charged cinematic imaginary, both as an idealised beloved and as a glamourous *bhadramahila* refashioned as a recluse.

NOTES

1. Suchitra's married woman roles included films such as *Boloygrash* (1954), *Saajghar* (1955), *Mejo Bou* (1955), *Shubho Ratri* (1956), and *Amar Bou* (1956).

2. It is important to note that Uttam's Bombay tryst started only in the late 1960s, that too with his own production of *Chhoti Si Mulaquat*, which was a box-office disaster. In a personal letter written in 1954, he referred sarcastically to Suchitra's Bombay career (*Anandalok*, 27 July 2007: 15). Clearly the relationship between the two was also one of professional jealousy and star ego clashes. This ego clash has often been cited as one reason why *Saptapadi* took more than two years to be made. See the discussion about the romantic star text and its reception circuits in Chapter One.

3. Uttam's 'affair' with Suchitra has recently resurfaced on television through the serial 'Mahanayak'. I shall discuss this serial and other retellings in Chapter Five.

4. The 1960s was a crucial decade for both superstars. In this decade, they reinvented their screen personas and moved away from their iconic romantic screen image to essay different figurations of selfhood. I shall discuss this shift in Uttam's text in Chapter Four.

5. This particular relationship between the star text and the melodramatic text, which has been discussed by Gledhill (1991) and elaborated by Majumdar (2009), has been referred to in some detail in the Introduction.

6. The 1963 October issue of *Rupmancha* was dedicated to Suchitra and carried extensive coverage and interviews with her directors and associates. The newspapers too gave wide coverage to the award and the various felicitations.

7. *Ghare Baire* was written by Tagore against the backdrop of the 1905 Bengal Partition and was eventually made by the maestro in 1984 with a different cast. He never made the Bankim adaptation, though Suchitra did perform Dinen Gupto's *Devi Chaudhurani* in 1974 opposite a much younger Ranjit Mullick.

8. This particular publicity picture was clicked by Dhiren Deb in the 1960s and had created a furore. In this photo, Suchitra posed with her shoulders bare, a big hair do, and the words 'no kiss' written on her cheek in lipstick. Her eroticised image was further consolidated by this picture.

9. This *sadhika* image has been written about extensively by G. K. Ray and I discuss this reinvention in Chapter Five.

10. Biswas uses the phrase 'aura of loneliness' in connection to the peripheral location of the family in the love films of the 1950s with the star pair. He suggests that these narratives of displacements, separation, and the presence of near states of neurotic breakdown are central to the Suchitra–Uttam love films (2000: 125). I, however, feel that this term is more productive to read the individual star texts where they do not act as the romantic couple. Even in Chapter Two, where I read marriage and its staging primarily in terms of the trope of discord, the filmic end still concludes with their iconic embrace. This embrace, which was central to their romantic coupling, was staged even in the Saratchandra text, *Grihodaho*, the ending of the film having been modified to suit the box office. Similarly, as I have said in Chapter One, *Saptapadi* too was modified to include the coming together of Krishnendu and Rina.

11. Limit situations can be understood as deeply tragic and fraught scenarios where the characters encounter terrible circumstances that force them to choose between their desires and social conventions.

12. I have used their intervention to locate my readings of the romantic couple films within this discursive regime in Chapter One (Biswas 2000, 2002; Chatterjee 2007; Gooptu 2010; Vasudevan 2000).

13. *Dweep Jele Jai*, *Saat Paake Bandha*, and *Uttar Phalguni* ran for twelve, eleven, and fifteen weeks, respectively, at a stretch. All three films were big hits and had successful Hindi remakes as well, as *Mamata* (1966) *Khamoshi* (1969), and *Kora Kagaz* (1974). Moreover, these three films brought awards for the leading ladies in both versions.

14. The traditional Hindu wedding rite involves circumambulations around the fire, where the couple take seven rounds as the priest chants the wedding vows.

15. It is worth noting that Suchitra essayed the role of a cabaret performer in *Fariyaad* (1970), who is also a single mother. I shall use this figuration as a counterpoint in my discussion of *Uttar Phalguni*.

16. Doane's work analyses a set of films made in Hollywood from the silent era to the early 1950s and 1960s, but concentrated more heavily on films in the 1930s–40s which were targeted at women spectators. Her work seeks to recover a feminine subjectivity via a reworking of psychoanalysis in her book, *The Desire to Desire* (1987).

17. These films were commercially huge hits; it cannot be argued that only women audiences were responsible for their commercial success. Suchitra's performances also brought awards, both international and national.

18. Byars argues that in the 1950s Hollywood melodramas: 'The Woman Alone came to embody the threat of female emancipation; the Woman alone became suspect. The Wife, the Mother, the Daughter—in their many manifestations—became the only truly viable alternatives in the film melodramas of the 1950s' (1991: 77).

19. This particular form is part of the classical repertoire and allied to the *thumri*, a style of light classical singing. It is

> an endearing lyrical form of Hindustani classical music that is rooted in the erotic love-play and *viraha* (separation), conditions of love between Radha and Krishna. Written in *Braj bhasha*, *Awadhi*, *Bhojpuri* and also with Urdu words *thumri* compositions privilege the lyrics even as, when sung, the notes are musically enunciated and performed with great virtuosity. (Bhaskar and Allen 2009: 55–56)

Hori is a particular form of *thumri* 'which celebrates the spring festival of color, Holi' (ibid.: 56).

20. Chaudhuri summarises Silverman thus: 'Embodied voiceovers are tied to characters on screen, often used to cue flashbacks. These characters are often marred by trauma and speak from extreme situations' (2006: 51).

21. This idea of gender as a performative act is central to Judith Butler's intervention in 'Gender as Performance'. Mukherjee has aptly summarised this feminist intervention that productively engages with both discourse and power, not in a monolithic or hegemonic manner, in her discussion on Devika Rani (2009: 24).

22. The woman patient in Doane's formulation is also sexually frigid and hence the love cure enables the staging of the erotic, which aids the patient's recovery (Doane 1987).

23. Doane refers to the Hitchcock film *Spellbound*, 'where precisely the opposite may appear to be the case since Ingrid Bergman is the doctor and Gregory Peck her patient, it can in fact be demonstrated that she is ultimately constituted and analysed—she suffers from a frigidity constantly associated with intellectual women in cinema' (1987: 46).

24. Suchitra's look was heavily glamourised in her films. She used Max Factor pancake make-up; her dark kohl-lined eye make-up and manicured fingernails added to her photogenic appeal and created a heavily star-like appearance. This star-like look was routinely criticised for being 'unrealistic', but was nevertheless part of her star persona.

25. Suchitra had been experiencing marital discord with Dibanath; it was during the shooting of *Saat Paake Bandha* later in the decade that she ultimately separated from him. During the late 1950s, there were rumours of Dibanath's anger and rage, which had reportedly translated into some form of physical violence as well (Chattopadhyay 2005: 19, 25, 41).

26. Hemanta Mukherjee scored the music for both films. He used a particular kind of melodic tune that is romantic and soulful and is deployed to cue us to the intense memory of the past that impinges upon both Radha's and Archana's present.

27. Suchitra's fashionable appearance is quite marked; the sheer white raincoat, her manicured hands clutching her purse create an unmistakably glamorous look even without jewellery. Of course, Ajay Kar's lighting and camera and the magic of black-and-white photography are superb in creating the cinematic charge of this star.

28. A 'good' marriage involved upward social mobility for the woman; marrying below her social status was considered foolish and sentimental and a terrible fallout of 'love marriages'.

29. Panja (2004) has astutely argued that these depictions of the well-managed household usually mask the labour and work that the woman has to perform. She has addressed this aspect in her discussion of Binodini and Asha in Tagore's *Chokher Bali*.

30. In this film it is the foppish Nanimadhav, Archana's rich suitor who is her elder brother's friend, who is unable to attract her enough to agree to a marriage. This is one of the reasons for her mother's anger; according to the mother, Archana could have aspired to a rich and comfortable lifestyle if she had agreed to marry Nanimadhav.

31. I have discussed how the Suchitra–Uttam films stage marriage through the song in *Indrani* or as a private vow in *Pathey Holo Deri* in Chapter One.

32. Kar did not use any song in *Saat Paake Bandha* and the two marriage scenes are layered over with the chants. The Hindi version, *Kora Kagaz*, directed by Chetan Anand, used songs.

33. There are eight kinds of marriage under the Vedic marriage (Chatterjee 1998: 58–59). The most common form is the 'Brahma' marriage ritual that we witness in this film.

34. This is part of the Bengali marriage ritual. Both the bride and the groom are supposed to fast through the day as the Vedic rites demand a complete purification of the soul and body before the ritual fire worship can be performed. The holy fire is symbolic of the celestial fire and is evoked as a witness to the earthly union.

35. The story was written by Niharranjan Gupto, who was known for his detective fiction. He was one of the popular writers whose stories and novels were regularly adapted for films.

36. Some notable instances of maternal melodramas across film cultures that stage the trope of suffering mother are *Imitation of Life* (1959), *Mildred Pierce* (1945), *Dancer in the Dark* (2003), *Stella Dallas* (1937), and *Volver* (2006).

37. One of the most iconic of these films is Kamal Amrohi's *Pakeezah* (1971), starring Meena Kumari in a double role of an abandoned mother and courtesan daughter.

38. Bhaskar and Allen explain the intricacies of the thumri repertoire as well as the classical use of folk forms such as *hori*, *kajari*, *chaiti*, etc., that 'were forms of folk music which [were] drawn into the institutions like the *kotha* and reconstituted within the *raga* and the *tala* structures of classical music' (2009: 55–56).

39. I will summarise the core arguments of Bhaskar and Allen's intervention as it pertains to this particular film. As the *thumri* performance unfolds, it is clear that the woman performer is marked in the visual plane as a courtesan, with heavy *kundan* jewellery and clothes derived from the *mujra* tradition of women performers, which do not draw upon the court dancer tradition, but rather upon what has been termed as the 'baithaki mehfil' tradition of the

mujra repertoire. In this performance, the courtesan sits 'in full attire for her performance, and (presents) her musical repertoire by articulating the meaning of her songs through abhinaya (expressive hand and facial gestures)' (Mishra 2009: 47, cited in Bhaskar and Allen 2009: 53). In this particular form, the woman draws upon 'her virtuosity as a vocalist and the forms of her musical heritage (that) are highlighted' as it foregrounds the '*baiji* or the singer-performer' (ibid.: 54).

40. Lucknow is an important space in the imaginary of the courtesan film. The nawabi culture of this city provides an interesting template for the genre to map the life of these performing women who thrived on the patronage of the nawabs and the feudal lord (ibid.: 44–46).

41. In Manish Gaekwad's recently-released memoir on his mother Rekhabai, a performing courtesan, Gaekwad writes about a similar kind of upbringing, where his mother was able to fund his boarding school education. However, unlike Suparna in *Uttar Phalguni*, he was able to visit her during school vacations and was aware of his mother's liminal status. See Gaekwad (2023).

42. Suchitra was effectively a single working mother after her separation from her husband Dibanath. She raised her daughter alone and provided her with a boarding school education. She was reportedly a strict mother who was seen to take her maternal responsibilities very seriously (*Television* magazine interview 1980).

43. The screen names in the three films are quite significant. Suchitra is Radha in *Dweep Jele Jai*, Krishna's lover who never achieves union with him, the symbol of unrequited intense love; Archana in *Saat Paake Bandha*, a modern Bengali name; and Debjani in *Uttar Phalguni*, one who is pure and close to the gods.

44. *Saat Paake Bandha* was released in March of the same year so audience recall would be greater, while *Dweep Jele Jai* released in October. Suchitra's Moscow Film Festival award was also declared in October. I have discussed earlier the film and its significance in staging the conflictual pull of affiliations that the modern woman experiences between her natal and marital identities and loyalties.

45. It could be speculated that this particular film was responding to and drawing on the tremendous popularity achieved by Miss Shefali, the noted cabaret dancer who was a rage in Kolkata. Suchitra had reportedly said that she had taken on this role as a challenge to beat Bombay heroines who were known for their bold roles (Gupto 2003: 107). Asha Bhonsle's playback for her in this film was deployed quite effectively in the two cabaret songs that Suchitra dances to.

46. The space of the modern club was mostly staged as a morally degraded space even in the 1960s films such as *Chowringee*, *Subarnarekha*, etc. See my discussion of partying in the context of *Nagar Darpane* in Chapter Four.

47. Suchitra had essayed some other maternal roles as well. In the 1950s, she did *Boloygrash* (1955), in which she acted as an unwed mother who is forced to raise her daughter as a servant in her married home. She had conceived before her marriage but could not bring herself to tell her lover/husband about her pregnancy. In *Chandranath*, a pregnant Saryu is turned out of her marital home due to her mother's licentious past. She refuses to kill herself and raises her child till her repentant husband accepts her back. In *Hospital* (1960), she is a doctor who raises her son on her own when her doctor lover cannot bring himself to marry her after she becomes pregnant. She walks away from her dithering lover and declares that she would give her own name to her child, and not be thwarted by fear of social scandal. Her father disowns her and the film stages the struggle of the single mother who fights all odds to bring up her child. In *Fariyaad* (1971), we see her as a cabaret dancer who is also an abandoned wife raising her son on her own.

48. The song *Aguner Parashmoni* has been chosen from Tagore's *Gitabitan* and appears in the 'Puja' section. Tagore's songs are divided into specific sections, each organised around a particular emotion such as Puja (prayer/offering to god) or Prem (love).

49. This particular figuration of the younger generation of the educated urban *bhadralok* is differently constituted from the older *bhadralok* characters such as Saibal/Ashok Kumar in *Hospital*, who did not have the courage to stand by his pregnant lover due to fear of social scandal, or Kuntal/Basanta Chaudhuri in *Megh Kaalo*, who cannot go against his father's promise and is forced to marry his lover's cousin. Both films saw Suchitra play strong women-centric characters who stand alone to map their individual trajectories after their lover abandons them. Both Saibal and Kuntal are doctors, but their education and supposed scientific rationalities do not translate into a liberal social outlook.

50. This particular trope of *bhadralok* youngsters taking to a life of petty crime was a terrifying fallout of the deteriorating social conditions of 1970s Kolkata. I have briefly discussed one aspect of this narrative in my discussion of Narayani and her son Raju in Chapter Two, in the context of *Nabaraag*. I shall discuss this particular urban phenomenon in greater detail in Chapter Four.

51. *Rupmancha* Editorial (October 1963, 17).

4

Disenchanting Modernity*

The Crisis of the *Bhadralok*

In Chapter Three, I argued for using the trope of the 'woman alone' to situate a dialogue between the feminine and the social, via the persona of Suchitra and her star text. In this chapter, I turn my attention to Uttam and his self-fashioning in the 1970s. The 1960s and 1970s defined the *mahanayak*, 'superstar', as he became virtually a 'one-man industry'. His career continued on an upward swing during this time when, along with romantic matinee idol roles, he experimented with and delivered hits in films where he appeared as a 'character actor', industry shorthand for him not being the hero in these films. Some big hits such as *Chowringee* (1968) and *Nishipadma* (1970), as well as *masala* films made in Hindi and Bengali like *Amanush* (1974) and *Ananda Ashram* (1977), were made in this period. He also capitalised on his star status to navigate different genres such as comedy, and even essayed negative roles as wastrels and villains.[1] It is pertinent to keep in mind that despite the declining 'standards' plaguing the popular, Uttam still managed a substantial box-office draw and remained a strong and profitable star in terms of economic returns.[2] After the heady possibilities of the 1950s where a certain kind of individuated modern love formed the primary locus of subjectivity, to the staging of marital discord,

*A condensed version of this chapter was earlier published in the journal *BioScope*. See Banerjee, S. 2019. 'Evolution of Dada Uttam Kumar: Performing Masculinity and the Disillusioned Bhadralok Mahanayak in the 1970s' Popular Melodramas'. *BioScope* 10 (1): 52–74. Screen South Asia Trust. Available at journals.sagepub.com/home/biohttps://doi.org/10.1177/0974927619855452 (accessed March 2023).

to Suchitra establishing herself as the lone female superstar, it is equally important to signpost that it was the 1960s that saw a reinvention of Uttam, the matinee idol, in interesting ways. It was in the post-romance phase, after his pairing with Suchitra entered a state of hiatus, that the most talked-about re-invention of his career took place. His casting in Satyajit Ray's *Nayak* (1966) and *Chiriakhana* (1967)[3] was responsible, to a large measure, for the grudging critical acceptance of his acting capabilities. However, even Ray was critiqued for 'selling out' to the diktats of 'commercial cinema' for his casting choice.

As I have mentioned earlier, unlike the 'golden 1950s', considered the heyday of this pair, the turbulent 1970s has not been at the forefront of sustained critical engagement in writings on cinema, at least in Bengal.[4] Suchitra's international award for *Saat Paake Bandha* and Uttam's National award for *Nayak* caused huge ripples in the popular press, but seemed to have been largely ignored by the film society critical engagement, which I will discuss in the next chapter. The popular, which was always the *bête noire* of this discourse, became more so in this decade, evident in the derisive tone in which reviews wrote of popular films' 'hackneyed' and 'stultifying' narratives. This was also noted in the film journalism discourse of the 1950s, and with the radical turn in film society politics, the scathing criticism acquired a more strident tenor.[5] It was a methodological and ideological trap that radical film society discourse was prone to. Uttam in particular was at the receiving end of harsh criticism as he was doing too many films and was accused of participating in a star monopoly.[6] I shall discuss this aspect of film criticism in Chapter Five.

What are the contours of Bengali self-fashioning that can signify the dystopic decade of the 1970s, if one tracks this male star? What specific form of masculine subjectivity can be used to signpost the dialogue of the social and the personal if Uttam is placed at the centre? How can one formulate a cinematic map of a certain beleaguered subjectivity that haunts Bengali people's memory of that time? What if the commercial model did not follow either the radical route of protest and revolution or the Ray/Sen map?[7] These are some questions that I address in this chapter by analysing three films starring Uttam: *Ekhane Pinjar* (1971), *Jadu Bangsha* (1974), and *Nagar Darpane* (1975).

Ekhane Pinjar (*The Cage is Here*) is a film about a middle-class family whose eldest son Nabendu/Dileep Chowdhury[8] is a *shikhita bekaar*, the educated unemployed (Gooptu 2010). Nabendu's family lives in a moffussil town, Birpur. His father is bed-ridden and ill, his mother is a housewife. Nabendu's three younger sisters and younger brother have gained a great deal of notoriety in their small town. His older sister Nila/Aparna Sen works as a night courier for a smuggling gang. The youngest brother Subho makes bombs for the neighbourhood gang. Nabendu is a graduate but he moves to Kolkata, the dream city of the *bhadralok*, not only for employment but also to acquire culture and urbanity, both crucial for their fashioning. But this move does not enable him to secure a job; he drifts into a life of criminality and dies in a police encounter as he is caught breaking into train wagons, one of the petty criminal activities undertaken by *bhadralok* youth during this time of acute shortages and black marketeering of coal. Amal/Uttam is a successful writer who meets Nabendu in a police lock-up and is drawn to this young educated man who has drifted into the nether world of petty crime, but still dreams of realising his *bhadralok* identity at some point in the future. After Nabendu's death, Amal visits his home to inform the family of the death of their eldest son, but cannot bring himself to disclose the real reason for his visit. The family ekes out an impoverished living of genteel poverty, neither aware of the eldest son's crime-related death, nor of the middle daughter and youngest son's criminal activities. Amal soon 'takes' the place of the absent/dead son and steers the family to a better life. He helps Nila, who is a smuggler, to move towards a respectable lifestyle. His *bhadralok* persona is able to provide the moral and economic stability for this particular family and enables its regeneration. He is able to exert his influence over the younger generation, converse with them, and convince them to give up their disreputable ways.

In *Jadu Bangsha*,[9] we encounter Uttam as the 'brooding, melancholic decrepit failure Gana *da*' (Biswas 2007). He is not the protagonist in this film, but it is his overarching presence as the elder brother figure in the neighbourhood that haunts Surya and his friends' imaginary. The film narrates the story of Surya/ Dhritiman Chatterjee and his three friends, Buli, Abhay, and Kripamoy, a group of drifters, jobless young men from *bhadralok* families who spend their days in a drunken stupor. This group of despairing youth uses violence and intimidation to make their presence felt. Gana *da* is the most potent victim of their violence and is forced to commit suicide as he is unable to live with the insult and humiliation that accompanied his confrontation with Surya's gang. While the narrative is invested in staging their anger and frustration, at the same time, the underlying moral economy is governed by despair at their purposeless and often anti-social or asocial activities.[10]

Nagar Darpane[11] stages the apogee of the 'actual elder brother figure' (Biswas 2007: 4). The film narrates the story of Anupam Chakravarty, a well-reputed and popular writer who also works in an advertising agency, and his family of two younger brothers and widowed mother. The first half of the film chronicles Anupam's work, his increasing isolation due to the amoral dealings of his manager, his refusal to collude with the manager in siphoning off money, and his forced resignation. From being the *karta* (head) of his *ekannavarty parivar* (joint family), he becomes dependent on his younger brother, Aju, who is a police inspector. As Aju rises in rank at his job, we slowly see him taking over the reins of the family, eroding Anupam's position and decision-making ability. Losing his job leads to the loss of his authoritative status in his family. At this point, we see Anupam slide into a spiral of 'entropy and inertia' (Rodowick 1987), an apt term that I borrow from the analysis of Hollywood domestic melodrama of the 1950s. He is besieged by madness and ultimately incarcerated in a mental asylum.

THE *MAHANAYAK DADA*

My analysis will examine Uttam's figuration as the 'putative or actual elder brother figure' (Biswas 2007: 4) in the three films mentioned above, expanding upon Biswas' formulations to argue that it is this figuration of the superstar as the *dada*, the elder-brother figure, that lets us see how Bengali self-fashioning was giving shape to its beleaguered dystopic communitarian subjectivity in the 1970s. This *dada* figure is an important constituent of Uttam's star persona along with his romantic image; in fact, this figure carries immense cultural valence. In the context of family relationships and hierarchy, the elder brother is significant as he stands in for the father figure and is usually the locus of authority in patriarchal family structures. According to Soumitra Chatterjee (2001), Uttam played the role of elder brother extremely well. In his film career, he essayed this role thirty times, almost the same number of times that he has acted opposite Suchitra or Sabitri or Supriya, the three heroines with whom he co-starred from the 1950s until the 1980s. This figure is therefore quite important as a marker of his screen persona.[12]

Beyond the diegetic, he represented the putative elder brother figure for the Bengali film industry as well. In popular film magazines, his personal status as the eldest son was conflated with his status as the figurehead of the entire industry. Not only was he responsible for carrying the burden of delivering hits, but he was also equally known for trying to look after the interests of junior artists and technicians.[13] If in the studio period—at least in Bengal—the New Theatres was run as a 'family' (Gooptu 2010: 65–114), then in the next decade of the star system, it is Uttam who emerged as the figurehead of authority. He inhabited the *dada* persona and, like an elder brother, provided a sense of direction and steered the industry to a better position.[14] As in many star biographies, his patronage of the technicians, his charity work, and his fundraising were part of public folklore.[15] Before discussing the figurations of the *bhadralok dada*, I will describe the turbulent social and political landscape that served as the background to this subjectivity in the period under consideration.

With the disillusionment arising from the failure of the Nehruvian developmental vision (referred to in Chapter Three), the late 1960s and 1970s, which saw two wars (in 1962 and 1965), divisions within the Congress, a food crisis, and the Bangladesh war in 1971, came to be marked by a tense and turbulent social polity. The period of the 1960s–70s was one of social turmoil in Bengal as well. Disenchantment with the political and social gave rise to the Naxalite movement, which sought to bring about social change through revolution.[16] The turbulent socio-political situation made the Bengali *bhadralok* self-imaginary fraught, disaffected, and disgruntled (Chatterjee 1990: 27–33; Thoraval 2000: 255). I suggest that in the popular Bengali cinema of the 1970s, the youthful anger and violent turn against the establishment that saw its culmination in the Naxalbari movement[17] can be read via a certain discursive formation of the *bhadralok* and its confrontation with the *changdas*, that is, the mostly middle-class street youth and their demotic youth culture. In the playing out of disjointed times, these *changdas* eschewed the turn towards radical politics associated with Naxalism, but their frustration and disavowal of *bhadrata*, or genteel, civil, and refined behaviour, was siphoned off to other routes. What follows is a summation of some critical interventions that scholars such as Gooptu, Biswas, Bhowmick, and others have made regarding this middle-class cinematic imaginary and its articulation in the late 1960s cinema, and the shifts that can be seen in the figurations of Uttam as a star.

THE *BHADRALOK* AND HIS WORLD

Gooptu has argued that 'the distinctiveness of a cinema which constructed an exclusionist ideology: one that was based on the Bengali *bhadralok's* worldview, and whose essence was "Bengaliness" and "Bengali culture" gives way to its "other" [in the 1960s]' (2010: 14). Tapan Sinha's *Apan Jan* (1968) is seen as the trendsetter for this shift, closely followed by *Teen Bhuvoner Paare* (1969), which starred Soumitra as the leader of street youth who gave voice to their failures and disillusionment (Biswas 2007; Gooptu 2010: 254–261).[18] This cinema displays what Biswas terms a 'generic shift' in the popular, where the 'lone romantic hero gives way to groups of drifting, despairing, angry youth, the street protagonists' (Biswas 2007: 4). The youth in these films come from the educated middle classes and lower-middle classes, but have no jobs and have either drifted into or chosen to be part of neighbourhood *mastaan* groups or petty gangs indulging in railway wagon-breaking and smuggling. These figures are not similar to the *tapori* figure of Hindi cinema (Mazumdar 2007) as the former are mostly educated with college degrees. They are liminal figures who do not see middle-class values as worth emulating; their rage is directed at everything the previous generation had stood for. Described by the middle class as uncultured, 'loafers', or 'good-for-nothings', they do not aspire to the earlier model of *bhadralok* identity or behaviour.

The preferred mode of self-fashioning of these youngsters is marked by a certain 'lumpenisation of the self' (Biswas 2007), visible in their derision for *bhadrata*, being street-smart, debunking middle-class social mores; these youths were variously described as *changdas*, impudent, flippant youth; *chhotolok*, rude, uncivil persons; *itar*, vulgar; and *asabhya*, ill-mannered, indecorous persons. Gooptu suggests that they can be categorised as '*bhadralok loafer* and the *shikhita bekaar* (educated unemployed)' (2010: 257).

However, we need to keep in mind that the ideal of *bhadralok* identity is not to be limited to a particular class; rather, it rests on a certain idea, 'an ethic or a sentiment' (Bhattacharya 2005: 52), a belief in a code of conduct which rests on 'a broad spectrum of ideas: nationalism, and liberalism and humanism of sorts' (Ghosh 2004: 251) that underlined this particular sense of self-fashioning. The notion of *bhadrata* or what it means to be *bhadralok* is understood as being characterised by genteelness, humaneness, refinement, and unselfishness, which are primary markers that constituted the defining features of the Bengali middle class's sense of self (ibid.). This sentiment rested on a certain idea of cultured Bengaliness and was not limited to any specific class, and as Bhattacharya points out, '[i]t appears as a subjective social code of comportment, style, morals' (2005: 7, 52–53). The heterogeneity of those who comprised the category of *bhadralok* made it possible for varied groups to lay claim to this category (Ghosh 2004: 248).[19] I suggest that it is not that late 1960s and 1970s popular cinema 'has given way to its other and therefore cinema itself changes its contours to cater to other dominant audiences' (Gooptu 2010: 14), that is, the *bhadralok* giving way to its other, the *chhotolok*, as a dominant social group. This interface between the *bhadra* and *abhadra* (the opposite of what *bhadra* stands for) is not an either/or situation, between the *bhadralok* self and its 'other'. The final demise of the *bhadralok* and the appearance of a subaltern protagonist in popular Bengali cinema occurred in the 1980s.[20] Uttam's death in 1980 is one of the crucial factors that marked this shift in the primary product of commercial cinema. I shall discuss this aspect in Chapter Five.

Moreover, in this period the *bhadralok* constituency further broadened its ambit to include a wider number of people who could lay claim to being *bhadralok*. This widening of the social base was possible due to certain social transformations in the 1960s and 1970s.[21] Education and *chakri* [job] were always central to this self-imaginary; in this period there was a perceptible enlargement of the core constituents of the group, 'the emergence of a growing number of people... at the lower end of the middle class, who or whose children have been to college, (but) who in no way can be compared to the *bhadralok* of yesteryears' (Ghosh 2004: 250). The spread of some form of social prosperity resulted in a larger number of even lower-middle class first- or second-generation learners who could afford college degrees. Hence, the acquisition of at least a college degree, even among the lower classes, became an essential tool of the newer classes of the *bhadralok*. A more productive engagement, then, would be to consider how the interface between *bhadrata* and *abhadrata* functions and what it might imply for the beleaguered self-fashioning of the *bhadralok* in this period. In popular cinema, the groups of young people whom we encounter belong to this diverse stratum of the *bhadralok* and consciously adopt the markers of *chhotolok*, the opposite of the *bhadralok*. The display of derision and anger at institutional authority/elders is one manifestation of the youth in the popular cinema of this period. The displacement of *bhadrata* and its interface with the *bhadralok* is one particular figuration that this chapter marks.

The cinematic staging of this conflict between *bhadrata* and its other is mounted as a confrontation between the Uttam figure and the younger generation. To quote Biswas, 'The moment where Uttam comes to confront the younger generation, mostly the disaffected youths in these films show that the standard melodrama was indeed undergoing a transformation... (2007: 6)'. He rightly points out that in popular melodrama, it is important to follow the star persona, rather than filmic enunciation directly. I argue that it is more productive to investigate the changing figuration of Uttam's iconicity during this period, since as the matinee idol he still provided the popular with its primary product identification, despite the antipathy to his stardom in radical film society discourse. Following the star figure's circulation can alert us to a cluster of subjectivities and enable a productive engagement with the particular melodramatic formations that speak for/to the times. The question that Biswas (2007) poses of the relationship between film and history is interesting in this context. He asks if the 'encounter between cinema and political history', the 'voices that cinema sifts out of a time, and makes them narrate to us a story that was there in the films but not told' can serve as a frame to formulate the narrative of the late 1960s and 1970s Bengali cinema. Biswas's nuanced intervention of excavating the political history of a particular time is essential to decode how the popular melodramas under discussion were mapping the fraught historical conditions of the 1970s. Even if this venture is in the mode of a 'retro' history, it still enables a nuanced reading of the varied subjectivities being staged in the cinema of this period. In a certain cluster of films from the late 1960s to the 1970s, Uttam undergoes a significant transformation; he becomes old and seems unable to cope with the varied shifts in values confronting the young. As Biswas observes, he is a brooding and melancholy presence in these films, often in confrontation with the younger generation. As the elder brother figure, in these films he is often held responsible for the predicament facing the youth; he fails to have the kind of dialogue or conversation that he so desperately seeks, or remains silent, not least because he has begun to recognise his own hand in the destruction of the youth.

I argue that it is this confrontation that allows us to glimpse the changing dynamics of the *bhadralok* and the transformations within their ranks. There seems to be a marked shift in this ethic or sentiment defining this group, which was undergoing a transformation in its self-imaginary, and I explore that shift in terms of this actual or putative elder brother figure and his interactions or confrontations with the youth in these three films. Confronted by generational differences, he seems unable to come to terms with his space and the increasingly antagonistic familial/social situations. In some other films, we see Uttam in similar roles that stage the conflicts experienced by the beleaguered middle-class husband and father. Films such as *Shesh Anka* (1963), *Jotugriho* (1964), *Jibon Jigyasa* (1971), *Bikele Bhorer Phul* (1974), *Baghbondir Khela* (1975), *Hotel Snow Fox* (1976), etc., saw him in roles that foregrounded the deep-seated anxieties that are constitutive features of the domestic melodrama, namely the vicissitudes experienced by the middle-class husband, the clash between father and son, the failure of the father figure, the negation of the father's authority by the son, the loneliness of the male figure, etc.[22] It is important to note that in this cluster, we also see the staging of certain motifs of the domestic melodrama that have been discussed in the context of 1950s Hollywood melodrama by critics such as Elsaesser (1987), Nowell-Smith (1987), and Rodowick (1987). A domestic melodrama usually narrates the vicissitudes of a middle-class family engulfed by a crisis, very often brought about by intergenerational conflict and psychological trauma, and implies covert social and political critique. The other significant generic constituent that can be applied to these films is of the 'male weepy', a term used by Thomas Schatz (1981) in his discussion and analysis of Hollywood melodrama in the 1950s. A male weepy, which is characterised by the lonely male protagonist, very often a social rebel, facing adversities, driven by emotional strife, and looking for affective, emotional fulfillment that is often denied to him, can also be termed as a male tear-jerker (cited in Mercer and Shingler 2004: 8–10).

The generational conflict at the heart of the domestic melodrama is played out to its fullest in these films. Commenting on the importance of the family as the site of narrative focus, Schatz says that the family unit is important

> ...for two fundamental reasons. First it is a pre-established constellation whose individual roles (mother, father, son,

> daughter, adult, adolescent, child, infant and so on) carry with them larger social significance. Second it is bound to the community by social class (father's income, occupation, location of family home etc). Ideally the family represents a 'natural' as well as a social collective, a self-contained society in and of itself. But in melodrama this ideal is undercut by the family's status within a highly structured socio economic milieu, and therefore its identity as an autonomous human community is denied—the family roles are determined by the larger social community. (1981: 227–28)

Following Elsaesser, we know that the world of domestic melodrama stages the crisis of the family besieged by intense social pressures, and the frame of respectability is so sharply defined that the range of strong action is limited (Elsaesser 1987: 56). Further, we know that '[t]he domestic melodrama is attentive only to problems which concern the family's internal security and economy and therefore considers its authority to be restricted to issues of private power and patriarchal right' (Rodowick 1987: 270). Similar to America's discovery of Freud in the 1950s (ibid.: 58–59) and the playing out of the conversion hysteria afflicting the family (Nowell-Smith 1987),[23] one can argue that in the crisis-ridden socio-political world of the mid-1960s and 1970s Bengal, this particular form was mobilised with spectacular contemporary resonance. Obviously this family in crisis is symbolic of the state of the community and the body politic. Furthermore, the worlds of these domestic melodramas are marked by 'ennui, inertia and social entropy' (Rodowick 1987), from which the characters seem unable to break away. Using the Rodowickian perspective, it is possible to argue that the father figures in these Bengali films are either paralysed, ill, or bed-ridden as in *Ekhane Pinjar* and therefore unable to exert any authority on the family, or dead as in *Jadu Bangsha*, or figures who acquire authority but fail to create any affective empathy with the family, as in *Nagar Darpane*. In *Ekhane Pinjar*, the crisis-ridden family is significant as it requires the putative *dada* figure for its survival; Amal provides that to his adopted family.

REDEEMING THE *BHADRALOK* FAMILY: THE PUTATIVE *DADA*

In *Ekhane Pinjar,* the ill and bed-ridden father can only stare helplessly at the tribulations experienced by his family. The interpersonal relationships between the older parents and the children are underscored by tension and resentment. Nabendu, Nila, and Subho are deeply troubled by their father's inability to look after his family. In their conversations with Amal at different times, they acknowledge the failure of the family to ensure their 'respectable' status. It is the intervention of Uttam's character, Amal, that is able to bring stability to this family, which is in the throes of disintegrating under the fraught internal dynamics caused by social and economic pressures. This figure thus emerges as the 'putative elder brother figure' (Biswas 2007) and, more significantly, as the 'male intruder-redeemer figure in a world of women' (Schatz 1981: 228). The generic elements of this narrative figuration, as explained by Schatz, revolve around 'the aging patriarch in a female dominated household, the search for the father/lover/husband by the anxious offspring, the male intruder-redeemer figure who regenerates and stabilises the family' (ibid.: 229).

In the closed world of *Ekhane Pinjar,* the most important transformation caused by the 'intruder-redeemer figure' happens to be in Nila's case. This transformation is signalled through a song sung by Nila, deployed to articulate her innermost feelings and sentiment, which she has otherwise kept in check. As she sings the opening lines, the camera moves to frame Amal, sitting in Nabendu's room. His presence in the room designates the locus within this reconstituted family. There are many such instances that place him in the elder son/brother category. He brings sarees for all the women, he steps in when Avinash Mitra tries to lure the middle daughter to sing at his garden house, and he pays off the mortgage and gives money to Nabendu's mother, pretending that her 'son' had sent the money through him.

The lyrics of Nila's song speak of how she has taken her boat alone, and of the sudden appearance of someone who will help her row her boat.[24] Visually, the frame is arranged with the father lying supine on his bed, Nila leaning at his side.

It is important to mention the lyrics in some detail to make clear their symbolic meaning:

> What was an imagined image, has taken shape;
> Who has put my sterile garland round your neck?
> Why did you not come during the morning of my youth?
> Did not become my companion in the first flush of my youth,
> Have you heard my plaintive song and come to take me to the shore?

It is through the lyrics that we glimpse the repressed desires of this young woman who is unable to articulate her fears and feelings in everyday speech or encounters. In the space of this heavily coded articulation, her unspoken desires burst forth. As she continues singing, we see Amal slowly enter the room to stand at the threshold. The symbolic takes over at this point. The inarticulate desires this song has staged remain withheld from her father. In a series of looks exchanged between her and Amal, we see Amal realise the intended meaning of her song. This subtext was absent in Nila's previous nocturnal conversations with Amal as she had avoided declaring her attraction for him and had refused his offers of help. As she finishes her song, Amal confesses to the bed-ridden father that he has done something which can be construed as crossing his limits as a houseguest. He has literally taken charge of this family. As he admits to Nabendu's father, he is aware of having overstepped his position as a guest; however, the mother is relieved that it is her son's friend who has made it possible for them to reclaim their mortgaged house. She has no qualms about accepting Amal in the absence of her own son. The family is still unaware of Nabendu's death. The father is ashamed of his incapacity and says despairingly that he is like Dhritirashtra, the blind king, who could not keep his family and clan together.[25] Amal's consolation refers to the changed and disjointed times, where the older generation has become incapable and has to give way to the new. At least in this film, the Amal figure can step into the space vacated by the sick father and the dead son to aid the younger generation in finding its own path towards life and survival.

Besides being the conduit through which Nila expressed her deep-seated desire to be rescued, the song also enables Amal to step in and assure Nila that she should accept his presence and take his help. Nila's transformation, which could not be signalled in the realist mode, can still be resolved at the level of the melodramatic plot. The film swiftly moves to its dénouement as Nila decides to give up her criminal work. With predictable plot twists, including her being subjected to attempted rape, and her trial for smuggling, the narrative resolves the crisis of this family through Amal's assurance that he will wait for Nila to finish her jail term.

The scene is set in the prison where Amal goes to meet Nila. We see them sitting inside and once visiting time is up, she gets up to leave. Amal reaches out and holds her hand; the shot cuts to them embracing and he assures her that he will wait for her. The ending seems staged, but what Schatz says about the domestic melodrama is important to note: '...all the contradictions cannot be resolved as they need to be resolved within the existing social structure i.e. the family itself. There cannot be an elimination of opposing forces nor can it show a transformation of social reality' (1981: 228).

Nabendu's desire for a respectable job cannot be realised as it is dependent on the existing social conditions, but Nila's rehabilitation can be hinted at as it involves personal action on Amal's part. He is the locus around which the family's regeneration can be mapped.

NAVIGATING WORK, SPACE, AND LOVE: THE *BHADRALOK* AND THE 1970S

In this cluster of 1960s–70s popular melodrama, the shifts in the pattern of work and middle-class life need to be kept in sight to understand the shifts in the self-perception of the *bhadralok*, signposting the changing dynamics of the self-fashioning that I have investigated in this book. If the cinema of the 1950s invested in projecting aspirational subjectivities in terms of the trope of middle-class respectability vis-à-vis the professional and educational space, then 1970s cinema saw a marked shift in terms of the images of work that were presented. As I have remarked in Chapter One, we saw the two stars appearing as teachers, doctors, engineers, and architects; in short, the whole gamut of what was perceived as conducive to upward social mobility and status for the *bhadralok* and *bhadramahila*, their aspirations and desires. According to Biswas, in the 1950s, popular melodrama tried to

> ...synthesise a vernacular version of the citizen largely by refracting the urban experience through the 'body' of Uttam. His body: his soft lilting voice, toned physique, his walk, made him into the most familiar middle class hero, the guy next door, the dependable brother, friend, husband, companion, and the dutiful son. It is important to talk of elements that went into the making of his 'body'. His voice, and diction, its melodic specificity, as also the compounded entity with Hemanta's playback for him gave materiality to the fantasy of a middle class Bengali male figure. (Biswas 2007: 4–5)[26]

The configuration of middle-class work and educational pursuits that governed the space of the 1950s films is also transformed in the 1970s filmic world. I have discussed how the 'new melodrama' enacted the conjoining of the lovers through the trope of both love and work in Chapter One. In the 1970s film cluster, too, Uttam carries over the aspirational symbolic capital of two professions that were crucial for defining the *bhadralok*: the writer and the railway job. His professional status as a writer imbues him with self-confidence in his interaction/confrontation in *Ekhane Pinjar*, but in the other two films he loses his stature as he is unable to make a success of his business in *Jadu Bangsha* and is unemployed in *Nagar Darpane*. Barring the first film, we see a different Uttam confronting a world in which he is a misfit and has nothing to say or affirm. This is especially poignant as he confronts the younger generation, who are unemployed as well, or have drifted into a world of petty crime and asocial activities. The 'intruder-redeemer figure'[27] (Schatz 1981) in *Ekhane Pinjar* becomes an ineffectual elder *dada*/male protector figure in *Jadu Bangsha* and eventually morphs into an elder brother who 'finds it difficult to maintain his overbearing persona and is afflicted with failure, desolation and even madness' (Biswas 2007: 12) in *Nagar Darpane* (Rodowick 1987).[28]

In the disjointed social conditions of the late 1960s and 1970s, the Bengali youth was no longer assured of the *bhadralok* trajectory of social mobility characterised by Uttam. Increasing urbanisation and the widening of the educated base also meant a narrowing of the job market.[29] The spectre of joblessness was a critical social problem that haunted the educated youth in this period.[30] The varied economic reasons led to certain interlinked symptoms described by Goswami, which included,

> The growth in urban population, especially among the middle-class refugee families, the increased demands for white collar jobs.... Neither the state government, public sector nor private sector expanded fast enough to absorb this potential labor force... very soon students with bachelors' degree were fighting and losing battles for jobs that needed no such qualification... resentment among the youth found expression in the political violence of the late 1960s–70s. (Goswami 1990: 95)

The horror of the job interview and its attendant farcical situation as shown in Satyajit Ray's *Pratidwandi* and Mrinal Sen's *Interview* are among the most well-known cinematic articulations of the middle-class youth's work-related debacles in the 1970s. Popular films were articulating and responding to the shifting terrains of subjectivities that the Bengali middle classes were trying to negotiate. Nabendu and his siblings are unable to enter respectable professions in *Ekhane Pinjar*, while in *Jadu Bangsha* we see the four friends trying to get a job in a factory owned by the neighbourhood factory owner, and finally, in *Nagar Darpane*, Anupam's youngest brother Amu needs the networking and social contacts of his Police Commissioner brother, Aju, in order to get a job. While the youth in the first film express their anger at their inability to become *bhadra* through their work, the four drifters in the second film can only resort to smashing teacups and issuing veiled threats to the local businessman when he refuses to help Abhay get a job. In *Nagar Darpane*, Anupam refuses to adopt corrupt practices while he is employed, resulting in his dismissal, while his two brothers prefer to adopt any means to further their economic and professional prospects. The clash in sensibilities between the Uttam characters and the younger generation drives the narrative conflict by deploying polarised selves of the *bhadralok* of yore on the one hand, and on the other, the newer, younger generations who are located firmly in their own historical/social context and respond to their own time. Another significant trope that defined the '*bhadralok* of yesteryears' (Ghosh 2004: 250) and was central to its self-fashioning, the spatial urban coordinate, also shifts shape in these films. This self, which has journeyed to the city to realise its full potential, had to confront an urban landscape that was itself besieged by violence and disintegration in the 1970s.

The 1950s 'city of joy', to use Kaviraj's formulation (2004), or what Biswas (2010) has suggested as an urban adventure, or the ambivalence of the urban gendered experience as described by Mazumdar (2009)[31] had all receed into oblivion in this decade. Pointing to the reality of post-independence India's urban life, Mazumdar comments on the emergence of 'a significant non legal urban subculture (filled with illegal supply chain, distribution and petty crime)... entrenching their tentacles in the eroding sphere of state presence and influence' (2007: 8). She refers to Jai Sen, who names this particular urban phenomenon as 'the unintended city', the obverse of the official or the planned city (Sen 1976, cited in Mazumdar 2007: 5).

The affirmative spaces of the 1950s post-independence city that I have analysed in Chapter One are unavailable in the 1970s as the city has morphed into its other. The state is absent and only appears in the form of the police force, the instrumental figures of state control. This point is made in all three films in different ways: Nabendu dies in a police encounter in *Ekhane Pinjar*, while police vans and sirens are heard starkly as they go around the streets to 'control' the spiralling violence in *Jadu Bangsha*; and in *Nagar Darpane* the police appear as agents of torture and state-sanctioned violence. *Ekhane Pinjar* brings into focus another aspect of post-independence India's small-town Bengali middle-class reality, where the erstwhile feudal lord of pre-independence India has been replaced by the local trader or small capitalists who are also involved in illegal economic activities.

In *Jadu Bangsha*, Gana *da* still dreams of a beautiful city, wide roads, fresh air, clean living; the *Suryotoron* imaginary, which is chimeric in the present. This sequence is staged on the terrace of Naina's house. We see Naina hanging clothes on the clothes-line and Gana *da* chewing a *neem* twig to clean his teeth. The soundtrack resonates with an *alaap*[32] as he describes his dream of a beautiful city to Naina. He lyrically speaks of the beautiful blue autumnal sky and the chirping bird-calls. In the entire film, this is the only poetic scene, full of tenderness and beauty, of a man who still has dreams of a better life, who can appreciate the beauty of nature and dream of the modern well-planned city. The intertextual reference is worth recalling. Uttam had acted as Somnath in *Suryotoron,* the young visionary architect who creates the modern skyscraper. Here, as Gana *da,* he can only 'dream' about what he had accomplished earlier. Naina and Nabendu's subjectivities are placed in spaces that do not have a Rajsekhar, Somnath, Anita, Mastermoshai, Sudarshan, or Indrani, discussed in Chapters One and Two. The vision of utopia that was possible in 1950s melodrama in terms of the individual is unavailable in the present. The imaginary of modernity and its affirmative possibilities that we encountered in the 1950s films seems to have become an empty signifier as the subjectivities that housed them have grown old and decrepit, no longer able to carry the burden of that imaginary. The dream of nation-building, spearheaded by the young in *Indrani,* the vision of the new habitat for the middle classes that the young lovers were able to translate into reality in *Suryotoron* have become untenable for these youngsters who have no dreams, only nightmares.

As Gana *da* says to Naina, 'Where did our time get lost? It wasn't supposed to be like this. The youngsters are so strange now, what has happened to the young? They are physically weak and have no sense of purpose'. His pained observation clearly refers to the degeneration apparent in the younger generations, who have no achievements and cannot bring themselves to do anything constructive to change their situation. The present is the harsh and nightmarish reality of *Jadu Bangsha* or *Nabaraag,*[33] the city and its people are besieged by violence, despair, and ennui. In *Nagar Darpane,* Anupam is subjected to a vicious attack by a violent mob on the streets as his innocuous gesture of throwing a rejected manuscript is mistaken for a bomb. This senseless violence is the sign of the fearful psychology of the times as the city has become a daily battle-ground for explosions and violence, from the police, the street gangs, as well as the Naxals.

These 1970s films no longer stage the romance of the self with the city; the city has become the space where petty and organised crime syndicates, black marketeers, and smugglers exist and operate, and the *shikhita bekaar* get sucked into their world as this affords them easy ways of making money. These films also indicate the different emerging professions that men and women were taking up, such as the society hostess, the cabaret dancer, or the woman escort.[34] The seedy nightclubs, the railway yards where smuggling activities take place at night, hotels, and *thanas* (police stations) are the spaces where we see the characters engaged in their 'work', which are far removed from the youthful spaces of work, love, and romance that we had encountered in the 1950s love films. 'Love' itself undergoes a strange transformation. What is significant in these films is that the lonely spaces which were normatively associated with the enactment of the love track and the lovers' conversations are used for social discourse and confrontations that play out the ugliest face of male–female interaction. The idea of love is either laced with suspicion, as we see in Nila's reaction to Amal's overtures in *Ekhane Pinjar*, or there is an inability to find love as in Naina and Jamuna's experience in *Jadu Bangsha*, or we have portrayals of estranged marital relationships as in *Nagar Darpane*.

The urban spaces of the 1950s films where cross-gender encounters took place become scary and unsafe spaces in the films of the 1970s, and now function to stage the display of male sexual aggression morphing into scenarios where the *changdas* harass women. In all three films, we see women experiencing this ugly social phenomenon: Nila and her sisters in *Ekhane Pinjar* have to live with the constant threat of sexual advances from the local businessman; Naina and her sisters are continuously harassed by the neighbourhood *mastaans* in *Jadu Bangsha*; Srilekha and Shukla are married to Anupam and Aju after the two men save them from the clutches of the *changdas* in *Nagar Darpane*. This open and often fearless sexual harassment of young girls and women is one of the immoral attributes of the *changdas* and *mastaans*. In all three films under discussion, this particular social problem underlines the family's desire for a suitable male figure who can provide the requisite protection from these unsavoury elements. In *Ekhane Pinjar*, Amal as the 'intruder-redeemer figure' is able to step in and provide the direction and stability that Nabendu's family needs in his absence. In the other two films, we see the Uttam figure, the putative and the actual *dada*, failing to do so. In *Jadu Bangsha* and *Nagar Darpane*, he is similar to the protagonists in the 1950s Hollywood male melodramas that narrate the 'plight of the middle class husband/lover/father' (Schatz 1981: 239). In Nowell-Smith's formulation, in melodramas,

> ...where the central figure is a man there is regularly an impairment of his 'masculinity'—at least in contrast to the mythic potency of the hero of the Western.... For both men and women, however, suffering and impotence, besides being the data of middle-class life, are seen as forms of a failure to be male—a failure from which patriarchy allows no respite. (1987: 72)

In these two Bengali male weepies, we see the Uttam figure as an ineffective male. His sensitive masculinity, his passivity and reticence, a valued characteristic in the couple films with Suchitra, where he was primarily configured as the figure of the gentle lover (as discussed in Chapter One), now becomes a sign of the failed male protagonist who, despite being the normative *bhadralok* figure, cannot provide the required protection or direction to his adopted and real family. Gana *da* is unable to save Naina's family from disintegrating in *Jadu Bangsha*, while in *Nagar Darpane* it is Anupam's younger brother Aju who steps in to take over the reins of his family. The ineffectuality of the Uttam figure can be read as a sign that denotes the passing and waning of the self that Uttam, the star, typified. The waning of the self that had defined the *bhadralok* in the 1950s and its shift in the 1970s is located in an intergenerational schism, which is an important generic element of melodrama that enables these questions plaguing the social to be displaced onto the personal. The subjectivity that these Uttam figurations represent also brings the star's almost androgynous masculinity into sharp focus (Bandyopadhyaya 2010)[35] which is differently plotted from the younger male figures, who are aggressive and prone to violence.

The Inheritors of Malady: The *Bhadra Dada* and the *Abhadra* Youth

In this cluster of films from the 1970s, we see the trope of male violence acquiring a significant space within the self-fashioning of the younger male characters. The canonical discourse of masculinity, according to Jenny Rowena, is one that is defined by its 'other', the feminine. Quoting Michael Kimmel, she says:

> Masculinity and femininity are relational constructs... one cannot understand the social construction of either masculinity or femininity without reference to the other.... Therefore, in order to establish its power, masculinity counters the feminine 'other' with oppressive messages of subordination, subjugation and dependence. Nonetheless power can never be absolutely and persistently captured by any given category. Thus the ideology of masculinity also creates a constant feeling of powerlessness in men.... The crucial paradigm of power/powerlessness invariably drives men towards certain rigid postures of control and authority. Male identities come to be crucially situated on performance—a performance of mastery and command that stretch from the workplace to the bedroom. Male (hetero) sexuality... treats the female body as a site for the endorsement of male identity. (Rowena 2010: 127–28)

The youngsters in these films fashion their 'maleness' by drawing on the blatant display of sexual aggression and seem to thrive on using their maleness to show off their 'power', while in reality they have no social locus or authority. They 'perform' virility while they are actually 'impotent' and hence can only perform power. This ineffectual performance of sexual aggression and power also governs their 'romantic' relations: Surya's lover Mala does not satisfy him, Abhay can only lust after Jamuna, Buli leers at his sister-in-law; they attempt to mask their lack of affective intimacy by cultivating gestures and attitudes that designate them as *changdas* who get their sexual kicks by threatening or harassing women. However, the most terrifying display and consequence of this aggressive maleness is staged in the final confrontation between Gana *da* and the gang. This display of male aggressive behaviour is in contrast to the genteel and *bhadra* male persona that Amal, Gana *da*, and Anupam embody in the three films under discussion.

In these films, the Uttam *dada* figure is confronted by the degeneration of the younger *bhadralok*, exemplified by the use of uncultured language and violence deployed by the disaffected youth. One of the defining features of *bhadralok* identity is that of cultured self-hood (discussed above), where language is a crucial marker. The peppering of everyday language with slangs and expletives is a marker of the 'other', the *chhotolok* or the *changdas*. Bhattacharya's work has demonstrated how, in the nineteenth-century discourse on language, the form of Bengali language was a deeply contested issue. The debate between the *sadhu*, *chalit*, and *moukhik* bhasha was resolved unequivocally in favour of the 'spoken voice', the 'cultured and educated voices of the Chaudhuries and Tagores' and not the 'unrefined parole of the peasant' (2005: 218). The use of slangs, expletives, and the open display of abusive language that we encounter in these films demonstrate the chasm between the 'cultured language' of the *bhadralok* and its disavowal by the *changdas*. The sense of disenchantment with the defining linguistic characteristics of the *bhadralok* that the young feel cannot be more pronounced and disturbing. *Ekhane Pinjar* articulates a similar idea, particularly in Amal's interaction with Subho, Nabendu's younger brother. Subho's sarcastic observation that he is no Vidyasagar[36] and has no desire to be one is reflective of this disavowal of polished language and the merits of education. But ultimately Amal is able to 'speak' to him and Subho at least promises to refine his language. In *Jadu Bangsha*, that possibility seems nonexistent. Surya and his friends cannot be bothered with the polished niceties of speech and language.

In *Ekhane Pinjar*, Amal's conversations with the educated but unemployed youth are used to reveal the shifts in the self-perception of the older, successful writer and the young *bhadraloks* who have no aspirations to become *bhadra*. Amal's first encounter with Nabendu stages the conversation between the successful, feted, and popular writer and the educated criminal who 'looks' like a *bhadralok* but is not one of them. This particular category of educated middle-class youth was an important constituent of the interaction between generations. The dominant tropes in these films play on the disintegration of the dreams of the middle classes, the ennui, the dejection, and the constant confrontation between *bhadralok* and the *abhadra* youth. As I have said above, this othering of the self is not enacted as a class confrontation but as an intergenerational schism. The younger generation has internalised the *chhotolok* attributes and hence is in constant collision with the demands and desires of respectability. The film narrative posits various conversations that revolve around the futility of being *bhadralok* in the given social circumstances. Amal's encounters with Nila and Subho are used to present the growing chasm between ideas and ideals that is inflicting the *bhadralok*, and reflect on why the younger generations are drifting away from their social and familial responsibilities to the nether world of crime and petty smuggling. In these encounters with the elder, more successful figure, the young do not accept his views. They question, critique, and are unapologetic about the errant and deviant ways that they have chosen.

The clash in *Nagar Darpane* is staged between Anupam and his brothers Aju and Amu, as well as Shukla, Aju's wife, as an intergenerational strife and a clash of *bhadrata* versus *abhadrata*. The values that Anupam believes in are not the normative ones that the younger family members choose to imbibe, and this leads to the narrative collision that culminates in the horrifying psychoses that Anupam experiences. The favoured cosmopolitan life of the younger generation is equated in the film to socialising, drunken parties, and dancing. In fact, 'partying and dancing to Western music' is a recurrent trope that makes a moral statement; in many of the 1970s films such as *Chowringee* (1968), *Fariyaad* (1971), *Hotel Snow Fox* (1976), and even in Ritwik Ghatak's *Subarnarekha* (1965), frenzied scenes of drunken partying and cabarets are represented to signpost the aspirationally Westernised, urban middle-class life, which is regarded with moral opprobrium. In *Chowringee*, we see Uttam/Sattay Bose, the suave manager of a five star hotel, observe the peccadilloes of the urban elite with a growing sense of bemusement. In *Nagar Darpane* we see the 'foreign-returned' Amu and his sister-in-law, Shukla, embark on a frenzied round of socialising and partying which bodes ill for the family. Aju's job makes it impossible for him to provide Shukla with the intimacy and time that she needs; Amu steps in to fill that gap. As we are confronted with their developing intimacy, we see a bewildered Anupam witnessing the affair with alarm and a censorious gaze. But what is significant is that this 'look' is denied to the others in the family. We gaze at the close dancing and developing sexual attraction between the two through Anupam's point-of-view shots.

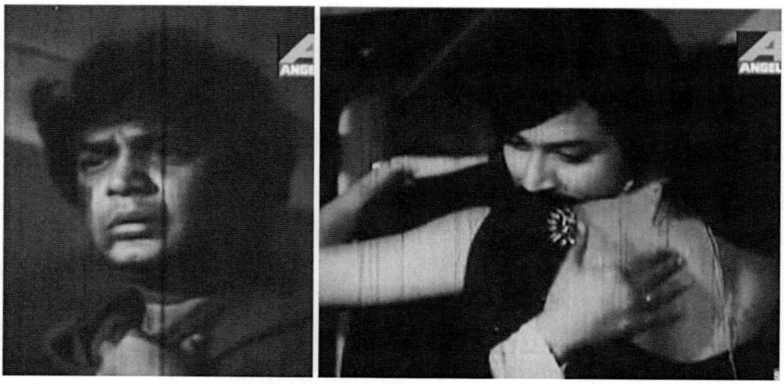

FIGURE 4.1: The Bhadra *Dada's* Gaze

It is his gaze that defines the '*bhadra* look', aghast at the unfolding events. Anupam's bewilderment is psychological, social, and political, and he increasingly becomes isolated and lonely in this familial space. In both *Jadu Bangsha* and *Nagar Darpane*, the interaction between the youth and the *dada* takes on darker tones, resulting in the *dada's* suicide and madness.

I shall analyse the physical intimidation and use of slang and expletives in the violent encounter of the gang with Gana *da* in *Jadu Bangsha* and in Anupam's experience of familial violence resulting in his psychotic breakdown in *Nagar Darpane*, to further illustrate the intergenerational schism that is central to the world of the domestic melodrama (Schatz 1981), and the waning of the *dada's* influence as the locus of authority, both moral and familial. In these two films, we encounter another constitutive figure central to the male melodrama, the ineffectual male figure unable to be the locus of his adoptive and real family, staging the crisis of the *bhadralok* male and his descent into suicide and insanity. Both Gana *da* and Anupam are forced to cede their locus of authority to the younger generation. This delimitation of patriarchal rights is similar to what Rodowick has described for 1950s Hollywood melodramas. As pointed out by Rodowick (1987), domestic melodrama is only focused upon the family's internal security and economy and hence limits itself to 'issues of private power and patriarchal right' (ibid.: 271). It is concerned with its power over inheritance rights and the reproduction of its 'network of authority' (ibid.) in the domains of sexual and social identities of the family.

Anupam loses his position as the family's legitimate centre of authority when he loses his job. The symbolic opposition between Anupam and his middle brother is staged using the tropes of work, family authority, and Aju's blatant display of disrespect towards Anupam as the former rises in stature. Gana *da* cannot claim any power as he is a failure; he has no job, no income, and is forced to live off his adoptive family, where Naina's work provides the family with the bare minimum economic sustenance.

In *Jadu Bangsha*, the terms of this conflict are brought out in two sequences that show the waning influence of the dada and the intergenerational schism. The first is when the gang comes to confront Gana *da* in his shop. Their childhood idol has been transformed into a 'pathetic loser', 'the owner of a rundown business' (Biswas 2007: 6). They subject him to horrible humiliation, making snide remarks, casting aspersions on his relationship with Naina, making fun of his adopted family and 'home', and extract the last five rupees he has. We see Gana *da* sitting with his face behind the typewriter, amidst the pile of 'worthless commodities' (ibid.).

As the group approaches him, the camera slowly zooms in to him, closing in after we see the overflowing shelves of goods that he has been unable to sell. He appears before us, unshaven, unkempt, with a cigarette dangling from his lips, writing to some *ayurvedic*

FIGURE 4.2: Gana *da*

agency offering to sell their products. This is the sad detritus of his business; either he does not get paid, or people do not want his merchandise as it is not manufactured by well-known companies. Surya and others continue to pressure him to give the money that is due for pawning an antique lamp. Viewers will recall that the gang had earlier given this antique gold lamp, which belonged to Kripamoy's family, to Gana *da* for safe-keeping. The young men were apprehensive that they themselves would be compelled to pawn it for ready cash. Their body language and gestures are extremely contemptuous, exhibiting derision. Gana *da* keeps quiet and remains seated in his chair.

His silence signifies his awareness of his culpability and responsibility in how the younger generation has turned out. Biswas observes that

> Conversation, face to face exchange, takes on a new vividness and intensity.... The star adopts a new speech, brings a new timber into his voice, and accentuates his age as he faces a generation that has come to question every legacy of its fore bearers. (2007: 6)

Surrounded as he is by the stacks of worthless merchandise, he appears to represent a devalued, scarred body. This erstwhile *bhadralok*, fallen on hard days, is the signifier of the '*bhadralok* of yesteryears' (Ghosh 2004: 250), one whose time has begun to wane. The gang leaves after bullying him and snatching the paltry five rupees he had. The next shot frames them on their cycles, victorious in their ability to corner and inflict abject humiliation on their childhood hero. This empty pride, the use of derisive sarcasm, display of sadistic pride, and aggressive maleness is enacted again towards the end of the film when the gang goes to confront Gana *da* at Naina's house, which results in his suicide.

Surya and his friends visit Gana *da* on the first day of Durga Puja.[37] The sequence opens with the sound of hoof-beats and martial music that resembles a marching tune, as if connoting soldiers going into battle, while in the visual field we see the four friends riding their cycles, framed from the back, a cemetery in the foreground with one big grave on which the cross is prominently visible. The camera then cuts to shots of slipper-clad feet climbing stairs while the marching tune and the hoof-beats continue in the aural register. The unfolding scene stages a battle between the childhood hero, whom the gang now views as a relic of the past, one who is accused of being a thief and a liar, and the young men drunk on spirits as well as their physical prowess, who thrive on the display of naked aggression and virility. At the beginning of the sequence, we see Gana *da* sitting on his bed while the four friends, led by Surya, stand facing him. The conversation begins innocuously, though the tense expression on Gana *da*'s face, his jerky movements as he smokes his *beedi*, and his attempts to make polite conversation are juxtaposed against the supercilious body language of the gang. As the conversation starts acquiring dangerous overtones with a blatant display of derision and aggression, we see Gana *da* becoming more and more agitated and he starts to raise his voice. As the tension mounts, the camera moves back and forth between Gana *da* and the youths. Surya repeatedly calls him a liar and a cheat, accuses him of pretending to be Yudhistira,[38] while actually pawning the gold lamp.

In the visual plane, Gana *da* still stands taller than Surya and dominates the frame's foreground, while Surya's close-up appears only as a reflection in the small, square mirror on the rear wall. This composition, with Gana *da* appearing larger and taller than the four youths, signifying his stature and placing him above the callow youths, is repeated through the sequence till we get to the culmination. As the tension mounts, so does the sense of dread. Gana *da* frantically searches his suitcase to return the lamp, but is unable to find it. In an earlier scene we had seen him wiping and cleaning the lamp and carefully putting it back. Gana *da* is puzzled, and we see Surya charging into the room to demand an explanation for the lamp's disappearance. As Gana *da* tries to convince them that he has not sold the lamp, they remain unconvinced, and suddenly start beating and punching him. In a series of intercuts we see their faces in close-up, sweating, panting, and raising their fists as they keep punching the prone figure on the bed. Throughout the beating, the soundtrack resounds with the rising beats of the *dhaak*, drum, and cymbals, the traditional music associated with Durga Puja. The shocked inserts of Naina and her youngest sister's scared reaction signals to us the bloody beating that Gana *da* is receiving. After a while they decide to leave, and the camera cuts to a shot of their feet climbing down the stairs as the *dhaak* music changes to the sound of hoof-beats and the marching tune with which the sequence had begun. The framing takes us back to the same composition of the four figures cycling and the grave with the cross

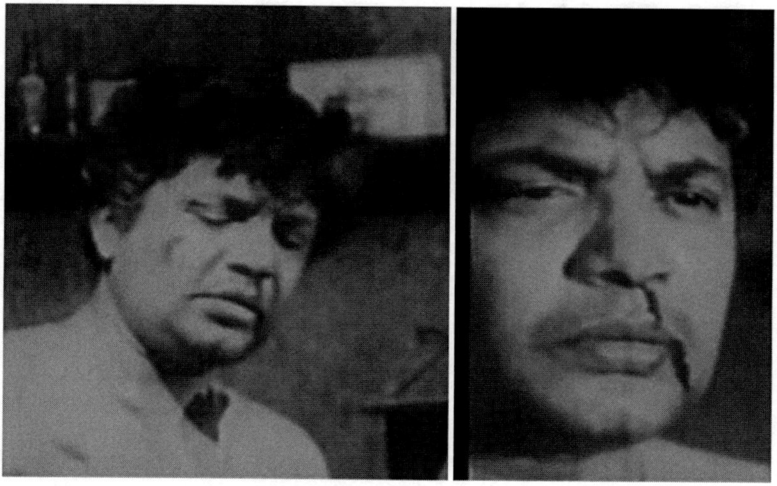

FIGURE 4.3: The Bruised *Dada*, Gana *da*

seen in the foreground. The 'victorious' warriors have achieved their victory and leave behind their vanquished adversary, the *bhadralok dada* who was their childhood hero.

The shocking consequence of this aggression and violence is visible in the close-up of Gana *da*'s face, blood-smeared, with a bloody nose and gashes on his cheeks. His torn kurta and broken spectacles are a sad reminder of the dangerous overtones of this interface of the *bhadra* and the *abhadra* that the film explores. This is further signified in Gana *da*'s gesture—an insert of his hand picking up a plate of sweets to throw it away. The sweets had been served to the guests as a mark of respect and in a spirit of joy to mark the auspicious day of the Puja, but the entire episode has shattered the veneer of *bhadrata* that the sweets connoted. It is significant that it is Gana *da* who throws it, and the import of his gesture is made clear by his observation to Naina. Gana *da* remarks, 'I probably deserved this; I had tried to make them understand....' We see Gana *da* smile,[39] and the camera slowly zooms in to a close-up and then a freeze shot of his bruised and bloodied face fills the frame. His culpability and dejection, coupled with his abject humiliation, results in the overdose of opium that takes his life. The *bhadra dada* can no longer bear the guilt or the responsibility for the crisis engulfing the young, and since he himself is a failure, he can only signal his protest by taking his own life.

Dystopic World: Scarred Body

In *Nagar Darpane*, the intergenerational chasm that Anupam experiences morphs into a psychological nightmare within the diegetic world, a portent of his imminent psychotic break. The camera frames him as a solitary figure lying on his easy chair or pacing up and down his verandah, disconnected from both his space and his writing. The use of his voiceover increases as well. This film deploys the 'embodied voice over' (Silverman 1988)[40] that tells us that he is in the *krishnapaksha*[41] of his life, a dark phase which he has to live through. But unlike the phases of the moon, he does not emerge from this dark fortnight. We see intercuts of

Aju surrounded by his busy work schedule and Anupam sitting without any work at his writing desk. The sequence shows that it is the younger brother who has now taken over the mantle of the head of both the family and the city as he has become Assistant Police Commissioner. In contrast, Anupam has lost his job in advertising as well as his market as a writer. His visit to his publisher makes it clear that his manuscripts have been rejected since they no longer sell, as they are not 'thrilling and lack sex'. In the current world of instant gratification, his writing espousing human emotions finds no takers and he has become passé. If work or *chakri* is a significant construct of the middle-class Bengali self, then its absence seems to create a vacuum within the self that cannot be bridged (Bhattacharya 2005; Sarkar 1997). Even his other profession/his creative muse, his writing, seems to have deserted him. It is not merely the loss of creativity that plagues him, but also the loss of his market. He can no longer translate his creative capital into viable economic capital.

Anupam becomes a caricature of his former self as he withdraws into himself, almost becoming mute. He morphs into a voiceover layering the visual track. When he speaks, it is a frenzied speech, a mix between a snarl and a scowl. We see the physical deterioration of the once suave and elegant figure. Anupam looks unkempt, with a stubble, dark circles under his eyes, and a jowly face that appears to be a grotesque version of what he once was. His conversations are marked by a puzzling inadequacy to grapple with the situation, or turn into aggressive confrontations where he becomes an object of fearsome loathing and terror. Whether it is his attack on his sister-in-law, Shukla, or his rage at his wife, Srilekha, and his brother, Anupam either shouts or becomes hysterically violent. He also starts peering at himself in the mirror, scrutinising the lines on his face, which appears shabby and unkempt. The uncombed hair and dark circles add to his desolation. We see the rapid deterioration of this ineffectual male, which is expressed as an inward violence, a characteristic of the melodramatic form that struggles to articulate individual or social disintegration. It would be productive to use David Rodowick's analysis from a different context to understand the irrational incoherence directed by Anupam at his family and its outward expression. Rodowick has eloquently pointed out that

> Melodrama is... characterized as a centripetal form which directs these forces inward... the expression of violence can only be regulated by an economy of masochism which often gives the narrative a suicidal thrust, channeling the expression of sexuality as violence against the text in a manner which maximizes the potential for disruption and incoherency. In this manner the melodramatic text is balanced on the edge of two extremes, one of which is inertia (the paralysis of the system, its resistance to change or any form of external development) and the other which is entropic (where action is expressed only as an irrational and undirected surplus energy). (1987: 273)

Since Anupam cannot lay claim to the space of authority at the symbolic level once his position as head of his family has been given over to his middle brother, he can only slide into madness. His descent into madness seems similar to what Rodowick views as the failure of authority in the domestic melodramas of 1950s Hollywood. To quote Rodowick: 'The structure could thus resolve on the symbolic level (acceptance of authority), or hermeneutic (which accepted madness and usually self-destruction)' (1987: 273). His snarling speech and frenzied, hysterical outbursts make his family despair of his state.

Anupam's slide into madness is juxtaposed with incidents in the city, thus equating his insanity with the madness unfolding outside. We see him looking at newspaper clippings and reports of the violence and shootings in the city, of youth being killed in cross-fire, explosions, etc., and we overhear phone commands that Aju gives to keep the violent and volatile city under control. But crucially, it is his body and his self that bear the marks of the pain and suffering of both his madness and the torture that the city is experiencing. It begins one night as we see Anupam overhear a woman's crying, beseeching voice and we cut to an old woman holding Aju's feet, pleading with him to spare her son who has not committed any crime. The ferocious scowl on Aju's face denotes his rage, and he brusquely asks his junior to remove the old woman. As she is dragged away, we see Anupam barge into the office and question Aju about the extent of violence that will satisfy his lust for control.

FIGURE 4.4: Delimiting Anupam's Authority, *Nagar Darpane*

As the sequence continues, we see Anupam back in his room, pacing. The subdued lighting and dark corridor visible outside the open door of the balcony adds to the sense of gloom. In a series of shots, we see Anupam clutching his stomach with his face contorted in a grimace, as if he is in pain. He is restless; he stands briefly looking at his sleeping wife, and then moves to the far end of the room, where the camera cuts with his point of view to his mother's picture on the wall. It again cuts back to a close-up of him, and now we see tears streaming down his cheeks. The gesture of holding and pressing his stomach is repeated and then he slowly walks to the balcony and sits on the easy chair. His distorted grimace, tear-stained face, and his gaze toward his mother's picture intensify the pain, anguish, and suffering that the old woman—who has probably lost her son in the violence engulfing the city—has experienced. Anupam's insomnia and stillness make him appear as the mute witness who cannot stop or even protest the horrific urban dystopia unravelling before him. This dystopic city, which seems driven by its display of violent aggression, is caught in its own entropic spiral which has desensitised it to death. The tragic news of a stampede that had occurred before the start of a cricket match played in the city, in which five youths were killed by surging crowds trying to enter the stadium, is cued via Anupam's shocked expression in response to the radio commentary. The camera moves to a close-up as he slowly raises his face to hear the news of their death, while the soundtrack resounds with the wild roar of the crowd now enthralled by the cricket match.

The prominent bruise on his cheek and the roaring, cheering crowds create a sense of dissonance that foregrounds the poignancy of the situation. The roaring resembles the noise of baying crowds at some blood sport, wildly cheering a death. We stay with Anupam in the visual field, sitting still while the radio loudly blares the match commentary, interspersed with the noise of the cheering spectators. Anupam's anguish and anger are unleashed on his youngest brother Amu, and Aju's wife Shukla, who had been to the match and return home happy and oblivious. The scene cuts to an evening shot of a drenched and happy Shukla and Amu at the foot of the stairs, back after the match and their dinner. The reverse shot of Anupam shows him at the top of the stairs, ready to confront the two. The framing now positions him at a height, looking down at the almost shrunken, cowering figures at the base of the staircase.

FIGURE 4.5: The Admonishing Elder Brother

His position above them with the shawl draped over his shoulders is almost the symbolic posture of the father-figure/ elder brother, admonishing the recalcitrant errant youngsters, who demonstrate no shame at their blatant display of immoral attraction, nor show any sympathy at the senseless death of the five youngsters in the morning stampede. He slowly climbs down, snarling, asking them how they can continue to enjoy themselves while young lives were snuffed out.

Anupam's fits of rage are symptomatic of his advancing insanity, but in his insane and hysterical moments, he asks pointed questions. He asks Aju, 'Would you hit me to keep me under control? Would you become the bogeyman to my fearful insanity?' The questions symbolically connote the larger issues that the film raises for us regarding the state-sanctioned violence unleashed by Aju on hapless people caught in the maddening spiral of violence engulfing the city. Aju is able to impose some control over the mad city, but at home, his elder brother seems to slide further into a nether world of insanity. In the familial space, Anupam's insanity is a threat, it too needs control; it cannot be allowed to disturb the lives of his family. Since medication proves ineffective, he has to be removed, apparently for his own good and his family's peace.

As we see Anupam being dragged down the stairs, Srilekha, Shukla, and Amu stand quietly in the room. Suddenly, Aju enters the room and Anupam rushes to him, asking Aju to save him from the asylum orderlies. He beseeches his brother not to send him away. The scene is a deep space composition: we see the elder brother cling to Aju in his uniform, with the asylum orderlies looking on as the family members in the background observe the scene. Suddenly we see Aju snarl and hit out with his baton as he shoves Anupam away. Aju becomes a frightening figure, keeping the law and order, but that is a front for state-sanctioned surveillance and violence. Anupam's bewildered expression is shown in close-up and then he becomes absolutely still. The orderlies now move to flank Anupam, who puts up no resistance and meekly walks out with them. The bruises on Anupam's body, whether from the marks left by the attacking mob mentioned earlier, or at the hands of his younger sibling, scar him and render him mute. The injuries

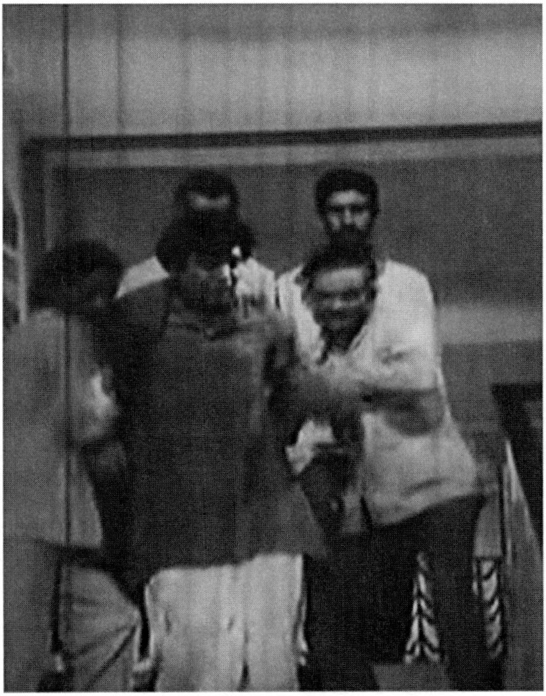

Figure 4.6: The Insane *Dada*

and marks of the changing times that he carries on his person can hardly be more evocative. The elder brother in this film is thus reduced to a redundant figure. He has to give up his space to the younger generation that is taking over; his time is up. The star who epitomised the romance of an era is now this broken, insane figure removed forcibly and locked up in a mental asylum. His body bears the marks of all the violence overwhelming the city, whether intended, sanctioned, or accidental. We see Anupam again in the penultimate sequence of the film, inside a cage in the asylum. As the scene unfolds, the camera cuts to his profile in a close-up.

We see Anupam's vacant eyes with their huge dark circles, the face bruised, unshaven, hair uncombed, and with an unblinking stare. His look is unfocussed; his body drooping even in his sitting posture. As Anupam slowly raises his head inside the room and the camera tracks back, we see him sitting still, looking like the decrepit human being he has become. The long journey of the emotionally and physically violated *dada*/star thus ends in the empty look, the stare that fixes us with its unblinking horror. The epitome of the romantic hero is now this battered body, displaying the bruises of the times on his face and self.

The figure of the bruised male star, the ineffective male of these two films within these male weepies, eloquently voices the loss and suffering of the region. This dystopic narration is accentuated through performance, changes in speech patterns, and sartorial elements adopted by the star. The melodic and elegant speech favoured by Amal changes to a hurried, tense cadence as Gana *da*, and to the frenzied snarl of Anupam as Uttam tries to give body to the beleaguered sense of subjectivity that he is enacting. The change in the timbre of his melodic voice to a high-pitched stutter and snarling dialogue delivery, and the visual of his bearded, unkempt, harassed look add to the sense of despair that the films articulate.

It is also important to discuss the sartorial elements that add to the performance of the *bhadralok dada* in these films. In all three films discussed here, Uttam is dressed in '*dhuti panjabi*' (dhoti-kurta), the traditional attire of the Bengali male. This attire is important as it is a significant visual marker for the self-imaginary of the Bengali *bhadralok*. In *Ekhane Pinjar*, Amal's cultured *bhadralok* identity is cued through his culturally coded dress and the *dhuti*-clad Amal dominates the visual field, striding through the frame with easy grace and felicity. There is a constant reiteration of Amal's *bhadralok* 'Bengaliness'. This figuration marks out the space of the *bhadralok* self who is able to vanquish the local villain, Avinash Mitra. As he negotiates with Avinash Mitra, one glimpses a strong will that can deal with the local henchman and come away victorious without resorting to violence. In this film, he is still in control of the changing situations of modern city life that he encounters, including deteriorating social conditions (see the discussion above on work and space). In a charged scene, he barges into Avinash Mitra's office and by sheer grit and fast thinking is able to fool the businessman into releasing the mortgaged property papers of Nila's family home. As the local lord fumes, Amal calmly tells him that he has not used force to enter, but has done so because he wanted to do so. He makes a distinction between the use of force that operates on the premise of power which oppresses, and that which is individual, motivated by necessity. On being threatened with forceful eviction, he calmly informs the lackey that his suitcase contains explosives which he will use if his words are ignored. Thus, by dint of inventiveness and the appearance of strong-arm tactics, he is able to get back the papers of Nila's mortgaged house. He sets the system right, not by taking on the persona of the avenger on a spree of retribution, but by retaining his core identity as a middle-class writer who will not compromise on his values.

In the other two films, we encounter the beleaguered male, the failed *dada* wearing unkempt clothes in *Jadu Bangsha*. His crumpled *kurta* and dirty clothes stage the detritus that Gana *da* has become, far removed from the elegant, suave Amal of *Ekhane Pinjar*; ultimately, he is seen in a torn *kurta* as he gets beaten up by a mob and descends into insanity in *Nagar Darpane*. The shocking sequence of familial violence where Anupam is slapped by Aju is made more poignant as we see the star dressed in dirty *dhuti-kurta* and a shabby shawl, being dragged barefoot by the asylum orderlies.

In these weepies, Uttam's genteel sensitivity is a sign of the failed male protagonist who, despite being the normative *bhadralok* figure, cannot provide the required protection or direction. Gana *da* is unable to save Naina's family from disintegrating in *Jadu Bangsha*, while in *Nagar Darpane* it is Anupam's younger brother Aju who steps in to take over the reins of his family. In his romantic couple films with Suchitra, Uttam was primarily configured as the gentle lover. He could be the compassionate companion for the strong, independent woman; his androgynous masculinity was not seen as a sign of failure. The ineffectuality of the Uttam figure in later films can be read as the sign that denotes the passing of the *bhadralok* subjectivity that Uttam, the star, once typified. For films in the 1970s, the waning of this self is located in an intergenerational schism, expressed through a central trope of the family melodrama, displacing the questions plaguing the social onto the personal, as I have demonstrated in my reading. The morphing of the superstar into the ineffectual *dada* figure, whose inabilities force him to yield space to the younger generation and their aspirations, is brought out with remarkable resonance in the three films discussed here. As the region itself spirals into an implosion of violence, the star who gave the region an affirmative and aspirational locus dwindles into a scarred body, embodying in his tragic cinematic denouement the tragedy of the region itself.

NOTES

1. Uttam's comedic roles in films like *Mouchak* (1974) and *Dhonni Meye* (1971), paternalistic roles in *Sabyasachi* (1977) and *Agnishwar* (1975), negative and villainous roles in *Aparichita* (1969), *Kuhok* (1960), *Shesh Anka* (1963), etc., added to the range of characters he played. His star status thus spanned varied genres across the three decades, with 200 released films.

2. Uttam was very conscious of the burden of being the only bankable star in the industry. Especially after his collaboration with Ray, he gave many interviews in which he claimed that he was tired of doing the same kind of cinema and hoped that directors would give him challenging roles (Kumar 2001: 46-47). He was equally conscious of his crowd-pulling capability and knew all the tricks of his trade to consume footage in shots and dictated editing patterns that would showcase him as the superstar (Sen 2003: 9, 11, 26). But the point remains that he was still able to make money for his producers, and in any case was forced into doing too many films despite his ill health due to the box-office disaster of *Chhoti si Mulaquat* (1967) (Chattopadhyaya and Ghosh 1980), and also on account of his financial troubles (Ghosh 2001).

3. Both films won many awards. *Nayak* won the National Award for Best Bengali Film, Best Screenplay and Story in 1966; Jury award at Berlin and International Critic's Prize in 1966. *Chiriakhana* won the Best Actor award and Ray the Best Director at the 1967 National Awards.

4. Most accounts of Indian cinema of this period focus on Hindi cinema and the Bachchan phenomenon. It is true that Hindi cinema had become a huge box-office success. In Bengal, the industry was reeling under the effects of heavy taxation as well as the problems of releasing their films alongside Hindi films. In the mid-1960s, Uttam's foundation, the Shilpi Sangha, was dealt a severe blow by the rival Abhinetri Sangha, which was promoted by Satyajit Ray and others. This schism led to a sense of gloom as this divide was considered detrimental to the larger interests of Bengali cinema.

5. As Rochona Majumdar (2012) has demonstrated in her analysis of this discourse from the mid-1960s, the definition of 'political' cinema was being

mobilised in a narrow manner. What is 'political' has of course acquired very different meanings in the post-Foucauldian sense.

6. I have in mind journals such as *Chalantika*, *Chitrabhav*, *Dekchi Shunchi*, etc., though in 2001 one of the most respected film societies of West Bengal, the North Calcutta Film Society, brought out a special issue of *Chitrabhash* dedicated to Uttam. This was one of the first endeavours by a film society to engage with the popular.

7. The popular films of the period, especially those starring Uttam, have not been on the radar of film scholars. Existing scholarship on Bengali cinema of the 1960s–70s mostly focuses on the auteurs, Satyajit Ray, Mrinal Sen, and Tapan Sinha. Ray's city trilogy *Pratidwandi* (1970), *Seemabaddha* (1971), and *Jana Aranya* (1975); Sen's Calcutta films, *Interview* (1970), *Calcutta 71* (1972), and *Padatik* (1973); and Sinha's *Apan Jan* (1968) and *Teen Bhuvoner Paare* (1969) are the most iconic examples that are cited to speak of this decade. Supriya Chaudhuri (2006) decodes the politics of middle-class complicity in her essay 'In the City' on Ray's Calcutta trilogy in Moinak Biswas's edited volume, *Apu and After* (2006). Other scholars who have written on the 1960s–70s parallel cinema include Anuradha Ghosh (2012) and Moinak Biswas (2006, 2007). Shormishtha Gooptu has discussed Tapan Sinha's *Apan Jan* and *Teen Bhuvoner Paare* (2010).

8. *Ekhane Pinjar* was directed by the collective Yatrik. Tarun Majumdar, Sachin Mukherjee, and Dileep Mukherjee had formed this collective, but they also made films separately under their individual names. In the late 1960s and 1970s, the Yatrik collective, along with Parthapratim Chowdhury, Tarun Majumdar, and Tapan Sinha, were prominent directors who made films that were known for the staging of the fraught social conditions of the times. This film starred Dileep Chaudhuri, who was one of the directors of the collective. The story was written by Prafulla Ray (1934–).

9. *Jadu Bangsha* was directed by Parthapratim Chowdhury and the story was written by Bimal Kar (1921–2003). The name of the story is derived from the myth of the slaying of the Yadava dynasty by Lord Krishna and his elder brother Balaram. According to the *Vishnupurana*, this dynasty was cursed by a Brahmin to self-destruct. The analogy of self-destructive centripetal forces is applicable to all the characters in the film as they carry the seed of their own destruction.

10. See Gooptu's analysis of some other films such as *Teen Bhuvoner Paare* and *Apan Jan* (*Mere Apne* by Gulzar, 1971, in Hindi), where the drifting youth gangs become the street protagonists and enact the rage and despair that the times witnessed (Gooptu 2010).

11. *Nagar Darpane* was directed by the directors' collective, Yatrik. The story was written by Ashutosh Mukherjee (1920–1989). Parthapratim Chowdury, the director of *Jadu Bangsha*, and Yatrik collaborated on the screenplay.

12. Other well-known films where Uttam enacted the elder brother include *Bosu Paribar* (1952), *Dui Prithibi* (1980), and the omniscient putative elder brother figure in *Chowringee* (1968). For detailed elder brother character taxonomy, see Chattopadhyaya (2008: 135–38).

13. Uttam established the Shilpi Sangha in 1968 after he broke with Abhinetri Sangha. He wanted to do a housing project for industry people in need of support and was known for his philanthropic endeavours. This is in keeping with the nurturing and paternalistic role that was expected of him. His junior actors, such as Shubhendu Chattopadhaya, have publicly acknowledged his *dada*-like stature and his contribution towards their filmic careers (Chattopadhyaya 2011).

14. It is important to keep in mind that in the popular imaginary, the auteur director Ray was not given this recognition of being the *dada* figure. Ray's commitment to 'good cinema' was seen as a self-promoting exercise; it got him international recognition but that did not translate into better working conditions for the technicians, the artists, or the infrastructure of the industry. To be fair to Ray, he was actively involved in the Abhinetri Sangha, but that was perceived as detrimental to the larger interests of the industry as it exposed its internal divisions.

15. After Uttam, Mithun Chakrabarti, Prosenjit Chatterjee and Jishu Sengupta have been accorded a similar stature. But Uttam's shadow haunts these two stars as well. Mithun modelled his walk on Uttam's in *Shukno Lanka* (2010), and part of his character was based on Uttam's life story. Prosenjit's *Autograph* (2010) too cited Uttam's stardom in concrete terms as we see his huge blowup hanging prominently in Prosenjit's drawing room. Prosenjit plays a lonely superstar in the film. He has also enacted the role of a mahanayak, Arun Chatterjee, in the television series *Mahanayak*, based on Uttam's life story, which I discuss in Chapter Five. Both Prosenjit and Jishu appeared in a contemporary adaptation of the Uttam-starrer *Antony Firangee* (1967), titled *Jaatishwar* (2014); Jishu portrayed the mahanayak in the film *Mahalaya* (2019).

16. In 1962, independent India fought the first war with its 'close *panchsheel* ally' China (the Suchitra-starrer *Sandhya Deeper Shikha*, released in 1964, briefly discussed in Chapter Three, staged the psychoses of the war widow Jayanti, whose husband had died in active combat in this war). I have discussed the fallout of political developments in the 1960s–70s in

my discussion of *Nabaraag* in Chapter Two. In 1964, the Communist Party of India split into two factions, the CPI and the CPI (Marxist). In 1967, the Bengal Congress party fought the elections divided into two camps, one led by Prafulla Chandra Sen (the old guard of the Congress affiliated to the Indian National Congress), and the other led by Ajay Mukherjee. This sociopolitical map demonstrates the rising disenchantment within the state that found expression in the varied subjectivities of the radical youth as well as loafers and street youth (P. Chatterjee 1990).

17. The Naxalbari peasant uprising in 1967 resulted in the rise of the Naxalite movement, which espoused the cause of revolution to end social inequities. The state repression and killing of twenty-seven farmers spurted the rise of Naxalism and engulfed the Bengali urban youth, who resorted to violence to bring about social revolution. A large number of students and young people joined the movement. In Kolkata, the state machinery deployed its might and unleashed a brutal and violent regime of imprisonment and shootings to curb Naxal violence (Donner 2008).

18. Gooptu provides an interesting analysis by arguing that this film stages the eruption of the anger of the street youth, the *shikhita bekaar*, who were one of the visible casualties of the 1970s. However, in this film, after a lot of tribulation, Montu/Soumitra Chatterjee is able to become a *bhadralok* with the help of his lover Swarashi/Aparna Sen. Dhritiman Chatterjee as Siddhartha in Satyajit Ray's *Pratidwandi* and Samit Bhanja and Swarup Dutta in *Apan Jan* as leaders of two *para* (neighbourhood) gangs, Ranjit Mullick in Sen's *Interview* as well as the three films discussed in this chapter all articulate the anger and frustration of the educated unemployed youth, with some variations. Other films where we see a group of disaffected youth include *Ekhoni* (1971), *Raja* (1975), *Ajker Nayak* (1972), *Chhera Tamsuk* (1974), and *Chander Kachakachi* (1976).

19. Ghosh (2004) and Bhattacharya (2005) both point out that the social range of people who could be called *bhadralok* is wide-ranging and diverse, although, as Ghosh remarks, it presupposed 'primarily upper caste Hindus, with some property or access to some degree of wealth, claim to liberal education and some profession or employment in government or commercial office' (2004: 248).

20. Anjan Chaudhuri's *Shatru* (1984) is generally accepted as the single most important film that enabled the shift from the middle-class audience to the rural hinterland of West Bengal. This film changed the face and generic configuration of popular Bengali cinema. The film catered to the moffussil town and its constituents, moving away from the previous urban-centric imaginary of the popular.

21. Ghosh points out that in West Bengal, certain state initiatives pertaining to the Land Reform Act of 1955 (later the 1978 Operation Barga) vested the sharecroppers with certain rights that protected them from summary eviction, and agricultural technologies of the 1960s–70s such as high-yielding variety of seeds, chemical fertilisers, and pesticides resulted in a widening net of people with surplus income than before. This resulted in a larger number of people who could access college education. It is this social transformation that impacted the *bhadralok* and its self-imaginary, its habitat, and the changing map of Kolkata as a city (Ghosh 2004).

22. In Chapter Three, I had analysed Suchitra's re-fashioned star text as she moved away from her iconic lover image into maternal melodramas, or staged death and insanity and created a subjectivity that could not find affective fulfillment. Uttam too was attempting something similar in the 1960s–70s.

23. Nowell-Smith argues that at certain emotional moments, hysterical conversion takes place, the repressed starts to appear, and these excessive emotions and conflicts are siphoned off into the *mise en scène* (1987: 73).

24. '*Eka mor gaaner tori bhashichilem, nayan jole... sohosha ke ashilo, tori mor baibe bole...*', 'I have rowed my boat alone, suddenly someone has come to row my boat'. It is a modern Bengali song composed by Atul Prasad Sen.

25. Unlike the Hollywood family melodrama, it is not the Freudian frame that is evoked to signpost the failure of the ageing and sick patriarch: *Ekhane Pinjar* uses the mythic reference to the *Mahabharata* and the failed, impotent blind king, Dhritirashtra, the patriarch of the Kauravas, who could not prevent the destruction of his family. In the film, though, Amal will steer the family back into the social.

26. Biswas's assertion about Uttam's appeal and his tangible charisma corresponds with the views of Bhowmick (2001) and Bandyopadhyaya (2010).

27. The intruder-redeemer has been identified by Thomas Schatz as an important character type in the standard Hollywood family melodrama. Typically, this male figure is an outsider who arrives mysteriously into a family beset by crisis and manages to steer it away from impending disaster, very often through a love track, and restores the family's fortunes. The crisis of the family is usually precipitated by the absence of the father, who is dead, ineffectual, bed-ridden, or absent (see Mercer and Shingler 2004: 8–13).

28. The trope of madness, as discussed by Rodowick (1987) in his analysis of 1950s Hollywood family melodramas, is particularly useful to read the specific characters that Uttam essays in these films from the 1970s. According to Rodowick, the domestic melodrama runs the full gamut of psychological disorders as the figures of patriarchal authority try to resolve

their crisis of identity: '...male characters, whose conflicts devolve from the difficulty of attaining an active sexual identity in which patriarchal power can be confirmed and reproduced...' (ibid.: 272). This trope can be productively used to read Gana *da* or Anupam as failed male characters within their familial spaces who are undergoing a crisis of authority and are besieged by failure and madness.

29. Comparing the 'figures pertaining to Industrial production computed from the Annual Survey of Industries from different years', S. C. Ray (2011) provides a glimpse into the dismal state of affairs in the state. He shows the steady decline in the state's 'share in Industrial Production and Employment'. From 1955–56, West Bengal's share in industrial production was 24 per cent and employment rate was 27 per cent; in 1966–67, production was 20 per cent and employment was at 22 per cent. In 1970–71, they fell to 13.5 per cent and 16.2 per cent, respectively.

> It is beyond dispute that labor trouble at the factories and political unrest throughout the state hurt industry in West Bengal. In 1965 there were 179 strikes and 49 incidents of lockout in factories. In 1970, by comparison, there were 678 strikes and 128 lockouts. (ibid.)

These factors put paid to the Nehruvian developmental vision, resulting in an explosion of rage, violence, and turmoil in the state. Many among the educated youth turned to the Naxalite movement, while others took to a life of petty crime and illegal activities. The state used extreme force and violence to control anti-establishment activities, while the political schisms within the Communist groups and the Congress made governance difficult. See Ray's (ibid.) analysis for a succinct summary of the troubled political climate of the state and the abysmal economic situation.

30. Goswami (1999) provides a detailed analysis of the decline of Kolkata's economy from around 1955. The first reason was a shrinking agrarian hinterland; the second, a lack of adequate public-sector investment to arrest the agrarian downswing; the third, inadequate manufacturing activities and lack of employment generating potential in the factory sector; the fourth, low levels of private-sector investment; the fifth, the growth of competing industrial locations outside Kolkata, which took away investment from West Bengal; and finally, the failure of the city to tax its own wealth (1990: 95).

31. Kaviraj (2004) and Biswas (2010) make the argument that the anonymity of the modern city enabled male characters to have a certain *joie de vivre* and the moral economy of the narrative was not bothered about the immoral activities of the protagonists. Mazumdar (2009) maps the spatial mobility of the woman in the 1950s city films such as *Taxi Driver* and

Nau Do Gyarah to show how the woman in these films escaped normative feminine roles by cross-dressing.

32. *Alaap* is a musical composition that only uses the notes.

33. See the discussion on *Nabaraag* in Chapter Two. This film stages the dysfunctional marriage of Reena and Vipulananda as a trope to reflect the social turmoil in the 1970s, which can be seen as strife in the city, labour unrest, and lockouts in the factory.

34. Some of the notable roles that we see in the popular films of this period include Suchitra as a cabaret dancer in *Fariyaad*; Supriya Chaudhuri as a high society hostess in *Chowringee* and as an advertising professional who trades on her body to get promotions in *Nagar Darpane*; Uttam as a male cabaret singer who runs an escort service, and Mithu Mukherjee as an escort in *Hotel Snow Fox*; Aparna Sen as a cabaret performer/escort in *Sonar Khancha*, and as a smuggler in *Ekhane Pinjar*. In Bombay cinema, Parveen Babi and Zeenat Aman essayed these non-traditional female roles in the mid-1970s.

35. Bandyopadhyaya (2010) provides an interesting analysis of the lack of Uttam's physical attractiveness, which can be coded as normatively handsome. His thick lips, pudgy hands and slack jaw line (as compared to a more rugged-looking Soumitra Chatterjee) still made him the heartthrob of his huge female fan base. Uttam's delicate demeanour and 'feminine' looks were attractive to women, who regarded him as an ideal romantic partner who would make them feel safe. Across his fan base, the oft-repeated phrase about him was that he was 'good', he would never harm anyone or be a villain (ibid.: 175–88). This idealised '*bhalo chele*', good-boy image, was carried along the '*bhadralok*' axis. Uttam's star image as a romantic icon resided in this middle-class *bhadralok* self. This image accreted despite his negative portrayals of a wife murderer in *Bicharak* and *Sesh Anka*, or of a drunkard, lustful husband in *Shankhabela*, or in films that deployed the trope of sexual aggression, such as that of a kidnapper and potential rapist in *Alo Amar Alo*.

Gender is performed both by men and women, especially in the context of stars; and if Uttam's romantic screen persona was generally that of the sensitive ideal male, then the 'normative' male stereotype of the sexually virile man was deployed beyond the diegetic. The biographies and fan letters in film magazines became sites where gossip about him, his peccadilloes with women, and the mad frenzy of his female fans was mobilised. In this extra-filmic domain of gossip, the various rumoured affairs, his marriage, and his long live-in relationship with Supriya Chaudhuri all created a tension that fed into his masculine image.

36. Ishwar Chandra Vidyasagar (1820–91), noted Bengali reformist writer and key figure of the Bengal Renaissance. He is credited with collating

the Bengali dictionary and is referred to as the father of the modern Bengali language.

37. This is a very important religious festival in Bengal, based on the worship of Goddess Durga as the symbol of female power, evoking the myth where she vanquished the demon Mahishasura. The beating and humiliation on the auspicious festival day overlays the pathos and irony of the scene, and the suicide on the last day completes the process begun by the gang on the *puja* morning. The pathos is further accentuated by an earlier scene in which Gana *da* describes his dream of a better world and comments on autumn and the impending festivity.

38. Yudhistira was the oldest of the five Pandava brothers from the epic *Mahabharata*. He was known for his allegiance to *dharma*, 'truth', and is thus a mythical figure representing truth and righteousness. In a sense, Gana *da* typifies the elder brother figure who adheres to truth and fair play and sacrifices his life for his values.

39. The insert of Jamuna, Naina's sisiter, fleeing with her lover shows us the truth of what Naina suspects. Jamuna had stolen the lamp and eloped with her lover.

40. This use of the 'embodied voiceover' technique has been discussed by Silverman in her work on the female voice in Hollywood films of the 1940s–50s (Silverman 1988). This principle of embodied voiceover is used to describe traumatic events related to the past, which impinge on the present. This particular strategy is useful in understanding the specific use of voiceover in this film and also in *Jadu Bangsha*. In *Jadu Bangsha*, all the violent events of the past related to Surya's family, madness, death, and suicide in Kripamoy's family, and violent events in Buli's family history are narrated via voiceovers and flashbacks.

41. The dark night, when the moon wanes.

5

Afterlives

Introduction

In this chapter, I shall track the circulation of the star texts of Suchitra and Uttam from the 1980s to the present, when the Suchitra–Uttam stardom and their 'love affair' reappeared in popular discourse, media texts, and imaginative literature. This mapping is crucial for unravelling the manner in which popular imaginaries travel across time. The 'travel of selves' signposts crucial articulations that can tell us 'what' of the self-imaginaries accrues over a period of time and 'which' of the selves acquires a mythic resonance. As I mentioned in the Introduction, their stardom has 'endured' long after their film careers ended; it has a *longue durée* and has continued to reappear in different sites. It has an afterlife: in Uttam's case, a posthumous reinvention and re-appropriation, and in Suchitra's case, a re-fashioned text predicated along her reclusive post-retirement image as a *sadhika*, or renouncer figure, and her posthumous stardom. The archive for this fragment is necessarily dispersed; it draws upon fan culture, star auto/biographies, television, fiction, etc.

In a city where culture and cultural artifacts are hierarchically categorised into high culture, which is deemed respectable, and the popular—including industrial and commercial cinema, which was the mainstay of these two superstars—with the latter often derided, it is interesting to note the attempted reconfiguration of the popular via a certain hagiography, especially around Uttam, that is now becoming available to the new political constellation that has come to power in West Bengal.[1] There seems to be a conscious move to appropriate the iconic presence of this popular hero, often pitted against the so-called cultural elitism of the previous political constellations.[2] The dice is loaded in terms of the hagiography around Uttam, especially due to his relationship with Supriya[3] and the fact that his family seems to be making concerted efforts, along with his Shilpi Sansad fans, to get him more public recognition and visibility posthumously.[4] Since January 2006, the Shilpi Sansad has been publishing a fortnightly fanzine called *Uttam Shilpi Varta*. The publication is nominally priced and is also sold at events organised by the Sansad. It very often carries a half-page colour photo of the star on the front page and many of the articles and reminiscences draw on his star power. The paper also carries current production news related to Tollygunj and news about forthcoming events organised by the Sansad, as well as features on older actors, especially around various anniversaries. Exhibitions held on Uttam's birth and death anniversaries too draw huge crowds. The first big event of this kind, the 'Uttam Mela', was organised by the star Prosenjit Chatterjee in 2005. Film posters and publicity booklets have also started appearing in exhibitions dedicated to him. One of the oft-repeated laments around Uttam's death refers to the refusal of the erstwhile Left Front state government to place his body at Rabindra Sadan[5] (Chowdhury 2012; Debi 2010: 910).

In fact, the image of Uttam as the popular star has been mobilised by the current political party in power, the Trinamool Congress (TMC), to position itself as a popular party in West Bengal. The leader of this party, Mamata Banerjee, released the first documentary about the superstar, 'Journey of a Megastar', and also inaugurated a commemorative function held to mark his death anniversary in 2009, which I had attended. Another documentary produced by the Film Division was released in 2011.[6] His life-sized statue stands at the intersection of Tollygunj; the Tollygunj Metro Station was renamed 'Mahanayak Uttam Kumar Metro Station' in 2009 by the West Bengal government, and the postal department has released a commemorative stamp. Suchitra's family, on the other hand, is assiduously committed to preserving her privacy and she was not at the forefront of a similar appropriation, although unlike Uttam, she was given a state funeral in 2014, attended by the Chief Minister. The state government also renamed a portion of the Ballygunj Circular Road as Suchitra Sen Sarani after Sen's death.

ADVOCATING THE STAR: THE AUTO/BIOGRAPHIES

As I have explained in the Introduction, my methodology involves deploying the star auto/biography as an important constituent of self-fashioning as I read it. I will briefly engage with two books: *Amar Ami*, Uttam Kumar's autobiography (Chattopadhyaya and Ghosh 1980),[7] and *Suchitrar Katha* (Ray 1992).[8] Very briefly, auto/biographies are accepted as narratives about the 'life story' of exemplary characters. They make certain 'truth claims' and provide evidence of historical contexts, and can be linear, chronological, or remain skeletal and partial narratives. But most importantly, auto/biographies evoke or construct the person for their readers. Even when they are hagiographic and attempt to deify the person, they still provide interesting clues about how that persona is being created for readers and which images are being circulated in the social domain. Auto/biographies are crucial in the field of star studies, not because they offer a glimpse of the 'real' person, but because they provide tools for decoding the star's image. Star studies are not about uncovering the real person beneath the image, but about analysing the star text.

One of the crucial questions is: How reliable are these auto/biographies as texts? If one reads these texts as a 'trace', a discourse that provides partial access to the image, to the context within which it is being constructed, and to how the advocacy of the subject is undertaken, then these biographies become important components of the star text. A close textual reading between the lines of even the mundane, formulaic, part rumour, part gossip, part historically verifiable, material facts can be an important tool to engage with the contemporary reconstruction of a segment of the star figure. Even autobiographies do not give unmediated access to the 'real' person writing about her/his life story. They are constructions of a particular persona and need to be read carefully to uncover their deletions and erasures, as indeed the method of how that subject is writing about her/his self.[9] Predictably, Uttam's version glosses over rumours and gossip. Suchitra's biographies, on the other hand, create a network of stories that had circulated as rumours and gossip and present them as facts. And as my project uses two specific stars who had attained remarkable popularity, and whose star texts did rely on the circulation of gossip and rumour, my deployment of their star texts does not shy away from relying on this particular rhetoric.

Before I discuss the two books, I turn to a brief summation of gossip as a useful rhetorical device that can enable a productive engagement with the circulation of stories and rumours, and their centrality to the fashioning of the star texts of Suchitra and Uttam.

The trope of gossip has been an object of study in literature and social linguistics, especially since the 1960s. Eschewing the commonplace understanding of gossip as malicious and slanderous, Spacks and others have demonstrated how this unofficial network can provide an alternative to official values (Holland 1996; Martin 2014; Spacks 1982).[10] Its complex nature is perceived as being harmful for the victims, but 'it retains value, in that it helps us navigate the social world' (Schmidt 2004: 1). According to Jack Shear, 'gossip is a "great delight", which has the power to "satisfy" a mutual desire to trade common currency and social speculation' (Shear 2008: 22). Spacks assigns the pleasurable characteristics of gossip to the realm of the erotic: 'Gossip even when it avoids the sexual, bears about it a faint flavor of the erotic' (cited in ibid.). It inhabits a liminal space, in that it seeks out and tests the boundaries of what can be said, what can be accepted as truth, and what constitutes public knowledge. It is constituted by a dual function, 'knowledge–play and pleasurable exchange' (Shear 2008: 23).[11] Gossip is particularly significant in any discussion of the public and the private as

> It carries within it an illicit tension or joy and it is different from the conversation of ordinary life in that its rules pierce the divide between public and private spheres... gossip challenges the notion of relegating information to either of the two separate spheres of discourse and calls into question the solidity of distinction between within and without. (ibid.)

Giselle Bastin (2005) quotes Spacks (1982), who insists that though '[g]ossip is not fiction', it nonetheless, 'in the form of memoirs and collections of letters, embodies the fictional'. Both Spacks and Bastin explicate the lexical meaning of the term to foreground its association with the feminine, its opposition to public discourse, and draw a parallel with 'history'.[12] Both terms, that is, 'history' (with a small 'h') and gossip, 'are often connected with the words "unruly", "transgressive", and "disobedient"' (Bastin 2005: 29). All of these formulations draw attention to the trope of gossip, as it inhabits largely an oral circuit of knowledge that circulates and creates a parallel discourse about the persons involved. It is evident that this particular rhetorical trope of gossip is crucial for unravelling the constructions and formations of self that comprise the star text since it can enable an entry into a space that is otherwise sealed off in public discourse. Drawing on these formulations, it is possible to suggest that the limits of all discourses are permeable and the desires and fictions embodied in star texts can be penetrated to yield more than simple voyeuristic/vicarious pleasures. Gossip ultimately produces knowledge; its circulation, therefore, works as a site where this knowledge is consumed.

Since I am interested in two specific stars, I argue that these circulations also signpost the forms of control that the fans and spectators choose to impose over the star texts and how their iconicity can be fashioned in public memory. If, as Shear suggests, this knowledge is part of social activity and functions with its own set of discursive limits, then surely these exchanges of knowledge ultimately cite our own embodied desires for the particular forms of control that we impose on star texts and their iconicity. Additionally, if gossip itself is feminine, then its absence or presence, as indeed its obfuscations, can alert us to the manner in which it is being mobilised and the uses of that mobilisation. As Suchitra's biographies rely on the circulation of uncorroborated stories, does this deployment then further the excess of femininity that she was known for? If Uttam had to consolidate his 'good boy', *bhalo chele* image, then what role, if any, did gossip (or its glossing over) play in that construction?

Further, if the star texts signpost the embodied desires of spectators, and since I have argued that these desires are not confined to either the filmic or the extra-filmic in its own time, but has a longer temporality, then which story/rumour/gossip is able to hold its sway and charm over others? Moreover, the circulation of these stories in biographies and autobiographies also need to be tracked to decode the manner in which images and selves are constructed for their readers. As I have argued in the Introduction, the star discourse in the Indian context, as well as most self-narratives, deploy the bracketing of the personal, the intimate, and the private. The circulation of the unofficial sites of gossip and fictional reconstructions are therefore significant tropes that I choose in order to decode the emergence of the private into the public. This slippery terrain of private discourse that spills out then enables an entry into the spaces of the liminal, unruly, and transgressive or suppressed-but-embodied spectatorial and fan desires that are being signalled.

Amar Ami [*Me Myself*] is a straightforward linear narrative, narrated in the first person in Uttam's own voice, beginning with his birth, his childhood, and his family. His abiding love for acting, his theatre experience, his struggle as an actor, and his stardom are interspersed with glimpses of his personal life—his first marriage to Gauri Devi, and his much publicised live-in relationship with Supriya Chaudhuri (who played the role of Neeta in Ritwik Ghatak's *Meghe Dhaka Tara*, and was Uttam's heroine in thirty films).[13] What emerges out of this text is the image of a gritty and determined middle-class person who is tremendously invested in the values of hard work, perseverance, and diligence; a person who entered the industry and worked his way up to the top, but never took his success for granted, was ever ready to work hard, and was continuously trying to better his craft. A large part of the narrative is devoted to descriptions of his endeavours to learn dancing, horse riding, Hindi and Urdu lessons to improve his diction for his stints in Bombay, and his tennis lessons. The book also reiterates his commitment to improve the working conditions of junior artistes and his life-long struggle to improve the status of the industry. There are long passages describing his meetings with various ministers and his charity fundraisers for various causes. The text makes constant references to Uttam being the *dada* [the elder brother figure] of the industry, who tirelessly strove to work for the betterment of Bengali cinema.[14]

The book features vignettes of Uttam as the devoted family man, who remained a good father to his son despite his live-in relationship with Supriya, and who was very fond of Supriya's daughter Soma, whose wedding he organised. Both these aspects of his troubled personal life form a significant section of the self-fashioning that this text attempts to create. However, this book glosses over the salacious gossip surrounding his troubled relationship with Soma (Chattopadhyaya 2005: 21). As discussed in Chapter Two, it was only in a special edition of the *Anandalok* magazine, brought out after his death in 1980, that Soma herself gave an interview about her attraction for her mother's partner (Bhattacharya 1980).[15] Of course, these erasures are in keeping with the demands of populist biographies. The idea that Uttam was a 'star' whom women could not keep away from, and that this was a necessary fallout of his profession, is alluded to only as an aside, if at all.[16]

This text is interesting not because it continuously peppers the narrative with actual dates and statistics, but because it creates the iconic figure and 'aura' of Uttam Kumar—the immensely successful romantic star, but also a tragic and lonely, angst-ridden modern individual grappling with the pressures of being a star,[17] and carrying the baggage of being the *dada* of the industry.[18] It is this *dada* figure that is significant for one fragment of his star text, his Shilpi Sansad, which remains an important fan organisation. This organisation was founded by Uttam in 1968 and still functions from the same building on Lenin Sarani that Uttam had initially rented. Uttam had envisaged it as an umbrella organisation that would protect the interests of junior artistes, older, out-of-work artistes, as well as people associated with music, jatra, etc. He was involved in regular call shows, plays, and private guest appearances to raise funds. In 1974–75, the Sansad had accumulated Rs 20,000 from Uttam's personal appearances. He used to charge around Rs 5,000 for private guest appearances; this money was also used to run the organisation. His film production of *Banpalashir Padabali*

(1973) was mounted to aid the cause of junior artistes and the huge cast and crew worked for a pittance to support the cause of destitute artists (Debi 1999: 267–68).

Suchitrar Katha [*Suchitra's Story*], written by G. K. Ray, does not claim to be an authorised narrative, mainly because Suchitra refused to give interviews after her retirement and is often compared to Greta Garbo, the famous Hollywood recluse. There were rumours and speculation about Suchitra after her retirement in the late 1970s; she starred in her last film in 1978, but had steadfastly refused to corroborate or refute any of these rumours. This text adopts a very intimate tone of voice as the author claims to be a friend of the star, one who had access to her home as a family friend and with whom Suchitra shared many hours of conversation after she retired from the industry; but, of course, their relationship dates back to her days as a star. Ray claims he decided to write the book for Suchitra fans who were keen to know how the star spent her days after her retirement, what transformed her into 'Suchitra' (her screen name) from Roma, her unparalleled rise as a star, and her relationship with her daughter Moonmoon Sen. This narrative created the persona of the exotic, moody, and often unpredictable, mysterious woman, who was extremely childish at times, but was also a caring and loyal friend and companion, who never engaged in salacious rumours and gossip, who sublimated her anger and rage into her devotion to her god, and who later spent her time at her puja, worship, and in being a doting grandmother to her daughter's children, Riya and Raima.

While this text signposts various dates and figures about her life and career, it is actually invested in creating the image of a retiring woman, a recluse who left her stardom behind her, more content to be a mother and grandmother; one who reluctantly became a star, but is essentially an elite middle-class woman looking for personal fulfilment; one who faced the personal trauma of a broken marriage, and yet juggled the requirements of a demanding career and motherhood singlehandedly. Suchitra's struggles as well as the handicap resulting from her East Bengal dialect are mentioned, but Ray seems more invested in glossing over these details. In fact, other accounts of her initial struggle mention the problems she faced because of this perceived handicap (Chatterjee 2002; Gupto 2003; Mukhopadhyaya 2000). She was even lampooned in a popular magazine.[19] As I mentioned in Chapter Two, unlike Bhanu, the popular comedian who made a very successful career out of his East Bengal dialect, the woman star could not use this identity to her advantage.

There are important erasures in the manner in which her star text was created. She had to mould her persona according to the demands of her geographical location after marriage. She participated in charity events regularly and donated at auctions organised to raise funds for victims of the 1967 floods. Suchitra is often regarded as the successor to Kanan Devi, who has been described as the first lady of Bengali cinema in the studio period, but Suchitra did not re-invent herself like Kanan Devi as a producer.[20] In this text, Suchitra remains the quintessential diva who had a successful stint as the *mahanayika,* the female superstar, but who also had the courage to turn her back on fame and popularity and withdraw into her world and her home.

Unlike Uttam's narrative, this text remains partial and sketchy as Ray does not follow a linear or chronological structure. In effect, this biography can be seen as an example of a fan memoir or described as anecdotal (Stacey 1994).[21] Ray writes it as a personal memoir of his interaction and conversations with Suchitra. Her successful industry stint is mentioned in passing, giving the impression that she has chosen to almost forget her professional life. In fact, Ray has nearly singlehandedly reinvented her image and created the new *sadhika* Suchitra, transforming the glamour queen of her times into a devoted Ramakrishna follower.[22] It is interesting to excavate this reinvention by drawing upon the life stories of earlier women performers, as seen in Sudipto Chatterjee's work on nineteenth-century theatre actresses, which discussed their devotion to Ramakrishna (Chatterjee 2007: 202). Since these women were generally seen as belonging to the world of prostitutes, they were considered to be fallen women, '*patitas*' (socially liminal). These women could lay claim to social acceptance through their devotional relationship with the seer, and found solace 'without fear of castigation, judgement or betrayal' (ibid.)[23] However, considering that Suchitra was not from this class, it is still pertinent that the only available trope for refashioning the woman performer known for an excessively sensuous and glamorous aura would be that of the devoted renouncer, the *sadhika* figure.[24]

As I have discussed in Chapter One, Suchitra's star text was deeply imbricated in her spatial and marital location of south Kolkata. Her reinvention into the renouncer devotee figure can be productively understood by invoking Swati Chattopadhyaya's (2005) work on the spatial location of respectable women and the public women performers in Kolkata in the colonial period as well as the gendered terrain on which the modernity discourse mapped itself. The emergence of the *bhadramahila* into the public sphere led to intense scrutiny of her attire, her education, her behaviour, and her comportment. Her access to modernity was controlled; she was expected to appear respectable in both demeanour and behaviour. The public woman, on the other hand, was the 'sexed body' who 'protected the freedom of the men to move between the two worlds of the prostitute and the *bhadramahila* without conflict' (ibid.: 254). Suchitra's public stardom, which rested on her 'sex-appealing capacity',[25] was in conflict with her 'respectable' marital and social location as the daughter-in-law, the *bonedi* ('elite') *bhadramahila*. All the problematics of this anxiety-ridden gendered spatiality, discussed by Chattopadhyaya, still seem to operate on Suchitra's star body in this post-colonial Bengali mode of self-fashioning. To quote Chattopadhyaya again: 'In examining the location of women in [the] Bengali public sphere, one is made aware of the stakes involved in the gendered marking of public space' (ibid.: 265). This glamorous female star's body could only be refashioned into a devoted renouncer figure, who lived a spartan life, totally secluded, which she chose of her own volition. Perhaps her seclusion is a form of withdrawal, a death-like imposition that the superstar herself chose after what was perceived as an earlier life of excess.[26] This excess of her star text was mobilised through glamour, fashion, a coalescing of her image with that of urban modernity, as well as her spatial and marital location within the elite city space,[27] which was then reconfigured via her subsequent self-fashioning as a recluse. However, the star text still manages to hold its space within public memory.

THE STAR TEXTS AND MEDIA SITES

If Suchitra's biography constructs an image of the *sadhika*, then what image emerges as we track other sites such as newspaper supplements and television? This reclusive image is further accentuated by these media sites as well. The thriving market for biographical accounts in weekly supplements and newspapers such as *Bartaman, Anandalok,* and *Anandbazaar,* television cable channels such as *Star Ananda, 24 Ghanta,* etc.; television programmes that undertake an endless analysis of the Suchitra–Uttam pair; and stories about her retirement or speculation about her reclusiveness are testimonies to her absent presence that still circulates in the public imaginary. The media frenzy surrounding her rare public appearances, and the intrusions she was subjected to, including attempts to sneak reporters into adjacent rooms in the private nursing home where she was often admitted due to poor health, provided fodder for gossip and paparazzi antics. News items on her would constantly talk of her ill health, her income tax dues, or how 'domesticated' she was in her private life. She thus inhabited a kind of everyday presence.

The other axis of her star text is predicated along an absence from the serious critical discourse of the older Little Magazines that I discuss in Uttam's context, or even from a collection on the lives of film actresses (Ghosh 2009). Sen's upper-class location as a *bonedi bhadramahila* and her fashionable glamourous looks were constantly evoked to critically examine her 'limited acting capabilities' as well as being a representative of an 'authentic' Bengali *bhadramahila*. In most accounts, she is compared negatively to her contemporary Sabitri Chatterjee (Ray and Raha 2002). Sabitri's long professional theatre career has assured her assessment as a serious actor;[28] even in the present, she has a very visible presence on television and in films. Her text is thus unlike Sen's, who had no experience of professional theatre performances or any art film in her career trajectory.[29] Uttam too had a successful professional theatre career; his performance in *Shyamoli*, staged at the famous Star Theatre in Kolkata with Sabitri as his romantic lead, was widely acclaimed and had a five year-long run. Sabitri's deglamourised, natural looks versus Suchitra's heavily made-up, glamorous appearances inhabit a polarised regime of evaluation informed by class-based perception, where Suchitra scores poorly against Sabitri.[30]

It is thus interesting to contrast the descriptions of the glamorous, made-up look favoured by Suchitra, with details of her fair skin glimpsed through sleeveless blouses and sheer chiffon sarees, her statement jewellery pieces, and elaborate hairdos, with Sabitri's appearance in a plain red chiffon saree, with minimal gold jewellery.[31] The photographs of her public appearances for various film-related events provided graphic evidence of her low-cut silk blouses and the drape of the saree, through which her bare shoulders and arms would be visible, and the reporter would ask the obvious rhetorical question: Is this the appropriate attire for a Bengali woman?[32] This would, of course, give the readers enough material to ask questions about her 'unseemly' dress sense and the excess of glamour that she displayed. Her figure certainly seemed to play out all the constituents of Dyer's formulation of the star persona, framed along the axis of this deeply gendered terrain which occluded the struggles and hardships that she might have encountered—these difficulties are glossed over due to her social position and her photogenic beauty. The latter, especially, which enabled her to construct her star text, has been considered essential in according stars a template of divinisation and is seen to add to their mythical aura (Morin 1961). According to Morin, the star's appearance, make-up, photographs, as well as on- and off-screen looks contribute to the construction of the image, which enables the accretion of an almost superlative iconic aura and renders that star extraordinary. This mythical aura is like a template of divinisation, bestowing a supra-human, almost god/goddess-like stature to the star. Suchitra's star text occupies a similar domain of divinisation, where her photogenic beauty and overtly sexualised, made-up appearance created an excessive template of veneration, voyeurism, and fetishisation over her 'sexed body'. The internet is one such site where the circulation of her fashion shoots and blogs added to her iconic image, and where her *bhadramahila* status and elite positioning are not seen as contrary to her star status in the contemporary. Perhaps the strident moralistic tenor visible in the immediate post-independence cultural nationalism has waned, allowing for a more inclusive acceptance of her star image.

I have foregrounded the fraught nature of the processes around the erotic/sexualised public image through which Suchitra's star text was constructed and consolidated. Suchitra was able to challenge the deeply patriarchal and hegemonic structures of the industry due to her box-office draw. By 1955, when *Saap Mochon* and *Saanjher Pradeep* released, the publicity material, song booklets, posters, film credit sequences, etc., gave her top billing and carried her name before her male leads. This included her films with Uttam Kumar. This was a singular exception to the usual practice in the 1950s—Uttam's name otherwise appeared after the female lead only if the lead could claim seniority, as was the case only with Kanan Devi or Sandhya Rani. Suchitra was able to make her Bengali producers follow this practice throughout her career; however, her Bombay stint did not adhere to this practice.[33]

I make this point to foreground the fact that Suchitra commanded a status that was quite at odds with the generally chauvinistic and patriarchal attitude of the industry. Kanan Devi's account of her career in the industry provides us an important insight into the deep-seated prejudices that women actors and stars encountered in the male-dominated film industry (Devi 1973: 124).[34] Devi's remark that Suchitra Sen needs to be seen as a rebel who embodied the struggles of women for successful professional and personal selfhoods is significant (ibid.). Clearly, Sen's continuous negotiations to increase her remuneration paved the way for later women actors and stars to get better financial deals (Gupto 2003: 91). An outsider like Suchitra commanding this status was certainly an anomaly. However, this particular fact has been erased from the contemporary domain as most references to the star pair follow the 'normative' practice of using Uttam's name before Suchitra's, except in some of her biographies where this fact is mentioned almost in passing.[35] In reconstructing the past through these retro histories, we seem to have lost a fragment that can provide an interesting entry into the fraught gender transactions that this woman negotiated in creating her star persona.

Biswas considers Suchitra as typifying the star versus the stereotype dialectic (1990: 309),[36] unlike Uttam, who represented the star versus the actor dichotomy. His trajectory as simply a matinee idol was redrawn when he was cast by Satyajit Ray in *Nayak* (1966) and *Chiriakhana* (1967), enabling him to challenge the negative connotations of his commercial superstar status. Ray's statement that Uttam was an instinctive actor as opposed to the cerebral actor (Ray 2011) cemented the star's reinvention as an actor.[37] In comparison, Suchitra is not accorded a serious assessment due to a lack of any art film performance or casting by Ray. There is an erasure here as Ray had expressed a desire to cast her twice: once for an adaptation of Tagore's *Ghare Baire* in the mid-1950s (which he ultimately made in 1985 with Soumitra Chatterjee, Swatilekha, and Victor Banerjee), and later for *Debi Chaudhurani*, his adaptation of the Bankim Chandra novel of the same name. Both these projects had generated considerable public interest at that time. However, the Ray projects never materialised; while Suchitra's *Debi Chaudhurani* (1974), directed by Dinen Gupto, opposite Soumitra Chatterjee had a mixed box-office reception. One may speculate that had the Ray films been made, Suchitra too could have been evaluated more positively. Suchitra was not accepted as an accomplished actor. On the contrary, her popular appeal and charisma was usually accorded negative valuation. This is not to suggest any definitive opinion on either Uttam or Suchitra's acting capabilities, but to draw attention to the multiple relays of discourses that shaped their stardoms, and to demonstrate how the public image of the erotic and highly glamourised woman star gets relegated to circuits of oral memories and populist biographies, which are dismissed as trashy products meant for quick sales, not to be taken seriously, while the male star gets some critical recognition in serious film journal discourses, especially the newer Little Magazines. It is to this discourse that I now turn to map the circulation of the Uttam star text.

POSTHUMOUS STARDOM: LITTLE MAGAZINES AND THE TWO STARS

FIGURE 5.1: Event Commemorating Uttam's Death Anniversary, 'Uttam Sarvottam', organised by Shilpi Sansad Kolkata in 2009

Source: Author's photograph.

In most of the film society material from the late 1960s and 1970s that I have been able to collect on Uttam, I did not come across any article specifically on Suchitra. She seems to not exist in this discourse on stardom. She appears tangentially, finding mention as one of Uttam's heroines. This erasure assumes importance in the present as there is renewed critical interest around popular cinema as well as the two stars, though the dice is loaded in terms of the hagiography around Uttam, as I mentioned in the opening section of this chapter.

The Bangla Film Society journals and Little Magazines are another critical site that has added to the aura of Uttam's star text in the present. The 1970s, when a few articles started appearing about Uttam, was an interesting period for the star as many of his breakaway or character roles belong to this time.[38] To my mind, the film society journals or Little Magazines prior to the late 1960s would not have found it important to engage with Uttam in any significant measure because of the ideological position that they espoused vis-à-vis the industry and their complete disavowal of the popular. Satyajit Ray's casting Uttam in his *Nayak* (1966) and *Chiriakhana* (1967) became the cause of a huge uproar at that time as Ray was seen to have sold out to commercial interests. Even though the film society journals began carrying reviews of his films, they still deployed the ideological grids of their film aesthetics.

This 'film sense' discourse was not new to the 1970s. I have mentioned in the Introduction that from the 1950s, the CFS critical template was responsible for debunking the popular film, with which the popular press and film magazines also concurred. It needs to be noted that 'good film sense' was an umbrella term used to signify the place of cinema in the Nehruvian developmental vision. If cinema had to participate in the necessary socialist enterprise of nation-building, then it had to reform itself to take its rightful place and position. This position has been described as being 'related to the formation of an art cinema' (Vasudevan 2010: 75–81).[39] This 1950s template was equally invested in exploring the aesthetics of good cinema which generally favoured the realist model. As I have argued in Chapter Four, following Rochona Majumdar (2011), the 1970s film society discourse had taken a radical turn, and hence the 'politics' of filmmaking itself had started becoming a crucial signifier of intent. Therefore, the 1950s aesthetic vision somehow took a back seat.

Given this template, it is not surprising that Uttam and his stardom became the most visible symbol of the 'rot' in the commercial model. There seems to be a palpable unease about engaging with the popular at the level of fan culture and following as his tremendous popularity is taken as indicative of the lack of discriminatory taste or *ruchi* among the masses. The tone of the reviews in magazines, especially the few that I found from the 1970s, is scathing and contain comments on the futility of Uttam's star power, since he was unable to deliver hits like earlier, as I mentioned in Chapter Four. These texts display a curious anger at his stature in the industry, and he becomes the scapegoat within whom all the wrongs of commercial cinema could be contained. In all these accounts, what is left unsaid is the fact that even after Uttam and Suchitra, other pairs were created in the industry, although they could not approximate the popular appeal that this pair enjoyed. The oft-repeated trope that was used to describe Uttam's popularity admitted that he was unquestioningly the superstar, but his acting abilities were underutilised in the commercial film as he had to work with mediocre directors. Therefore, his acting in the two Ray films was routinely cited as evidence of his capabilities, if he could only get good, competent directors. The critiques against Uttam seemed more invested in drawing attention to the problems of the popular form and the industrial structures of filmmaking, as opposed to the committed politics of art cinema. As the most popular star of the industry, he became the most visible object carrying the charge of the popular and could hence also be designated as the symbol of its failure. The superstar could escape this construction only in his death. It is interesting to note that the articles that appear after his death deploy the same tropes of star-versus-actor dialectic to suggest that this particular contradiction haunted the superstar and that he himself was troubled by this. The most cited among this lament is Uttam's interview after his association with Satyajit Ray (Chattopadhyaya 2001: 46), which I have cited in Chapter Four. I now map that specific moment which aided the fashioning and construction of this star, as well as Suchitra's death and its aftermath.

DEATH OF THE STAR: ACCRUING ICONICITY

Edgar Morin (1961) has noted that stars acquire a specific state of authentication and immortality in death since they are attributed with mythic status as they become stars. He analyses this process by examining the death of James Dean and remarks that death accorded Dean a cult status as a

> perfect star god, hero, model. But this perfection, if it has only been able to fulfill itself by means of the star system, derives from the life and death of the real James Dean and from the exigence which is his own as well as that of a generation which sees itself in him, reflected and transfigured in twin mirrors: screen and death. (ibid.: 133)

His death symbolises the heroic struggles of the mythical hero pitted against the inimical forces, but these struggles further symbolise his destiny that is 'the beginning of his victory over death' (ibid.: 123). Death seems to have bestowed the star figures of Uttam and Suchitra with similar cult status, through which their stardom has become more accentuated posthumously.

Uttam's death in 1980 seems to have framed the *mahanayak*, the superstar, with a halo that has still not lost its glow. The popular press at the time, of course, went to town with special supplements dedicated to the star. Newspapers carried half-page spreads of the sea of people who joined the funeral entourage. The sudden death created a vacuum which was sought to be filled with a new discourse of the popular mass appeal of the star. This mass appeal was considered significant enough to mask the problems that had plagued the star in his lifetime. A perusal of the special *Anandalok* issue is illustrative of the obfuscations that eventually enveloped the star figure. In one article that analyses the romantic pairing of Uttam and Suchitra, the author argues that the star couple created a map of innocent middle-class love, which aided the subsequent occlusion of the critical reception that these films had generated in the 1950s (Aniket 1980).[40] Even film critics who had written scathing reviews of Uttam's films in the 1970s began to re-visit his stardom via a nostalgic haze of memory and reminiscence.[41] The 'mis-remembrance' of the 'scandalous embrace' that appears subsequently (Subhajit Chatterjee 2007)[42] can actually be located in this moment, where death created and aided iconicity with different attributes. The Little Magazines too began to reconfigure their critical evaluations related to Uttam. His assessment as a star and his contribution to the industry became important considerations for some writers (Chattopadhyaya 2006; Sengupto 1987).

Other articles also foregrounded his star status and his pairing with Suchitra, which was now regarded as the only pairing that had stood the test of time. In one historical overview of Bangla cinema, Uttam was placed after Durgadass and Pramathesh Barua, and Suchitra after Kanan Devi. The writer did not deploy any particular critical position or evaluative mode.[43] The piece ended with a lament on the demise of the star system that dominated Tollygunj.

Both Suchitra and Uttam were described as the 'golden pair' of the industry (Ray 2001). In another article, the duo's dialogue delivery, use of film sound technology and cinematography were analysed by deploying the lens of Metzian semiology to decode the immense popularity of the star pair (Sengupta 2001).[44] These changing templates of critical engagement with the popular were getting mapped onto Uttam and his star text. In this re-configuration, his death was thus clearly a significant event.

I will now refer to two pathbreaking publications: a special issue of *Chitrabhash* on Uttam brought out in 2001 by the North Calcutta Film Society and the *Tehai* volume published in 2010. The first publication created a furore as people felt that a reputed film society, dedicated to the spread of 'good/serious film culture', should not have brought out a special issue on a matinee idol, who was just a romantic star. In this full issue of 111 pages with around forty-three articles, the reference to Suchitra appeared only as an aside in one article as someone who contributed to the creation of Uttam's star persona, or as the heroine with whom he had a commercially successful romantic pairing. Most others followed the pattern of close textual analysis, following the earlier model of film analysis, and surveyed his career through the films. They concluded that he successfully deployed his middle-class status to articulate the spectatorial fantasies and desires in the post-independence cinema of the 1950s, when common people in Bengal were grappling with the demands of living the dream of a modern, independent nation and were also dealing with the aftermath of the Partition, a traumatic experience that popular cinema had refused to engage with.[45] In this publication, only one piece by Someshwar Bhowmick tried to locate the text of the superstar within the grid of the box-office success of his films. This article foregrounded the necessity of keeping in view the strings of platinum, golden, and silver week runs, along with the estimated revenue that some of his biggest hits had earned. He rightly pointed out that unlike Pramathesh Barua, Uttam was the middle-class hero who could voice his ordinariness with ease to capture the hearts of his audiences. The context of the post-independence 1950s demanded a figure that was not feudal like Barua, but could inhabit urban, middle-class Kolkata or rural spaces with equal ease.

Figure 5.2: T-Shirt Print of a Sketch by Satyajit Ray, used in *Nayak*
Source: Seen by the author in Kolkata, 2009

The majority of articles in this volume framed their discourse around Satyajit Ray. His towering presence cast its long shadow over the industry in curious ways. His figure intersected with that of Uttam in the mid-1960s and occupied a polarised position. Acclaimed, feted both nationally and internationally, Ray has also been seen as part of the statist agenda, propagating the cause of realist cinema. But curiously, he is seen as having failed to support the industry during a period of crisis in 1968–69, when Bombay film distributors were holding Bangla film releases to ransom. Hindi films were being given priority releases, while Bangla films had to wait even after Censor clearance.[46] The controversy around the release of Ray's *Goopy Gyne Bagha Byne* and *Arogya Niketan* added to the schism. Despite prior Censor clearance, Uttam's film had a delayed release in December 1969 as the Minar–Bijoli–Chabighar chain released Ray's film first in May. This period saw the film fraternity split into two opposing camps, one led by Ray and his followers, the other led by Uttam and senior actors (Sanyal 2008). This spilt had emerged in preceding years and formed the context for Uttam's decision to create the Shilpi Sansad in 1968 to safeguard the interests of junior artists and technicians. The late release of the Uttam film further exacerbated the schism in the industry. Public memory is, however, short-lived; the schism between the two is now almost forgotten. What remains in cultural memory is the fact that Ray cast Uttam in two of his films. After 1980, this fact re-surfaced in the popular imaginary and has been touted as one of the reasons to evaluate Uttam's acting skills favourably. Ray's speech at the condolence meet at Technician's Studio in 1980 has acquired the status of the final word on Uttam's acting skills, especially within the discourse of actor versus star. His commendation that Uttam was an instinctive and not a cerebral actor is the most quoted statement in this evaluatory model. The unarticulated subtext is the inevitable comparison with Soumitra Chatterjee, the intellectual actor who was a Ray favourite. Ray's comment that it was not possible to say that one was necessarily superior to the other is taken as proof that both Uttam and Soumitra were believed to be on par by the master auteur.

The *Tehai* issue, though huge and unwieldy with its 918 pages, uses a more balanced and nuanced tone in its approach to the star; the articles set up the star as an important phenomenon who, despite being at the receiving end of disdain from 'intellectuals', has managed to remain in the cultural memory of the people thirty years after his death. The issue is a compendium of articles, songs, commemorative speeches, newspaper reviews, screenplays, etc. The editorial is in itself indicative of the shift in the terms of engagement with the popular. It offers a scathing critique of the problematic Left cultural hegemony that had held sway in the state. It claims that it aims to give due recognition to the kind of evaluation that this star deserved, and which had been denied as the communist government did not even deem it necessary to keep his body at Rabindra Sadan, the usual place where even small-time political leaders are brought so that people can pay their last respects. In this volume, there are at least five articles on the couple; melodrama debates also find a place here. The rest of the pieces are devoted to an analysis of Uttam's star power, his humane character, his greatness as an actor; and it is clear that the earlier polarised debates around star versus actor are no longer being deployed. Other Little Magazines such as *Ababhas* are also important in this enterprise. In a way, the popular seems to have been accepted on its own terms. However, we need to remember that it is with his death and the changing political/cultural map of the city that we see a certain refashioning of the popular via the star figure.

Suchitra's death in 2014 after a period of illness enabled a different reconfiguration of her star status. The earlier critical evaluations have shifted shape in the contemporary period. Given that the current political regime in the state is known for its populist appeal, it is not surprising that the *mahanayika* was given a state funeral after her death and a street renamed after her, as mentioned earlier in the chapter. Her complete withdrawal from public life after her retirement had accorded her an exotic, iconic status, which remained impregnable even in her death. Her dead body was not shown to the public as she had assiduously refused to be seen after her retirement from the industry. Some new publications, including a compilation of features that had appeared in *Anandlok,* the Sunday supplement issued with *Anandabazaar Patrika,* have been published. Fan sites and online platforms too have been flooded with her fashion shoot photographs, aiding the accretion. It is also noteworthy that she has appeared in two short volumes—*Suchitra Sen: The Legend and the Enigma* by Shoma Chatterjee and *Uttam Kumar and Suchitra Sen: Bengali Cinema's First Couple* by Maitreyee B. Choudhuri—as part of a series on women actors of Indian cinema. She has an official Facebook page as well! It is with this changing cartography in sight that I turn to the trope of nostalgia and television, which has played a crucial role in this contemporary re-mapping.

Nostalgia and the Stars: Lament for the Past

The kind of fan circulation visible after 1980 and in the present is akin to an experience of loss, a lament for the glorious cinematic imaginary of the golden 1950s and later through the iconicity of the two stars.[47] Nostalgia has been described as a specific postmodern condition where the nostalgia film operates as the only available mode to narrate the past. Jameson's decoding of the postmodern condition via the nostalgia film is an important intervention that needs to be factored into an understanding of how this mode of remembrance can circulate in a larger discursive terrain, and not remain merely limited to the specific instance of the nostalgic film described by him (Jameson 1991). These modes of remembering the past in terms of nostalgia may not, and most often do not, deploy the 'critical insight or questioning' that Linda Hutcheon (1988) describes in her reading of the postmodern condition. Hutcheon had argued that the postmodern draws on parody to self-reflexively narrate itself, as opposed to pastiche, which Jameson believes is quintessentially postmodern. However, Jameson's intervention is especially significant since he rightly points out that it is pastiche, not parody (which uses satire and is ironical), that signals a deep longing for the past as well as the desire to experience that past, which is unavailable in the present except via its image. In the postcolonial condition, too, nostalgia is crucial as '...it connects people across historical, national or personal boundaries. It works in a collective cultural space, and is "curious" in the manner in which it brings to the fore, individual and social desires that prompt the search for remembered times and sites' (Walder 2011: 1).[48] These collective cultural remembrances can be described as the *lieux de memoire* that Nora suggests are significant sites which function in the absence of actual lived memories (Nora 1989).

The uneven discursive terrain that I have signalled above in relation to the contemporary circulation of the star texts of Suchitra and Uttam is perhaps important for the creation of their *lieux de memoirs*.[49] The question that this nostalgic recuperation asks is: What is being recovered or cultivated via this need to retrieve a lost past? What specific desires are being projected in this act of 'going back' to the star figures and their filmic and non-filmic selves, and what does it signify for the present? The move from populist fan circulation to the critical regime of the Little Magazines, and the poster and publicity exhibitions (both in Kolkata and beyond) are vigorous attempts at creating an archive for the present.[50] The state is also trying to inveigle itself into this terrain; nostalgia culture around this recuperation needs to factor in the political impulses operating in the varieties of nostalgia, each with their hierarchies; we need to be cautious in our calibration of the same. Interestingly, nostalgia has a particular democratic impulse, since in its original enunciative meaning it was considered an affliction related to Swiss soldiers who were away from their homeland (Boym 2001, cited in Cronberg 2009–10: 163–64). This seventeenth-century disease was positioned as an affliction related to the masses, as opposed to melancholia, which was a condition afflicting the intellectual person (ibid.). In this sense, the mapping of nostalgia culture becomes an enabling tool to think through the circulation of the popular iconicity of the two stars who held sway over the masses, and not the 'classes' in the context of Bengali cinema. However, the present recalibrations through the nostalgia discourse do signpost newer constellations between the masses and classes. Nostalgia nonetheless remains a crucial trope for the circulation of this fragment of fan culture. I shall now turn to one significant visual site where this circulation functions in the contemporary, but often with strange outcomes.

Television has played a crucial part in the recuperation of the two stars. Biswas (2000) has rightly pointed out that both television and the cassette boom of the 1980s around film songs have played a big role in the circulation of the two stars' texts.[51] The Bengali cable channels and Doordarshan Bangla channel telecast re-runs of their films, including special packages[52] that are advertised across the city through huge hoardings.[53] ETV Bangla also telecast remakes of Uttam's films as tele-films, as part of a series called *Oti Uttam* which was a co-production between Arya Entertainment and ETV. Broadcast in 2005, the channel telecast these remakes in the Saturday 9.30 PM slot. The entire series included 104 films; in 2005–06, around twenty-six films were showcased, including films such as *Khokababur Pratabartan, Harano Sur, Saap Mochon, Pathey Holo Deri, Kuhak, Jotugriho, Mouchak, Baghbondir Khela, Ekhane Pinjar,* and *Nishipadma,* among others. These films were made in colour and starred newer Tollywood actors. The rationale behind this series was to remake the almost canonical popular films with contemporary actors, many of whom were children of Uttam's co-stars, like Shashwat Chatterjee, who is Shubhendu Chatterjee's son. These films tried to offer what Pam Cook, writing about a different context, calls a 'compelling emotional appeal to audiences via memories of these films which were themselves calculated to produce an affective response in viewers' (Cook 2005: 12). These films attempted to capture 'the loyalty' that Uttam inspired in his audiences and the '*probasi*' (Bengali people living outside West Bengal) and younger generation of viewers, many of whom had not even been born when the originals were made. However, it needs to be noted that despite high Television Rating Points (TRPs), the remakes generated a mixed and often hostile reception as audiences compared them unfavourably to the 'originals' and charges of 'commercial commodification' routinely appeared in the press to criticise the remakes. What added to the clamour of objections was the use of colour, and the subsequent 'lost' magic of the black and white originals. Most of the films also reconstructed the original films and did not merely remake them in a repetitive manner.[54]

Mahanayak was televised on Star Jalsha in June 2016 and ran for ninety-two episodes. It starred the well-known contemporary star Prosenjit Chatterjee, who is consciously reinventing himself as an actor by starring in more critically acclaimed films that are also part of the festival circuit. The actor had earlier starred in *Autograph* (2010), which also self-reflexively cited Uttam's stardom. He was also responsible for organising the 'Uttam Mela' in 2005, a large-scale commemorative exhibition that drew huge crowds in Kolkata. Therefore, Prosenjit's casting in *Mahanayak* is significant, as in public memory the star is seen as constantly citing his fan appreciation for the superstar. Pre-publicity campaigns for the serial drew huge attention; despite disclaimers about its fictional nature, the name 'Mahanayak' and the male superstar's name, Arun Chatterjee (Uttam's real name), were dead giveaways. The serial chronicled the protagonist's rise to superstardom and his relationships with three of his heroines, which were thinly-veiled references to rumours around Uttam's relationships with Suchitra, Supriya, and Sabitri. The personal lives of all the stars were depicted using stories that have circulated as gossip over the decades, including about the troubled marriages that had supposedly haunted both Uttam and Suchitra.

Predictably, the serial, despite high TRPs, drew scathing criticism from Supriya Debi, Uttam's live-in partner.[55] She blasted the makers for besmirching the memory of both Uttam and Suchitra and derided the salacious manner in which all the interpersonal relationships of the superstar were depicted. Interestingly, both the television productions, the remakes screened as *Oti Uttam* or this latest series, have not been received unconditionally. These sites of memory clearly did not garner acceptance as they were perceived to be inimical to the hagiographic impulse of commemoration that underscores public discourse. Television remakes in this particular instance thus did not generate an absolute acceptance of attempts to recreate the aura of the past and the two stars. Clearly, nostalgia for the past via the star figure could not be re-sited in new products; despite the repackaging, the 'original' held its emotive and symbolic space.

In his reading of *Harano Sur*, Biswas (2000) speaks about the feminine world that this film and other love films starring Uttam–Suchitra inhabit. He argues that the re-circulation of the films via television is perhaps a form of nostalgia for not only the lost modern, but also the lost feminine that the region can no longer lay claim to. Do these collective remembrances seek to capture the changing regional self in its cinematic manifestation? I have argued that it is Uttam's death that acts as a marker for the emergence of a new configuration of his self-fashioning and idea of the popular that has held sway in the post-demise period. Bhattacharya (2011) has argued that it was the superstar's death that saw the appearance of the lament narrative, which sought to read the crisis that had engulfed Bangla cinema in the late 1980s and 1990s as an important factor that finally consolidated the discourse of parallel cinema in the 1990s. It is only in the new millennium that other popular filmic configurations of the *bhadralok* cinema appeared in films by Rituparno Ghosh, Suman Mukhopadhyaya, etc. (ibid.). The interface with the young that Uttam staged in the 1970s films showed traces of different kinds of protagonists and heroes that eventually engulfed the popular, which staged the truly moffussil hero in the Bengali action film through the 1980s and 1990s, as I have mentioned earlier. Can it be argued then that with the deaths of Uttam and Suchitra, the cartography of the *bhadralok/bhadramahila* self that I have mapped in this book became the lost object of desire and could only be relocated as affect via these media sites? The dispersed sites function both as traces and as affective bridges, spread across space, time, and geographical locations. It is with these acts of remembrance that I turn to another crucial site where the star texts make their appearance and aid nostalgic recuperation, with remarkable resonances.

FICTION AND THE STARS

The 'end' of this chapter narrates three fictional scenes: one a short story, the second a novella, and the last a depiction of a scene at Uttam's ancestral house on the night of his death in 1980. As I have argued following Majumdar (2009), the appearance of the private in the star text cannot be limited to only official sites like biographies and star discourses, but gets displaced onto other sites such as fictional reconstruction. It is in the fictional sites that the contradictions, erasures, and deletions from the official discourse get displaced and reconfigured. These reconfigurations rewrite the 'stories' about the stars for the present. If one regards the star text as evolving and shifting, then it is imperative to mark these shifts through these fictional sites as well. The short story that I use validates Uttam's star stature as an actor who was able to move his audiences with his melodramatic acting. The other two reconstructions create imaginaries of the woman star's life, as well as draw on the personal, emotive relationship of friendship and rumoured love affair of the two stars. It needs to be reiterated that in the 1950s, film publicity campaigns had used the 'love affair' with startling effect, as I discussed in Chapter One. Even in the present, media speculations continue about the special relationship that the two stars shared.[56]

'Uttam Kumarer Kampuni' / The Shivering Uttam Kumar[57]

This is an imaginary reconstruction of Uttam's final appearance, staged after his death; the scene is set in Chitragupta's audience hall, the god before whom all Hindus have to appear after death to give an account of their lives. Uttam, a handsome old man, has been brought before him. As he is escorted by two soldiers, they break into applause and are joined by other ruffians, the menials of the *durbar*. Chitragupta asks Uttam to narrate his contribution to the betterment of cinema. He points to the rag-tag group of youths, one of whom starts talking. This young man, with long sideburns and wearing a garish shirt, is appalled at the god's question and says forcefully that '*Guru*'[58] was a top-notch actor who could do a smashing job; he was called *mahanayak*. He further claims that many women would willingly have become his widows. Chitragupta is terribly annoyed at this intrusion and asks the youth to keep quiet. He turns to the star and asks if he managed to work with world-renowned directors; was his name familiar to the big names of world cinema; and was he a member of the cine clubs of his country? Have people in other parts of the world seen his films? Does he find any mention in any film reference guide? Did stars such as Richard Burton, critics like Marie Seton, or directors like Antonioni know of him? They all reply in the negative (they are all present; hovering around in the firmament). Uttam acknowledges that he had only acted in two measly films directed by a world-renowned Indian director.

The god then calls the industry directors whom he worked with. As they enter, a stink wafts from their dead bodies; Chitragupta shoos them away saying, 'These are the dregs in whose films you acted? No wonder you are condemned.' Uttam, of course, is forced to accept all the charges of bad films, bad selection, and cheap popularity. He points to the hangers-on, the ruffians, and the young men, the foot soldiers who are cheering for him as the 'guru', and says that his films were targeted at this crowd. Uttam asks to be given one last chance to act. He then enacts the first and the last scene from a Manik Bandopadhyaya short story, 'Madan Tanti'.[59]

As he finishes, people are mesmerised at the display of emotional affect that leaves them spellbound. Both Richard Burton and Gregory Peck think, 'Thank God he did not act with world greats or in good cinema, else our domination would have suffered.' And Chitragupta is seen crying profusely, for the first time.

This short story captures the ineffable circulation of pathos that melodramatic acting can bring forth. In a nutshell, it collapses the entire derisive discourse mobilised by the proponents of serious cinema and re-positions the appeal of emotive affect. It is this power of emotion that Bhaskar (2012) has argued is the key to understanding the appeal of melodrama. Furthermore, the ironic manner highlights the highly hierarchical and hegemonic place that film society discourses occupied in Bengal. At least in this fictional retelling, the popular manages to circumvent that hierarchy to signpost its power, as well as celebrate the star power of Uttam, emphasising the need to take the large public, who found their idol in the star, seriously. It was this undifferentiated public who were thought to be debased by their exposure to the sentimental melodramas that were Uttam's forte. I think what the story manages to foreground very economically is the power of sentiment and the fact that the public knew what it wanted as affective sustenance from the star. In the concluding section, I turn to two other fictional sites: a novella on Suchitra, and her staging of affect and devotion on 24 July 1980 as she paid her last respects to her 'best friend'.[60]

The Erotic *Nayika* and Her Love: Suchitra and Her Story

The erstwhile glamour queen of the industry,[61] who, in a critic's words, is the woman one can desire but not possess (cited in Nag 1998), has also reappeared in the present. Her sensuality and erotic excess, which generated so much discomfort in her own time and became the object of derision for a while, was given a fresh lease of life in the novella *Suchitra Sen: Uttaran O Antaraal* [*Suchitra Sen: Evolution and Seclusion*] by Ranjan Bandopadhyaya (2009). Bandopadhyaya uses the descriptive and narrative tropes of the *vaishnav padabali's* erotic *nayika*[62] to describe her charged sensuous beauty and glamour. The cover of the novella is taken from a painting in the Radha series by artist Suhas Roy, a well-known portraitist specialising in depictions of mythical women. It is interesting to note that in Roy's painting, Radha's face is done using the Suchitra profile.[63] Descriptions of Suchitra's body fill up more than half of the 150-page book. The prose is quite lurid and voyeuristic as it dwells almost like a camera to frame and stage her sensuality and photogenic beauty. The rest of the novella is devoted to a fictional reconstruction of her marriage to Dibanath and her relationship with Uttam, with the latter narrated as a love story. The two stars declare their feelings for each other quite candidly, but choose to keep it un-legitimised and under wraps. The love scenes in the novella are staged under a tree in the New Technicians studio premises, replicating the *mise en scène* of a film set.

This purported love story between the two stars has always occupied centrestage in narratives around their love films and also the extra-filmic. In the 1950s, this 'affair' was also used for publicity, as I have shown in the discussion of *Sagarika*'s reception in Chapter One. Other than a 'candid confession' by Uttam himself, who acknowledges that he loved Suchitra but could not 'describe' his feelings, there is hardly any 'evidence' besides the gossip surrounding the love affair (Bosu 1998: 400). In Himanshu Chattopadhyaya's book on Suchitra, he refers to the special relationship that the two stars shared. Uttam had reportedly asked Suchitra to marry him. She had refused, saying that it would mean the death of their on-screen pairing. In fact, the night he walked out on his wife and family, he had gone to her house, but she turned him away. It is then that he went to Supriya, with whom he stayed for seventeen years until his death in 1980 (Chattopadhyaya 2005: 31). His romantic involvement with Sabitri has been written about by the actor herself in her biography and mentioned in numerous interviews that she has given. His long-standing live-in relationship with Supriya is equally in the realm of public acceptability. It is, however, the intense cinematic romantic pairing with Suchitra that defied all limits of acceptability, staging a love that titillated and disturbed but acquired its own life, circulating across time to now achieve a metonymic status. The Suchitra–Uttam romance still inhabits the public oral gossip circuit and the Bengali middle-class imaginary and remains the stuff of media speculation and romantic literature.

I conclude this chapter with the last encounter of this metonymic love. The scene is set in Uttam's ancestral house, on the night of his death. In a melodramatic twist, his companion of seventeen years, Supriya, was not allowed by his family to see his dead body;[64] mourners filed past his body the whole day. What has acquired the status of a mythic tale is the scene enacted late at night when Suchitra arrived; she had already withdrawn from the industry two years earlier. This account of her final goodbye was published in an issue of *Television*. In this account, there is a two-line description of her visit when she placed a garland over his dead body (Chaudhuri 1993: 37). It subsequently resurfaces in other biographies and starts accruing the status of a mythic retelling (Gupto 2003: 147; Ray 1992: 63).[65] She had a garland of *rajnigandha*, tuberoses, in her hands. The *rajnigandha* flowers are familiar to all spectators of their films, as discussed by Biswas (2000) in his article on *Harano Sur*. As she stood over his body, with tears in her eyes, she could not decide what to do with the garland, until Uttam's wife, Gauri Devi, told her, 'Roma, put the garland around his neck; after all you have done that so many times on screen'. The near-mythic 'love affair' gets its final legitimisation, the on-screen/off-screen romance comes to rest in its final space of devotion. His wife lets his 'cinematic lover' place the garland on his body (Chattopadhyaya 2005: 9).

What has not yet been laid to rest is the excess of that *ugra pranaya*,[66] the aggressive and erotic romance that keeps reappearing in many narratives across time and space, haunting us with newer possibilities that allow us to ask questions about illicit and legitimised desires and their afterlives. Neither has it laid to rest the 'emotion travel' (Bruno 2002: 7) that the stars signify. It is this travel that keeps circulating still to let us create utopian bridges of romance and desire. It is this charge of the popular and the post-independence modern embodied by the stardom of Suchitra and Uttam that gets articulated in this emotional retelling. The nostalgic gaze of the present manages to capture the past via the two iconic lovers and their submerged desire. As Moinak Biswas has said, the act of nostalgic looking back via the two stars is perhaps a search for the lost modern of the Bengalis. Nostalgia then works to recover the past, its memories, and their circulation, allowing the present to find some figure to anchor its own self-fashioning. I conclude this chapter with a quote from Walder, who says, 'Nostalgia begins in desire, and may well end in truth. It can and often does, serve as a key to multiple pasts that make us who and what we are, for better or worse' (Walder 2011: 3). I think it is the twin axes of desires and the 'truth' that the two star bodies signify that finds a space in the present via the multiple sites that I have attempted to signpost in my book.

Notes

1. The Left Front was defeated after thirty-three years of rule by Mamata Banerjee's Trinamool Congress in the state elections of 2011. I shall discuss the political appropriation of the star's hagiographic reconfiguration later in the chapter.

2. Sayandeb Chowdhury (2012) discusses the aftermath of Uttam's death in 1980 and presents an imaginative reconstruction of the Left Front state government's response in his article, 'The Heroic Laughter of Modernity'.

3. Supriya had given a detailed account of her relationship with the superstar in her autobiography, *Amar Jibon Amar Uttam*. She also appeared in television and newspaper advertisements for products that are advertised as being Uttam's favourite, for instance the Sunrise Mustard Oil ads. She also brought out a cookbook which contained his favourite recipes and carries an intimate picture of Supriya and Uttam.

4. See Bolton and Wright (2016) on the posthumous manipulation of star images, including the fashioning of the star texts by families for commercial purposes. They have remarked about the posthumous accretion of star images of Frank Sinatra and Grace Kelly. Something similar has happened with Uttam's star text after his death, especially his appropriation for political gains by the Trinamool Congress, as I have mentioned above.

5. Rabindra Sadan is a government-run cultural complex that carries a lot of symbolic capital.

6. Swapan Das (dir.). 2011. *Mahanayak: A Superstar Journey*. Films Division.

7. The book was co-authored by Gourango Prasad Ghosh, but is a first-person narrative of the star. The book carries a signed letter by Uttam, and as I have remarked above, was advertised as his *atmajibani*, his autobiography. It was supposed to have been released on his birthday in 1980, but since he passed away in July, it was brought out posthumously. This is the only authorised autobiography till date. Uttam had written a serialised autobiography which was published in 1961 in *Nabakallol*.

8. See the Bibliography for the list of published biographies that I have been able to track. This excludes books by other actors and contemporaries who mention the two stars. Wherever used, such material has been duly referenced in the text.

9. I have discussed Dipesh Chakrabarty's intervention about self-narratives in the Indian context and Majumdar's (2009) engagement with the rhetorical device of 'reticence' that governs star biographies in India. Gayatri Chatterjee, in her introduction to Shanta Gokhle's translation of Durga Khote's autobiography, also makes the relevant intervention that autobiographies do not provide access to truth. Udaya Kumar (2008) has made an extremely relevant point to critique Chakrabarty's position about the bracketing of the private. He suggests that in the Indian context, we need to understand that autobiographies are public utterances. As such, 'Insofar as (the) autobiographical act involves an exhibition of one's lived life before the gaze of a reading public, paradigms of spectacle and performance may be more relevant to the study of self-narratives than (the) model of authentic expressiveness' (ibid.: 422). See the Introduction to this book.

10. Holland (1996) and Martin (2014) harbour a different view of gossip, compared to Spacks (1982). According to them, gossip carries a censorious and moral tone that defines discourses of public morality specific to its time. 'Most commonly the subject of gossip is considered to be a failure of living up to the relevant standards (assumed to be), and is directly or indirectly criticised for this failure' (Holland 1996: 198). It is this aspect of gossip that has led sociologists to claim that it serves to enforce social norms. Drawing on Mill's *On Liberty*, Holland suggests that gossip's function to criticise involves moral censure and it can become a 'mechanism for policing the individual and society' (ibid.: 204). Martin too ascribes to this view: 'Gossip, like satire, is revealed… to be broadly conservative in intent. While acts of gossiping are invariably hypocritical and at odds with their implied moral purpose, [the] gossip nevertheless often claims to be acting as both the guardian and the censor of public morals' (2014: 138).

11. Shear defines knowledge play as a voluntary social activity that possesses its own discursive rules and communal limits.

12. Spacks has a more positive and affirmative view about gossip as a social activity that fosters a sense of community and affinity, especially its etymological connection with the feminine gender.

13. Other notable biographies include *Khanjanma Uttam Kumar; Uttam Kumar; Mahanayak Uttam; Uttam Sarvottam*, etc. Uttam's first serialised biography, which had appeared in *Nabakallol* in 1961, was re-published as a book and released at the Kolkata Book Fair in 2013.

14. I have discussed this *dada* figure and its centrality to Uttam's star text to read the 1970s popular cinema in Chapter Four.

15. In Supriya's autobiography, there is no mention of this troubled aspect of her daughter's infatuation. Soma's education and marriage occupies half a page (1999: 297). Recently, in a personal account, Sarbani Mukherjee too has written about her attraction as a teenager for the superstar who had a long association with her father, the well-known writer Ashutosh Mukherjee, many of whose literary works were adapted for films (*Anandolok* 2007).

16. In numerous letters from film magazines, it is possible to glimpse the fan following that he had amongst women. The story about a married woman chasing him in a car and other salacious gossip about his 'womanising' have not been able to dim the halo around his *bhalo chele*/good boy image. This discourse of middle-class values that Uttam typified still inhabits numerous sites; from a barber who named his hair salon after the star following his death in 1980 and firmly believes that the star would never have chased after any woman or misbehaved with her (Ray 2007: 75–78) to an anthropological study of young, Bengali middle-class women, all of whom dream about and romanticise the star (Ray 1993), his presence inhabits diverse sites and social locations. Uttam himself had acknowledged the vicissitudes that he had to face due to unwarranted fan intrusion and the salacious stories that circulated as a result (Chattopadhyaya 2010: 358–61).

17. Supriya describes the tortuous relationship that Uttam shared with her. Over half of her autobiography is dedicated to her relationship, its ups and downs, the anxiety of 'living together', and her devotion to his health, especially after his first heart attack in 1967 during the disastrous box-office failure of *Chhoti si Mulaquat*. This book also contains personal letters that they exchanged during their seventeen years together (1999: 198–99, 246–48, 337–72).

18. The industry during his stint was referred to as 'a one-man industry'. From being the 'flop-master general' during his initial period of struggle, he had managed to become the figurehead of the entire industry. I have discussed this figuration of Uttam in Chapter Four.

19. This short poem, called 'To Vichitra Sain' (the play on her East Bengal dialect was reflected in the distortion of her name, suggesting the nasal twang peculiar to this dialect), was published in a magazine called *Rupanjali* and the editor was slapped with a lawsuit by Suchitra. He had opened a donation account to fight the ensuing court case, but lost it and the magazine was eventually shut down (Gupto 2003: 66–67).

20. It was during 1966, when she was shooting for *Mamata* (the Hindi remake of *Uttar Phalguni*), that she was first compared to Kanan Devi (*Rupmancha* March 1966).

21. Despite the fact that Stacey describes the female spectator's relationship to the star image, this category is useful to describe the intimate style that Ray uses in this and his other books on Suchitra. Amitabh Chaudhuri too uses a similar narrative strategy in his book, *Amar Bondhu Suchitra*. Both Ray and Chaudhuri are veteran film journalists and were reportedly very close to Suchitra. These authors used this style to debunk the public perception that Suchitra was a haughty, proud woman star. The anecdotal account proved useful to narrate incidents of a personal and intimate encounter which provided the reader with 'personal' access to the reclusive and elusive woman star who was warm and friendly, and whose elusive nature and intense professionalism were often misunderstood as the behaviour of a proud woman.

22. In his latest book on Suchitra, *Onno ek Suchitra* (2008), Ray continues his reinvention of the star from where *Suchitrar Katha* had left off.

23. Kanan Devi too refers to her devotion to the seer in her autobiography, published in 1973.

24. Other biographies, such as *Tollywood er Greta Garbo*, *Je Jon Achen Nirjane*, *Mahanayika Suchitra*, *Amar Bondhu Suchitra Sen*, etc., try to track her charismatic glamorous diva image and self-consciously compare her to Garbo.

25. This particular phrase was regularly deployed in the readers' letters that I found printed in *Rupmancha* around 1956. See the discussion around *Sagarika* in Chapter One.

26. Her elite lifestyle after her marriage and her husband's foreign model cars were routinely part of photos in the film magazines. Moonmoon Sen referred to her mother as a 'party animal' who used to enjoy her partying and socialising, but chose to give that up (cited in Chatterjee 2002: 71). There are uncorroborated rumours of her drinking and smoking, as well as special men friends.

27. Her status as the daughter-in-law of the *bonedi* Sen family, her spatial location in the elite south Kolkata neighbourhood of Ballygunj, and her

daughter's marriage into the erstwhile royal family of Tripura together add to the aura of the elite, urban, modern *bhadramahila*.

28. Suchitra herself had acknowledged Sabitri as a better actor than herself (Ray and Raha 2002).

29. Sabitri provides a detailed account of this stint on stage in her autobiographical section, 'Parda Sariye' (Ray and Raha 2002: 80–82).

30. Marshall notes that cultural ideals of actresses as denoted by the use of 'artifice and cosmetics', as seen in the positioning of Sarah Bernhardt's looks versus the 'natural look' and 'simplicity' of Eleonara Duse, are two important constituents of the woman performer's gendered reception. These varied discourses throw light on the manner in which actresses' makeup, physical beauty, etc., are used as evaluative models, and 'stars' seem to fare poorly in these comparisons (Marshall 2007: 69–70).

31. *Rupmancha* (February 1959) carried this report for Sabitri's birthday celebrations. In comparison, all the reports on Suchitra highlighted her glamour and her see-through sarees. Even the special *Rupmancha* issue published after she won an award in Moscow referred to the inappropriate press coverage of her photographs, focusing on her dress and body, and the editor self-righteously commented that his magazine had desisted from publishing such scandalous images of the star (November 1963). However, I found enough evidence of the same magazine describing in great detail her public appearance at a felicitation ceremony organised by the producer R. D. Bansal at Indira Film Hall, where her dress and makeup was described in lurid prose. The reporter remarks that if he were the poet Kalidas, he would have been able to describe her better. The readers' letters after this news report drew attention to her dress sense, which was criticised for being too spectacular and not appropriate for a Bengali *bhadramahila* (ibid.: 51).

32. Film magazines such as *Ultoroth, Cinema Jagat,* and *Rupmancha* regularly carried photographs of Suchitra which added to her glamour quotient for the public.

33. For instance in *Hospital* (1960), in which she appeared as Ashok Kumar's heroine, the credit sequence and publicity in newspapers and magazines such as *Ultoroth* carried the male star's name before hers.

34. *Sobare Ami Nomi* (1973).

35. Gooptu (2010) mentions this aspect of Suchitra's star text but offers no analytical framework to read this.

36. Biswas (1990) borrows the term from Molly Haskell's work on female Hollywood stars and argues that Meena Kumari and Waheeda Rehman typified this dialectic in Bombay cinema. This dialectic is framed along the creation and consolidation of the star image along the axis of certain

stereotypical figurations, such as the strong but sexualised, domesticated woman star, or the girl next door, and the inability of the star to break out of that image. In contrast, the actor versus star dialectic can be described as the ability of a particular star to keep experimenting with different kinds of roles that would redefine his acting capabilities.

37. Ray had given a speech after Uttam's death at the commemorative meet organised at New Technicians Studio. This excerpt has gained wide circulation in the Little Magazine circuits (*Chitrabhash* 2001).

38. I have discussed one fragment of this reinvention in Chapter Four, where I read the 'elder brother or the putative elder brother' figure as an important component of the roles that Uttam essayed in this decade. Besides this, films such as *Chowringhee* and *Nishipadma* saw him enact roles that were different from the usual manner of staging the star.

39. Vasudevan's introduction to his volume, *The Melodramatic Public*, is an excellent summary of this 'idea of better cinema' that was central to film criticism in the 1950s (2010: 6–7).

40. It is in many of the articles written around 1980 that one can glimpse the accretion of the image of a highly romanticised version of the on-screen lovers' naïve, innocent love that, despite their passionate embrace, was pure and unsullied; their romance displayed '*parishilito o marjito prem*', or cultivated and refined love (Gupto 2010). This particular article had initially appeared in *Television* magazine. From the 1950s discourse of obscenity and scandalous modernity that I discussed in Chapter One, the shift to a refined, cultured display of love is interesting to note.

41. Ranjan Bandopadhaya, who used to write film reviews in *Desh* in the late 1970s–80s, wrote a series of articles in *Aajkal* in the mid-1980s where he re-evaluated his own critical position on the star. These articles have been published in a collected volume of his works (Bandopadhyaya 2010).

42. Chatterjee (2007) argues that one of the first articles that aided this 'mis-remembrance' was Dulali Nag's article in *Economic and Political Weekly* (1998).

43. However, it is interesting to note that this assessment of the star was part of the popular discourse, as *Rupmancha* had carried an article where Kaalish Mukherjee, the editor, had deployed a similar historiographical model (October 1961: 174–92).

44. This article offers an analysis of the film craft of important directors such as Satyajit Ray, Ritwik Ghatak, Tarun Majumdar, and Tapan Sinha.

45. This idea has recently been contested by interventions mounted by Bhaskar Sarkar's recent book *Mourning the Nation* (2010), which reads these elisions and gaps in popular cinema as a sign of trauma work. Biswas (2010)

too argues that the dislocated figures in the 1950s popular films can be regarded as reflective of the larger dislocation associated with the Partition.

46. Uttam had written an article about the sorry state of the industry and urged the state government to help upgrade studio facilities and infrastructure (Sanyal 2008). Bengali film magazines such as *Rupmancha* and *Ultoroth* used to carry big advertisements urging their spectators to watch Bengali films. Asit Chaudhuri, a well-known distributor, spearheaded a campaign to promote the cause of Bengali films.

47. This lament seems to surface mostly in the mid-1980s to the mid-1990s, when popular Bangla cinema went through a particular phase of representing the proletariat hero figure. Films made by Swapan Saha, Haranath Chakrabarty, and Anjan Chowdhury, and films made as joint productions with Bangladesh were partly responsible for this lament (Bhattacharya 2011). I have discussed this shift as it emerged in the 1980s in Chapter Four.

48. Walder uses the term 'curious' as, according to him, he cannot find a better term to express the "'strange, even uncanny mix of individual and social desires" that drive "the search for remembered time"' (Walder 2011: 1).

49. Most of the contemporary critical discourse on nostalgia is undertaken to study diaspora, the role of memory, and history in the context of the reunification of the two Germanys, or as a reflection on Hong Kong's identity crisis after the Sino-British joint declaration.

50. Nora argues that the contemporary epoch is an epoch of the archive. In the intensely ephemeral and visual cultural regime, these sites of memories—anniversaries, events, etc., as well as commemorations, museums, and archives—are important because spontaneous memory and lived memory is no longer available (Nora 1989: 12).

51. The hit songs from the love films were repackaged and had tremendous success, especially during Puja and festival seasons; now, audio CDs have taken the place vacated by cassettes. I have found a CD that has an artist whistling tunes of Uttam's hit songs!

52. The Doordarshan Bangla channel had broadcast a special retrospective of Suchitra's films in 1993 to mark her fourteenth retirement anniversary. The reason provided for this special package was that it was a 'nostalgic look' for the older viewers and to make younger viewers aware of the golden period of cinematic heritage. *Television* magazine brought out a special issue to mark the occasion.

53. When I travelled to Kolkata for archival work during 2006–10, I came across these advertisements, with Uttam's face covering almost half the billboard and the channel's name and telecast days in smaller font, displayed at

Gariahaat Flyover or near Park Circus Flyover, two major traffic intersections in the city.

54. Films such as *Jotugriho, Kuhok,* etc., were reconstructed keeping in mind the contemporary times, but garnered negative criticism. The reviews of the series were published in *Bikeler Pratidin* (selected issues 2006).

55. See https://www.anandabazar.com/supplementary/anandaplus/an-interview-with-supriya-devi-about-mahanayak-serial-1.485866 (accessed March 2023). The relationship between Uttam Kumar and Supriya Debi has been at the forefront of further controversy since the 2019 docudrama *Jete nahi Dibo* was stalled by the actor's family as being disrespectful to his memory. For further details, see https://bengali.indianexpress.com/entertainment/alipur-court-issues-stay-order-on-uttamkumars-documentary-by-prabir-roy-jete-nahi-dibo-163226/ (accessed March 2023).

56. Supriya Debi mentions the special relationship that Uttam and Suchitra shared (*Saptahik Bartaman,* 25 July 2010). Uttam's brother, Tarun Kumar, has also mentioned their special bond. In the 1950s and 1960s, film magazines would regularly publish photographs of the two stars sitting together, laughing, at various film functions. The photo caption would say, 'the romantic superstars in "*antaranga*", private/intimate moment enjoying themselves'. I was able to find many such photos with similar captions in *Ultoroth* and *Rupmancha.*

57. This short story was published in the Little Magazine *Dekhchi Shunchi,* but the torn copy does not have any date and no writer's name. I was able to only locate the name of the editor of this volume; Ramaprasad Dutta. The Temar Lane Little Magazine library has this volume in its collection. The summary is my translation from the original Bangla story.

58. This diminutive was an affectionate name bestowed on Uttam by his fans; as he would appear on-screen, the halls would ring out with shouts of '*guru, guru*' ('boss, boss'). This fan name probably started around 1966 during the screening of *Rajdrohi,* in which Uttam had enacted a Robin Hood character who would loot foodgrain from the rich landlord and distribute it to the poor. We need to remember that the mid-1960s witnessed a terrible food crisis. I have discussed this social problem in Chapter Two, in the section on *Nabaraag.*

59. This short story narrates the plight of Madan, a weaver, and his struggle to save his art from excruciating poverty. However, the writer seems to have got the name of the story wrong as the short story published by Manik Bandopadhyaya in 1947 is called 'Kanai Tanti' and is collected in the short story collection titled *Khatian,* that is, ledger, account book.

60. Suchitra had described Uttam as her best friend in the excerpt published in *Anandalok* after Uttam's death in 1980.

61. In the mid-1960s, a photograph of Suchitra clicked by Dhiren Deb raised a furore, as I have mentioned in Chapter Three. This photo has been reprinted in her biography, *Tollywood er Greta Garbo*, with a detailed account of Dhiren Deb's remembrance of this photo shoot (Chattopadhyaya 2005: 58; Gupto 2003). This photo also circulates widely on the internet.

62. This particular literary or descriptive category usually narrates the sensuous beauty of Radha as Krishna's paramour, typically in the form of songs or lyrics, *padabali*.

63. In the 1960s–70s, many clay idols for Laxmi and other goddesses, used for celebrating festivals, were cast and made with recognisable resemblance to Suchitra's profile (Gupto 2003: 31). This practice, of course, added to the popular circulation of her image and its iconic accretion.

64. The interview published in the August issue of *Anandalok* mentions this in passing; the report of his funeral cortege in the same issue mentions Supriya and Soma paying their respects at the New Theatres Number 2 Studio (*Anandalok* 1980: 77).

65. Most people whom I met and who are self-confessed fans refer to this story, although, as Professor Shohini Ghosh commented during my workshop presentation, she had not heard about this particular incident (JNU Workshop, November 2010). This underscores my argument about the centrality and significance of some stories, which then acquire mythic proportions.

66. This phrase was used to describe the charged romance of *Sagarika* in the publicity ads.

Conclusion

This book has analysed a particular imagination of the post-independence modern cinematic self-fashioning that emerges via melodrama in popular Bengali cinema of the 1950s–70s, as seen through the star texts of Suchitra Sen and Uttam Kumar. As I have shown, their stardom, with their purported status as the only two superstars that the Bengali film industry has seen, is significant as a fragment of the popular Bengali cinema and its history. Their star texts, which defined the popular during the 1950s–70s, reappear as a residual imaginary that still inhabits the cultural and emotive spaces of the popular in Bengal. This imaginary continues to circulate in the form of commemorative events and other sites that I examined in Chapter Five, clearly tapping into the nostalgic, looking back at the emotive desirability inherent in the two stars, which remains powerful in its affective possibilities.

In Chapter One, the analysis foregrounded the trope of modern love as it emerged via individual subjectivities seeking emotional sustenance through love and work, invested in the utopian possibilities of love and couple formation. The self-fashioning that both women and men participated in brought to the fore the issues that complicated the coming together of the romantic couple. These issues were located in the fraught social structures that these selves had to encounter as they negotiated their selfhoods to realise their love and achieve emotive and affective fulfillment. My examination of the self-fashioning of 1950s Bengali cinema was informed by my analysis of the middle-class characters representing the *bhadralok*. My analysis of the love films and the manner in which the question of region, community, identity, and the star texts of both Suchitra and Uttam were mobilised in the 1950s, demonstrated the complicated layers of negotiating *bhadralok* self-fashioning. This cinematic negotiation could not completely concur with a monolithic construct of the idea of idealised *bhadralok/*

bhadramahila identity, so central to middle-class self-fashioning in this period, especially as seen in the love films. As I discussed in Chapter One, it is important to keep in mind that the performative excess of Suchitra, the staging of the love of the desiring woman, the sensitive and sometimes reticent, inert male characters played by Uttam, and the spilling over of the erotic charge of love in the publicity machinery associated with *Sagarika* and *Ekti Raat* gave us a text that pulled in contrary directions and thus challenged the homogeneous construct of 'respectable' *bhadralok* middle-class subjectivity. Further, the constant reiteration of the regional imaginary via the discourse constructed by film magazines and readers' letters rested on disavowing the Bombay model and the *videshi* cinema or 'foreign', Hollywood model of 'titillating and sex appealing cinema'; however, through the love films, this regional cinema also created a product, centred on the two stars, that was able to match both these models. The particular cinematic self-fashioning of these romantic melodramas therefore inhabited a terrain of collision and conflict. Despite being at odds with the *bhadralok* communitarian impulse, these love films were spectacular commercial successes in their own time and also had successful re-runs when they were eventually re-released.

Chapter Two analysed marital discord as another significant constituent of the couple phase of Suchitra and Uttam's films. I navigated this marital imaginary across three moments: the first located in the playing out of marital discord in the 1950s, the second in the colonial modern period, and the third in the 1970s. The first film analysed the personal upheavals that the married couple experienced in the context of the working woman and her stay-at-home spouse. The new working woman, who was negotiating her selfhood tied to her marriage and her husband, encountered an uneasy terrain of gendered expectations in *Indrani*. The second film, *Grihodaho*, showed how the urban, educated Brahmo woman Achala negotiated her dislocation to a rural setting after marriage, and the attendant complications of an extra-marital relationship. However, the text's location in the nineteenth century left the new woman trapped within her circumscribed historical, social, and marital location. The last film, *Nabaraag*, dealt with ideological clashes of parenting and the emotive disconnect experienced by the trophy wife Narayani. Her marital status and her motherhood provided a point of entry to decode the fraught social conditions under which this married couple had to negotiate their selfhoods as parents to achieve emotional fulfillment. Despite the staging of marital discord, all three films were governed by the logic of the romantic couple text, insofar as the end had to show the embrace that was central to their romantic iconicity, even in the Saratchandra adaptation where the literary text did not end in the union of the estranged couple. In varied ways, the endings of these films showed symbolic resolutions that enabled the new married woman to achieve her emotional selfhood, tied to the figure of her partner. This imaginary participated in narrating the ideal of the companionate marriage, a significant coordinate on which the post-colonial modern mapped its social locus vis-à-vis the personal.

Chapters Three and Four analysed the individual stardom of Suchitra and Uttam. After the heady romantic phase of the 1950s, and the examination of marriage along an arc of discord, we saw Suchitra create a text of self that gave voice to the varied feminine subjectivities located in the 1960s: the figure of the doomed lover, Radha Mitra, in *Dweep Jele Jai*; the sacrificing mother and her daughter in *Uttar Phalguni*; as well as the divorced woman in *Saat Paake Bandha* who cannot forget her husband. All three films analyse the modern *bhadramahila* who defined her selfhood via love, education, and work, and yet could not attain affective union with her lover due to social and familial strictures. Chapter Four examined Uttam across the fraught 1970s and analysed the varied male figures of the saviour, Amal in *Ekhane Pinjar*, the failed suicidal male Gana *da* in *Jadu Bangsha*, and the insane Anupam in *Nagar Darpane*. Barring the male figure in the first film, the other two remained incapable of dealing with tense personal and social conditions.

The 1960s and 1970s cinematic map that I discussed in these two chapters brought forth the difficulties of forming affective unions as the individual subjectivities seemed to crumble under inimical circumstances with mostly tragic consequences. If the trope of suffering invested the woman/star with a self that still had cultural valence, the beleaguered male, however, could only die by suicide or stare inertly at his wife and family. In the gendered social terrain, masculinity can only be valued as a success story, with any deviation regarded as a failure. These gendered subjectivities, despite their 'stereotypical' figurations, remain powerful cinematic explorations that still retain their pull on the popular imaginary in Bengal. Whether it is Radha Mitra, Panna Bai, or Archana; Amal, Gana *da*, or Anupam, the enactment of each of these *bhadramahila/ bhadralok* characters is a powerful cinematic rendition that defined the self-fashioning of the region and its cinema in the 1960s and 1970s. The common feature of these melodramas remained the enactment of selfhoods that are tied to emotion and affect. It is the emergence of the individual's deeply felt desires, which were otherwise suppressed, that was voiced in these films.

This cinematic self-fashioning not only rested on the filmic selves of Suchitra and Uttam, but was also equally created out of the extra-diegetic, as is true for any star text. The star body and its attire were significant constituents of the mapping of the self. Suchitra's star text was created out of an axis that used fashion, make-up, and glamour to construct a highly charismatic aura of the sensuous diva. As I analysed in Chapter One, readers' letters displaying anxiety regarding Suchitra's attire and appearance were being used to assign negative value to her star text, deploying highly gendered language. The frisson between her on-screen and off-screen look created the text of a sensual woman who oozed 'excessive' femininity. This excess spilled over into the extra-diegetic, and her attempts at re-inventing herself in the 1960s, with roles that staged the woman alone as a figure of noble sacrifice and ended in extreme situations of madness, death, and loneliness, was inadequate to gloss over her charismatic presence and persona. The off-screen discourse around her public appearances mobilised the discussion about her class, social, and spatial location as the elite, married *bhadramahila* of south Kolkata.

In contrast, Uttam's star text was mobilised along the different axis of his middle-class location and appearances. In Uttam's case, his Western and Indian clothes gave credence to his middle-class social status. In particular, his traditional Bengali attire came in for praise and approval. It was an assiduously cultivated look and he carried it off with tremendous aplomb and élan. A lot of his public appearances saw him clad in elegant '*dhakka par*' *dhutis* and *mulmul kurta*. Photo captions in contemporary film magazines referred to the elegance with which Uttam could carry off the attire of the cultured 'Bengali Babu': and the distinct difference between his *dhuti* when he visited an acquaintance to commiserate a death and when he attended a celebration was reported in great detail. This can be attributed to the public demand for all information about the star's lifestyle, but what is crucial here is the accretion of the particular Bengali *bhadralok* self/body that was being mobilised. If Uttam repeatedly referenced his average middle-class Bengali upbringing, then it is equally this minutiae regarding his persona that enabled his easy translation as the *bhadralok dada* figure. In contrast, the letters and photo captions that I cited on the glamorous excess of Suchitra's off-screen appearances, as well as the letters objecting to the filmic display of 'unprincipled modernity' actually signposted the spilling over of the sensual and erotic excess of this woman star, who made her mark in a space that was not ready to accept her as a fashion icon, or as a woman who was not averse to the display of her glamorous, elite *bhadramahila* persona. In different ways, both stars became melodramatic texts, demonstrating an excess in their own time and beyond.

Chapter Five examined the various trajectories of the star texts of Suchitra and Uttam across time and space. I have argued that the impulse of the popular to converge on the star bodies created a heterogeneous archive and acquired varied manifestations; it produced new sites for the star body to reside in and make a home for itself. This multiplicity was read as a dispersed text and mapped as traces across time and space. The nostalgic culture around the stars and the display of fan devotion and loyalty bore the marks of that trace; equally, it allowed newer constellations of cultural remembrances to emerge. These memory sites may get congealed, or they may aid new accretions in the future. The contemporary accretion of romantic iconicity seems the most valued fragment of this star text, still reappearing in fictional romantic reconstructions years after its cinematic moment has passed to haunt the popular.

In their affective resolution, the stories create a palimpsest: leaving all the marks of their varied traces on each retelling, emerging at various times, acquiring new methods of narration. What remains is the star body, allowing the cinematic imaginary to map itself out, to let the popular find its space and place among the charmed objects of our desires.

Filmography

Deep Jwele Jai. 1959. Asit Sen (dir.). Badal Pictures. Suchitra Sen, Basanta Chowdhury, Pahari Sanyal, Dilip Chowdhury.

Ekhane Pinjar. 1971. Yatrik (dir.). Kalamandir Arts. Uttam Kumar, Aparna Sen, Dilip Mukhopadhyaya, Aparna Debi, Ratna Ghoshal.

Grihodaho. 1967. Subodh Mitra (dir.). Uttam Kumar Films (Pvt.) Ltd. Suchitra Sen, Uttam Kumar, Pradeep Kumar, Sabitri Chattopadhyaya, Pahari Sanyal.

Indrani. 1958. Niren Lahiri (dir.). H. N. C. Productions. Suchitra Sen, Uttam Kumar, Chhabi Biswas, Pahari Sanyal.

Jadu Bangsha. 1974. Parthapratim Chowdhury (dir.). Montage Films. Uttam Kumar, Aparna Sen (Double), Sharmila Tagore, Dhritiman Chatopadhyaya.

Nabaraag. 1971. Bijoy Bose (dir.). S. M. Films. Suchitra Sen, Uttam Kumar, Bikash Ray, Bijan Bhattacharya.

Nagar Darpane. 1975. Yatrik (dir.). Sree Giridhari Pictures. Uttam Kumar, Dilip Mukhopadhyaya, Koushik Bose, Supriya Debi, Kaveri Bose.

Saat Paake Bandha. 1963. Ajoy Kar (dir.). R. D. Bansal and Company. Suchitra Sen, Soumitra Chattopadhyaya, Pahari Sanyal, Chhaya Debi.

Sagarika. 1956. Agragaami (dir.). S. C. Productions. Suchitra Sen, Uttam Kumar, Jamuna Singha, Jiben Bose.

Saptapadi. 1961. Ajoy Kar (dir.). Alochhaya Productions. Suchitra Sen, Uttam Kumar, Chhabi Biswas, Tarun Kumar.

Suryatoron. 1958. Agradoot (dir.). Nabarun Chitra. Suchitra Sen, Uttam Kumar, Chhabi Biswas, Kamal Mitra.

Uttar Falguni. 1963. Asit Sen (dir.). Uttam Kumar Films (Pvt.) Ltd. Suchitra Sen (Double), Bikash Ray, Pahari Sanyal, Dilip Mukhopadhyaya.

Bibliography

Alam, Javed. 1999. *Living with Modernity*. New Delhi: Oxford University Press.

Allen, Graham. 2007. *Roland Barthes*. London and New York: Routledge.

Anderson, Benedict. 1991. *Imagined Communities: Reflections on the Origin and Spread of Nationalism*. London and New York: Verso.

Aniket. 1980. 'Uttam–Suchitra: Sei Basanta'. *Anandalok*, 16 August: 25–28.

Ashcroft, Bill. 2012. 'Bollywood, Postcolonial Transformation, and Modernity'. In *Travels of Bollywood Cinema: From Bombay to LA*, Anjali Gera Roy and Chua Beng Huat (eds): 1–18. New Delhi: Oxford University Press.

Bagchi, Jasodhara. 1999. 'Women In Calcutta: After Independence'. In *Calcutta: The Living City*, Vol. II: *The Present and Future*, Sukanta Chaudhuri (ed.): 42–49. Kolkata: Oxford University Press.

Bandyopadhyaya, Ranjan. 2009. *Suchitra Sen: Uttaran O Antaraal* [*Suchitra Sen: Evolution and Seclusion*]. Kolkata: Gaangchil.

———. 2010. *Gadya Samagra*, Vol. I: *Chalachitra*. Kolkata: Pratibhas Prakashan.

Banerjee, Smita. 2009. 'Revisiting Popular Bangla Cinema of the 1950s'. *The Book Review* 33 (2), February: 39–40.

———. 2015. 'The Making of Uttam Kumar: The Star, the True Bhadralok'. *Silhouette Magazine*, 3 September. Available at http://learningandcreativity.com/silhouette/uttam-kumar-the-star/ (accessed March 2023).

Banerjee, Swapna M. 2006. 'Child, Mother and Servant: Motherhood and Domestic Ideology in Colonial Bengal'. In *Rhetoric and Reality: Gender and the Colonial Experince in South Asia*, Avril A. Powell and Siobhan Lambert Hurley (eds): 16–49. New Delhi: Oxford University Press.

Barnouw, Erik and S. Krishnaswamy. 1980. *Indian Film*. New Delhi: Oxford University Press, 2nd edition.

Bastin, Giselle. 2005. 'From Grand Re'cit to Petit Histoire: Exploring Historical Cleavage in Kate Granville's Joan Makes History'. *Limina Journal of Historical Cultural Studies* 11: 28–37. Available at https://www.archive.limina.arts.uwa.edu.au/__data/page/186585/bastin.pdf (accessed March 2023).

Benjamin, Walter. 2008 [1969]. *The Work of Art in the Age of Mechanical Reproduction*. In *Illuminations: Essays and Reflections*: 19–50. New York: Schoken Books. Available at https://warwick.ac.uk/fac/arts/english/currentstudents/undergraduate/modules/fulllist/second/en229/benjamin_work_of_art.pdf (accessed March 2023).

Bhaskar, Ira. 2012. 'Emotion, Subjectivity, and Limits of Desire: Melodrama and Modernity in Bombay Cinema 1940s–50s'. In *Gender Meets Genre in Post War Cinemas*, Christine Gledhill (ed.): 161–76. Chicago and Urbana: University of Illinios Press.

Bhaskar, Ira and Richard Allen. 2009. *Islamicate Cultures of Bombay Cinema*. New Delhi: Tulika.

Bhattacharya, Shankerlal. 1980. 'Nana Ronger Din: Uttam–Soma'. *Anandalok*, 16 August: 41–45.

Bhattacharya, Sougato. 2009. *Shatabarshe Aurora*. Kolkata: Baishakhi.

Bhattacharya, Spandan. 2011. 'The Post Liberalization Bengali "Parallel" Cinema: Bhadralok Nostalgia, the Politics of Pastness, and the Discourse of "Difference"'. MPhil Dissertation, unpublished. New Delhi: Jawaharlal Nehru University.

Bhattacharya, Tithi. 2005. *The Sentinels of Culture: Class, Education and the Colonial Intellectual in Bengal (1848–85)*. New Delhi: Oxford University Press.

Bhowmick, Someshwar. 2001. 'Mahanayaker Akhyan'. *Chitrabhash* 36 (January–December): 15–18.

Biswas, Moinak. 1990. 'Modern Calcutta Cinema'. In *Calcutta: The Living City*, Vol. II: *The Present and Future*, Sukanto Chaudhuri (ed.): 302–15. Kolkata: Oxford University Press.

Biswas, Moinak. 2000. 'The Couple and Their Spaces: *Harano Sur* as Melodrama Now'. In *Making Meaning in Indian Cinema*, Ravi S. Vasudevan (ed.): 122–42. New Delhi: Oxford University Press.

_____. 2002. "Historical Realism: Modes of Modernity in Indian Cinema 1940–60". PhD Thesis, unpublished. Melbourne: Monash University.

_____. 2003. 'The Urban Adventure and the 1950s Melodrama'. Paper, Sarai Workshop, 23–24 October. New Delhi: Centre for the Study of Developing Societies.

_____, (ed.). 2006. *Apu and After: Re-visiting Ray's Cinema*. London, New York, Kolkata: Seagull.

_____. 2007. 'Speaking Through Troubled Times'. *Journal of the Moving Image*. Available at https://jmionline.org/article/speaking_through_troubled_times (accessed March 2023).

_____. 2010. 'Shohorer Pathe: Uttam Kumar O Panchasher Nabya Melodrama'. *Tehai*: 37–51.

Bolton, Lucy and July Lobalzo Wright. 2016. *Lasting Screen Stars: Images that Fade and Personas that Endure*. New York and London: Routledge.

Bose, Pradip Kumar. 1995. 'Sons of the Nation: Child Rearing in the New Family'. In *Texts of Power*, Partha Chatterjee (ed.): 118–44. Minneapolis: University of Minnesota Press.

Bosu, Robi. 1998. *Saat Rongo: Sritir Sarani te Bangla Chalachitrer Ardhashatabdi*. Kolkata: Dey's Publishing.

Bosu Roy, Iraban. 2001. 'Uttam Kumar: Romantic Nayaker Pratima'. *Chitrabhash* 36: 19–23.

Bourdieu, Pierre. 1986. 'The Forms of Capital'. In *Handbook of Theory and Research for the Sociology of Education*, J. Richardson (ed.): 241–58. New York: Greenwood.

Boym, Svetlana. 2001. *The Future of Nostalgia*. New York: Basic Books.

Brooks, Peter. 1984. *The Melodramatic Imagination: Balzac, Henry James, Melodrama and the Mode of Excess*. New York: Columbia University Press.

Bruno, Giuliana. 2002. *Atlas of Emotions: Journeys in Art, Architecture, and Film*. New York: Verso.

Byars, Jackie. 1991. *All that Hollywood Allows: Re-reading Gender in 1950s Melodrama*. Chapel Hill and London: The University of North Carolina Press.

Chakrabarti, Sambuddha. 1995. 'Changing Notions of Conjugal Relations in Nineteenth Century Bengal'. In *Mind, Body and Society*, Rajat Kanti Ray (ed.): 297–329. Kolkata: Oxford University Press.

Chakrabarty, Dipesh. 1993. 'The Differance–Deferral of (a) Colonial Modernity: Public Debates on Domesticity in British Bengal'. *History Workshop* 36 (Autumn): 1–34.

———. 1996. 'Postcoloniality and the Artifice of History: Who Speaks for Indian Pasts'. In *Contemporary Postcolonial Theory: A Reader*, Padmini Mongia (ed.): 223–47. New Delhi: Oxford University Press.

———. 2000. *Provincializing Europe: Postcolonial Thought and Historical Differnce*. Princeton: Princeton University Press.

Chatterjee, Monidipa. 1990. 'Town Planning in Calcutta: Past, Present and Future'. In *Calcutta: The Living City*, Vol. II: *The Present and Future*, Sukanta Chaudhuri (ed.): 133–47. Kolkata: Oxford University Press.

Chatterjee, Nilanjana. 1990. 'The East Bengal Refugee: A Lesson in Survival'. In *Calcutta: The Living City*, Vol. II: *The Present and Future*, Sukanta Chaudhuri (ed.): 70–78. Kolkata: Oxford University Press.

Chatterjee, Partha. 1989. 'The Nationalist Resolution of the Women's Question'. In *Recasting Women: Essays in Colonial History*, K. Sangari and S. Vaid (eds): 233–53. New Delhi: Kali for Women.

———. 1990. 'The Political Culture of Calcutta'. In *Calcutta: The Living City*,Vol. II: *The Present and Future*, Sukanta Chaudhuri (ed.): 27–33. Kolkata: Oxford University Press.

———. 1993. *The Nation and its Fragments: Colonial and Post-colonial Histories*. New Delhi: Oxford University Press.

———. 1997. *The Present History of West Bengal: Essays in Political Criticism*. New Delhi: Oxford University Press.

Chatterjee, Sabitri. 1980. *Chena Mukh*. Kolkata: Nandan.

Chatterjee, Shoma A. 1998. *Subject: Cinema, Object: Woman; A Study of the Portrayal of Women in Indian Cinema*. Kolkata: Parumita Publications.

———. 2002. *Suchitra Sen: A Legend in Her Lifetime*. New Delhi: Rupa Publications.

Chatterjee, Soumitra. 2001. 'Prosongo Uttam Kumar'. *Chitrabhash* 36 (January–December): 54–58.

Chatterjee, Subhajit. 2007. '(Mis)Reading Romance: An Enquiry Concerning Representation of "Love" in Bengali Literature and Cinema'. PhD Thesis, unpublished. Manipal: Manipal University.

———. 2010. 'Uttam–Suchitra and the Mise en Scene of Desire: Anatomy of a Screen Romance'. *Tehai*: 66–78.

Chatterjee, Sudipto. 2007. *The Colonial Staged: Theatre in Colonial Calcutta*. London, New York, and Kolkata: Seagull Books.

Chattopadhyaya, Himanshu. 2005. *Tollywood er Greta Garbo: Suchitra Sen*. Kolkata: Urbi.

Chattopadhyaya, Rinto (ed.). 2008. *Khanjanma Uttam Kumar*. Kolkata.

Chattopadhyaya, Sajal. 2006. 'Taraka Pratha O Uttam Kumar'. *Chitralipi* (May): 96–111.

Chattopadhyaya, Shubhendu. 2011. 'Uttam-Katha'. *Chitrabhash* (January–December): 60–62.

Chattopadhyaya, Swati. 2005. *Representing Calcutta: Modernity, Nationalism and the Colonial Uncanny*. London and New York: Routledge.

Chattopadhyaya, Uttam and Gourango Prasad Ghosh. 1980. *Amar Ami*. Kolkata: Dey's Publishing.

Chattopadhyaya, Uttam. 2010. 'Fan ebong Fan Letter'. *Tehai*: 358–61.

Chaudhuri, Amitabh. 1993. Interview with Suchitra Sen. *Dream Woman: Suchitra Sen* (special issue). *Television*, February.

———. 1995. *Amar Bondhu Suchitra Sen*. Kolkata: Dey's Publishing.

Chaudhuri, Nupur and Rajat Kanto Ray. 2005. 'From Beehive Cells to Civil Space: A History of Indian Matrimony'. In *Living Together Seperately: Cultural India in History and Politics*,

Mushirul Hasan and Asim Roy (eds): 250–81. New Delhi: Oxford University Press.

Chaudhuri, Shohini. 2006. *Feminist Film Theorists: Laura Mulvey, Kaja Silverman, Teresa de Lauretis, Barbara Creed*. London and New York: Routledge.

Chaudhuri, Supriya. 2006. 'In the City'. In *Apu and After: Revisiting Ray's Cinema*, Moinak Biswas (ed.): 251–76. London, New York, and Kolkata: Seagull Books.

Chowdhury, Indira. 1998. *The Frail Hero and Virile History: Gender and Politics of Culture in Colonial Bengal*. New Delhi: Oxford University Press.

Chowdhury, Sayandeb. 2012. 'The Heroic Laughter of Modernity: The Life, Cinema and Afterlife of Bengali Matinee Idol Uttam Kumar'. *Film International* 10 (4/5), Fall: 82–91.

_____. 2021. *Uttam Kumar: A Life in Cinema*. New Delhi: Bloomsbury Publishing.

Clark, Danae. 1995. *Negotiating Hollywood: The Cultural Politics of Actors' Labor*. Minneapolis and London: University of Minnesota Press.

Cook, Pam. 2005. *Screening the Past: Memory and Nostalgia in Cinema*. London and New York: Routledge.

Cronberg, Anja Aronowsky. 2009–10. 'Imagined Nostalgia and False Memories: Postmodernism and Fashion in the Late Twentieth Century.' *Vestoj.com*. Available at http://vestoj.com/postmodernism-and-fashion-in-the-late-twentieth-century/ (accessed March 2023).

Dasgupta, Chidananda. 1991. *The Painted Face: Studies in India's Popular Cinema*. New Delhi: Roli Books.

Dasgupta, Sushmita. 2010. 'Uttam Kumar: A Sociological View of the Bengali Culture in the Aftermath of Partition'. *Tehai*: 107–12.

Debi, Supriya. 1999. *Amar Jibon Amar Uttam*. Kolkata: Model Publishing House.

_____. 2010. 'Adda Shilpa'. *Tehai*: 899–916.

Devi, Kanan. 1973. *Sobare Aami Nomi*. Kolkata: M. C. Sarkar and Sons Pvt. Ltd.

Dissanayake, Wimal (ed.). 1993. *Melodrama and Asian Cinema*. Cambridge: Cambridge University Press.
Doane, Mary Ann. 1987. *The Desire to Desire: The Woman's Film of the 1940s*. Bloomington and Indiana: Indiana University Press.
Donner, Henrik. 2008. 'The Significance of Naxalbari: Accounts of Personal Involvement and Politics in West Bengal'. LSE Research Online. Available at http://eprints.lse.ac.uk/21343/ (accessed March 2023).
Dube, Saurabh (ed.). 2004. *Postcolonial Passages, Contemporary History Writing on India*. New Delhi: Oxford University Press.
_____. 2009. *Enchantments of Modernity: Empire, Nation, Globalization*. London, New York, and New Delhi: Routledge.
During, Simon (ed.). 1993. *The Cultural Studies Reader*. London and New York: Routledge.
Dutta Gupta, Sarmishtha. 2010. *Identities and Histories: Women's Writings and Politics in Bengal*. Kolkata: Stree.
Dwyer, Rachel. 2000. *All You Want is Love, All You Need is Money: Sex and Romance in Modern India*. London and New York: Cassel.
Dwyer, Rachel and Christopher Pinney (eds). 2000. *Pleasure and the Nation: The History, Consumption and Politics of Public Culture in India*. New Delhi: Oxford University Press.
Dwyer, Rachel and Divia Patel. 2002. *Cinema India: The Visual Culture of Hindi Film*. New Delhi: Oxford University Press.
Dyer, Richard. 1979. *Stars*. London: British Film Institute.
_____. 1987. *Heavenly Bodies: Film Stars and Society*. London: Macmillan.
_____. 1993. *The Matter of Images: Essays in Representation*. London: Routledge.
Elsaesser, Thomas. 1987. 'Tales of Sound and Fury: Observations on the Family Melodrama'. In *Home is Where the Heart is: Studies in Melodrama and the Woman's Film*, Christine Gledhill (ed.): 43–69. London: British Film Institute.
Forbes, Geraldine. 1996. *Women in Modern India* (The New Cambridge History of India). Cambridge, UK: Cambridge University Press.

Forbes, Geraldine. 2006. 'Negotiating Modernities: The Public and Private Worlds of Dr Haimabati Sen'. In *Rhetoric and Reality: Gender and the Colonial Experience in South Asia*, Avril A. Powell and Siobhan Lambert-Hurley (eds): 223–41. New Delhi: Oxford University Press.

Foucault, Michel. 1980. *The History of Sexuality*, Vol. 1, trans. Robert Hurley. New York: Vintage.

Ghosh, Anuradha. 2012. 'Bollywood, Tollywood, Dollywood; Re-visiting Cross Border Flowsand the Beat of 1970s in the Context of Globalisation'. In *Travels of Bollywood Cinema: From Bombay to LA*, Anjali Gera Roy and Chua Beng Huat (eds): 98–122. New Delhi: Oxford University Press.

Ghosh, Debiprasad (ed.). 2009. *Abhinetri Katha*. Kolkata: Urbi Prakashan.

Ghosh, Gourango Prasad. 1982. *Sonar Daag: Shatabarsher Aloye Bangla Chalachitra*, Vol. 1. Kolkata: Jogmaya Prakashani.

Ghosh, Jayanta Kumar (ed.). 2001. *Uttam Kumar*. Kolkata: Srishti.

Ghosh, Parimal. 2004. 'Where Have All the "Bhadraloks" Gone?' *Economic and Political Weekly* 39 (3), 17–23 January: 247–51.

Ghosh, Somen. 1997. 'Mool Dharar Bangla Chabi'. In *Bhartiya Chalachitrer Ruprekha*, Parthapratim Bandopadhyaya (ed.): 91–106. Kolkata: Banishilpa.

Ghosh, Srabasi. 2000. '"Birds in a Cage": Changes in Bengali Social Life as Recorded in Autobiographies by Women'. In *Ideals, Images and Real Lives: Women in Literature and History*, Alice Thorner and Maithreyi Krishnaraj (eds): 35–67. Mumbai: Orient Longman.

Gledhill, Christine (ed.). 1987a. *Home is Where the Heart is: Studies in Melodrama and the Woman's Film*. London: British Film Institute.

———. 1987b. 'The Melodramatic Field: An Investigation'. In *Home is Where the Heart is: Studies in Melodrama and the Woman's Film*, Christine Gledhill (ed.): 5–39. London: BFI.

———, (ed.). 1991. *Stardom: Industry of Desire*. London and New York: Routledge.

Gledhill, Christine. 2000. 'Rethinking Genre'. In *Reinventing Film Studies*, Christine Gledhill and Linda Williams (eds): 221–43. London: Arnold.

Gledhill, Christine and Linda Williams (eds). 2000. *Reinventing Film Studies*. London: Arnold.

Gokulsinge, K. Moti and Wimal Dissanayake. 1991. *Indian Popular Cinema: A Narrative of Cultural Change*. New Delhi: Orient Longman.

Gooptu, Sharmishtha. 2010. *Bengali Cinema: An Other Nation*. New Delhi: Roli Books.

Goswami, Omkar. 1990. 'Calcutta's Economy 1918–1970: Fall from Grace'. In *Calcutta, the Living City*, Vol. II: *The Present and the Future*, Sukanta Chaudhuri (ed.): 88–96. Kolkata: Oxford University Press.

Greenblatt, Stephen. 2004. 'Renaissance Self-Fashioning'. In *Cultural Studies*, Nilanjana Gupta (ed.): 243–57. New Delhi: Worldview.

Gupto, Sebabrata. 2010. 'Dui Swarnajug'. *Tehai*: 753–57.

Gupto, Suman. 2003. *Je Jon Achen Nirjane*. Kolkata: Sahityam.

Hall, Donald E. 2004. *Subjectivities*. London and New York: Routldege.

Harris, Thomas. 1991. 'The Building of Popular Images: Grace Kelly and Maryiln Monroe'. In *Stardom: Industry of Desire*, Christine Gledhill (ed.): 40–44. London: Routledge.

Herzfeld, Michael. 2005 [1997]. *Cultural Intimacy: Social Poetics in the Nation State*. New York and London: Routledge, 2nd edition.

Hill, John and Pamela Church Gibson (eds). 1998. *The Oxford Guide to Film Studies*. Oxford: Oxford University Press.

Hoek, Lotte. 2014. 'Cross-Wing Fimmaking: East Pakistani Urdu Films and their Traces in the Bangladesh Film Archive'. *Bioscope* 5 (2): 99–118.

Holland, Margaret G. 1996. 'What's Wrong with Telling the Truth? An Analysis of Gossip'. *American Philosophical Quarterly* 33 (2): 197–209. Available at http://www.jstor.org/stable/20009858 (accessed May 2023).

Hutcheon, Linda. 1988. *A Poetics of Postmodernism: History, Theory, Fiction*. London and New York: Routledge.

Jain, Jasbir and Sudha Rai (eds). 2002. *Films and Feminism: Essays in Indian Cinema*. Jaipur: Institute for Research in Interdisciplinary Studies.

Jameson, Fredric. 1982. *The Political Unconscious: Narrative as a Socially Symbolic Act*. New York: Cornell University Press.

———. 1991. *Postmodernism or, The Cultural Logic of Late Capitalism*. London: Verso.

Kaviraj, Sudipta. 1995. 'The Krishnacharita: The Construction of Krishna in the Works of Bankim Chandra'. In *The Unhappy Consciousness: Bankimchandra Chattopadhyay and the Formation of Nationalist Discourse in India*. New Delhi: Oxford University Press.

———. 2004. 'Reading a Song of the City: Image of the City in Literature and Films'. In *City Flicks: Indian Cinema and the Urban Experience*, Preben Kaarshom (ed.): 60–82. Kolkata: Seagull.

———. 2007. 'Tagore and the Transformations in the Ideals of Love'. In *Love in South Asia: A Cultural History*, Francesca Orsini (ed.): 161–82. New Delhi: Cambridge University Press.

———. 2010. *The Imaginary Institution of India: Politics and Ideas*. Ranikhet: Permanent Black.

Khote, Durga. 2006. *I, Durga Khote*, trans. Shanta Gokhale. New Delhi: Oxford University Press.

King, Barry. 1991. 'Articulating Stardom'. In *Stardom: Industry of Desire*, Christine Gledhill (ed.): 167–82. London and New York: Routledge.

Kothari, Rajni. 1968. 'Tradition and Modernity Revisited'. *Government and Opposition* 3 (3): 273–93. Available at https://onlinelibrary.wiley.com/doi/abs/10.1111/j.1477-7053.1968.tb01292.x (accessed March 2023).

Kosambi, Meera. 2000. 'Women, Emancipation and Equality'. In *Ideals, Images and Real Lives: Women in Literature and History*, Alice Thorner and Maithreyi Krishnaraj (eds): 104–44. Mumbai: Orient Longman.

Kuhn, Annette. 1982. *Women's Pictures: Feminism and Cinema*. London: Routledge and Kegan Paul.

Kumar, Udaya. 2008.'Autobiography as a Way of Writing History: Personal Narratives from Kerela and the Inhabitation of Modernity'. In *History in the Vernacular,* Raziuddin Aquil and Partha Chatterjee (eds): 418–48. Ranikhet: Permanent Black.

Kumar, Uttam. 2001.'Amar Abhinayer Mukti and Ekti Sakhatkaar er Uttare Uttam Kumar'. *Chitrabhash,* January–December 2001: 46–47.

Kelly, G. 2016. 'Robert Taylor: The Lost Star with the Long Career'. In *Lasting Screen Stars: Images that Fade and Personas that Endure,* L. B. Wright (ed.): 85–98. New York and London: Routledge.

Kundu, Abhijit. 2004. 'Changing Iconography of the Women in Bengali Cinema (1950s to 1990s)—A Sociological Study of Some Select Films'. PhD thesis, unpublished. New Delhi: Jawaharlal Nehru University.

Landy, Marcia. 1996. *Cinematic Uses of the Past.* Minneapolis and London: University of Minnesota Press.

Majumdar, Neepa. 2009. *Wanted Cultured Ladies Only! Female Stardom and Cinema in India, 1930s–1950s.* Urbana and Chicago: University of Illinois Press.

Majumdar, Rochona. 2011.'Debating Radical Cinema: A History of the Film Society Movement in India'. *Modern Asian Studies* 46 (3): 1–37.

Marshall, Gail. 2007. 'Cultural Formations: The Nineteenth Century Touring Actress and her International Audiences'. In *The Cambridge Companion to the Actress,* Maggie B. Gale and John Stokes (eds): 52–73. Cambridge: Cambridge University Press.

Martin, Nicholas. 2014.'Literature and Gossip: An Intoduction'. *Forum for Modern Language Studies* 50 (2): 135–41. Available at http://fmls.oxfordjournals.org/content/50/2/135.full.pdf+html (accessed May 2023).

Mazumdar, Ranjani. 2003.'The Bombay Film Poster'. *Seminar* 525 (May): 33–41.

_____. 2007. *Bombay Cinema: An Archive of the City.* Ranikhet: Permanent Black.

_____. 2009.'Cosmopolitan Dreams'. *Seminar* 598: 14–20.

Mazumdar, Ranjani. 2011. 'Aviation, Tourism and Dreaming in 1960s Bombay Cinema'. *Bioscope South Asian Screen Studies* (2): 129–55.

Mehta, Rini Bhattacharya and Debali Mukerjea Leonard (eds). 2014. *The Indian Partition in Literature and Films: History, Politics and Aesthetics*. New York and London: Routledge.

Mercer, John and Martin Shingler. 2004. *Melodrama: Genre, Style, Sensibiilty*. London: Wallflower.

Mishra, Yatindra. 2009. 'The Bai and the Dawn of Hindi Film Music (1925–1945)'. *The Book Review* 33 (2), February: 46–47.

Mitra, Kamal. 1989 *Flash Back*. Kolkata: Mondal & Sons.

Mitra, Smita. 2009. 'Mahanayika Madam'. *Seminar* 598, June: 41–46.

Morin, Edgar. 1961. *The Stars: An Account of the Star System in Motion Pictures*. London: Evergreen Books.

Mukherjee, Debashree. 2009. 'Good Girls, Bad Girls'. *Seminar* 598: 21–27.

Mukherjee, Madhabi. 1999. *My Life, My Love*. California: The Stanford Theatre Foundation, Palo Alto.

Mukherjee, Samrat. 2010. 'Sonar Juti (1962–67): Chabighar e Andhakar, Chabighar e "Grihodaho"'. *Tehai*: 52–57.

Mukhopadhyaya, Ashishtaru. 2000. *Mahanayika Suchitra*. Kolkata: Dey's Publishing.

Mukhopadhyaya, Chandi. 2010. 'Uttam Nirman: Bangla Cinemar Prothom O Shesh "Taraka"'. *Tehai*: 26–36.

Mulvey, Laura. 1996. *Fetishism and Curiosity*. Bloomington: Indiana University Press.

Nag, Dulali. 1998. 'Love in the Time of Nationalism: Bengali Popular Cinema of the Time of Nationalism'. *Economic and Political Weekly* 33 (14): 779–89.

Nandy, Ashis. 1981. 'The Popular Hindi Film: Ideology and First Principles'. *IIC Quarterly* 8 (1): 89–96. New Delhi: India International Centre.

———. 1983. *The Intimate Enemy: Loss and Recovery of Self Under Colonialism*. New Delhi: Oxford University Press.

———. 1995. 'An Intelligent Critic's Guide to Indian Cinema'. In *The Savage Freud and Other Essays on Possible and Retrievable Selves*. New Delhi: Oxford University Press.

Nandy, Ashis. 1999. 'A Critique of Modernist Secularism'. In *Politics in India*, Sudipta Kaviraj (ed.): 330–32. New Delhi: Oxford University Press.

———. 2001. *An Ambiguous Journey to the City: The Village and Other Odd Ruins of the Self in the Indian Imagination*. New Delhi: Oxford University Press.

Nora, Pierre. 1989. 'Between Memory and History: Les Lieux de Mèmoire'. *Representation* 26: 7–24.

Nowell-Smith, Geoffrey. 1987. 'Minnelli and Melodrama'. In *Home is Where the Heart is: Studies in Melodrama and the Woman's Film*, Christine Gledhill (ed.): 70–74. London: British Film Institute.

O'Flaherty, Wendy Doniger. 1980. *Sexual Metaphors and Animal Symbols in Indian Mythology*. New Delhi: Motilal Banarsidass.

Orsini, Francesca (ed.). 2007. *Love in South Asia: A Cultural History*. New Delhi: Cambridge University Press.

Pandian, M. S. S. 1996. 'Gendered Negotiations: Hunting and Colonialism in the Late Nineteenth Century Nilgiris'. In *Social Reform, Sexuality and the State*, Patricia Uberoi (ed.): 239–64. New Delhi: Sage.

Panja, Shormishtha. 2004. 'Rabindranath Tagore's Chokher Bali: The New Woman, Conjugality and the Heterogeneity of Home'. In *Signifying the Self: Women and Literature*, Malashri Lal, Shromishtha Panja, and Sumanyu Satpathy (eds): 211–25. New Delhi: Macmillan.

Petro, Patrice. 1989. *Women and Melodramatic Representation in Weimar Germany*. Princeton: Princeton University Press.

Ponzanesi, Sandra. 2007. 'Branding the Nation: Exporting Literature as Cultural Capital'. In *Focus India: Postcolonial Narratives of the Nation*, Harish Trivedi and Meenakshi Mukherjee (eds): 146–58. New Delhi: Pencraft International.

Powell, Avril A. and Siobhan Lambert-Hurley. 2006. *Rhetoric and Reality: Gender and the Colonial Experience in South Asia*. New Delhi: Oxford University Press.

Prakash, Gyan. 1999. *A Different Modernity, Another Reason: Science and the Imagination of Modern India*. Princeton, New Jersey: Princeton University Press.

Prasad, Madhav. 1998. *Ideology of the Hindi Film: A Historical Construction*. New Delhi: Oxford University Press.

Raghavendra, M. K. 2008. *Seduced by the Familiar: Narration and Meaning in Indian Popular Cinema*. New Delhi: Oxford University Press.

Raha, Kiranmoy. 1991. *Bengali Cinema*. Kolkata: Nandan.

Rajadhyaksha, Ashish. 1987. 'The Phalke Era: Conflict of Traditional Form and Modern Technology'. *Journal of Arts and Ideas* 14 (15): 47–48.

_____. 1993. 'Neo-Traditionalism: Film as Popular Art in India'. *Framework* 32 (33): 26–67.

Rajadhyaksha, Ashish and Paul Willemen (eds). 1995. *An Encyclopedia of Indian Cinema*. New Delhi: Oxford University Press.

Ray, Bharti. 1995. 'Female Rivalries and the Joint Family Structure in Bengal, 1900–1947'. In *Mind, Body and Society*, Rajat Ray (ed.): 364–90. Kolkata: Oxford University Press.

Ray, Bikash. 1985. *Ami*. Kolkata: Karuna Prakashani.

Ray, G. K. 1992. *Suchitrar Katha*. Kolkata: Ananda Publishers Private Limited.

_____. 2008. *Onno ek Suchitra*. Kolkata: Amiya Pushp Prakashani.

Ray, Manas. 2007. 'Uttam–Kumarer Saloon'. *Ababhas*, April–September: 55–105.

Ray, Manisha. 1993. *Bengali Women*. Kolkata: Stree.

Ray, Mrigankasekhar and Partha Raha (eds). 2002. *Sabitri Chattopadhaya: Chalachitrabhinayer Panchas Bachar*. Kolkata: Nandan West Bengal Chalachitra Kendra.

Ray, Satyajit. 2011. 'Uttamkumarer Smarane and the Nayak Uttam Kumar'. *Tehai*, January–December: 84–87.

Ray, Shivkumar. 2001. 'Bangla Chalachitrer Shatabarsha'. *Chitrabhavna*, November: 56–120.

Ray, Subhash C. 2011. 'The Political Economy of Decline of Industry in West Bengal: Experiences of a Marxist State Within a Mixed Economy'. Department of Economics Working Papers Series, University of Connecticut. Available at https://media.economics.uconn.edu/working/2011-10.pdf (accessed May 2023).

Roberts, Adam. 2007. *Frederic Jameson*. Noida: Routledge (Indian reprint).

Rodowick, David N. 1987. 'Madness, Authority and Ideology: The Domestic Melodrama of the 1950s'. In *Home is Where the Heart is*, Christine Gledhill (ed.): 268–80. London: British Film Institute.

Rowena, Jenny. 2010. 'The Laughter Film and the Reconfiguration of Masculinities'. In *Women in Malayalam Cinema*, Meena T. Pillai (ed.): 125–52. Hyderabad: Orient BlackSwan.

Sangari, Kumkum. 2011. 'Viraha: A Trajectory in the Nehruvian Era'. In *Poetics and Politics of Sufism and Bhakti in South Asia: Love, Loss and Liberation*, Kavita Panjabi (ed.): 250–87. New Delhi: Orient BlackSwan.

Sanyal, Amiyo (ed.). 2008. *Uttam Sarvottam*. Kolkata: Ritwik Publication.

Sarkar, Bhaskar. 2010. *Mourning the Nation: Indian Cinema in the Wake of Partition*. New Delhi: Orient BlackSwan.

Sarkar, Sumit. 1985. 'The "Woman Question" in Nineteenth Century Bengal'. In *Women and Culture*, K. Sangari and S. Vaid (eds): 157–72. Bombay: SNDT University.

_____. 1997. *Writing Social History*. New Delhi: Oxford University Press.

Sarkar, Tanika. 2001. *Hindu Wife, Hindu Nation: Community, Religion and Cultural Nationalism*. New Delhi: Permanent Black.

Schatz, Thomas. 1981. 'The Family Melodrama'. In *Hollywood Genres: Formulas, Filmmaking and the Studio System*: 221–60. New York: Random House.

Sharma, Aparna. 2016. 'From Angry Young Man to Icon of Neo-liberal India: Extra Cinematic Strategies that make Amitabh Bachchan India's Lasting Super Star'. In *Lasting Screen Stars: Images that Fade and Personas that Endure*, L. B. Wright (ed.): 11–25. New York and London: Routledge.

Siddique, Salma. 2022. *Evacuee Cinema: Bombay and Lahore in Partition Transit, 1940–1960*. Cambridge, UK: Cambridge University Press.

Sen, Anil. 2003. *Cinemar Gappo*. Kolkata: Satyajug Prakashan.

Sen, Samita. 1999. *Women and Labour in Late Colonial Bengal.* Cambridge: Cambridge University Press.

Sen, Shova. 2000. *Ora, Amra, Era.* Kolkata: Thema.

Sengupta, Judhajit. 2001. 'Chalachitra-Chitra O Chitrakalpa'. *Chitrabhavna,* November: 177–87.

Sengupto, Rana. 1987.'Prosongo: Uttam Kumar'. *F4*: 14–16.

Shear, Jack. 2008. 'The Reader's Idle Talk: Gossip in Henry Fielding's Tom Jones'. In *Literary and Cultural Intersections in the Long Eighteenth Century,* Mariana D'Ezio (ed.): 22–37. Cambridge: Cambridge Scholar's Publishing. Available at https://www.cambridgescholars.com/resources/pdfs/978-1-4438-0063-1-sample.pdf (accessed March 2023).

Silverman, Kaja. 1988. *The Acoustic Mirror: The Female Voice in Psychoanalysis and Cinema.* Bloomington and Indianapolis: Indiana University Press.

Sinha, Mrinalini. 1995. *Colonial Masculinity: The 'Manly Englishman' and the 'Effeminate Bengali' in Late Nineteenth Century.* Manchester: Manchester University Press.

Spacks, Patricia Meyer. 1982. 'In Praise of Gossip'. *The Hudson Review* 35 (1): 19–38. Available at https://doi.org/10.2307/3851309 (accessed May 2023).

Stacey, Jackie. 1994. *Star-Gazing: Hollywood Cinema and Female Spectatorship.* London and New York: Routledge.

Sunder Rajan, Rajeshwari. 1993. *Real and Imagined Women: Gender, Culture and Post-Colonialism.* New York: Routledge.

Sur, Anshu.1999. *Bengali Film Directory.* Kolkata: Nandan.

Tejani, Shabnum. 2007. *Indian Secularism: A Social and Intellectual History, 1890–1950.* Ranikhet: Permanent Black.

Thoraval, Yves. 2000. *Cinemas of India.* New Delhi: Macmillan Publishers India.

Vasudevan, Ravi. 1991. 'Cultural Space of a Film Narrative: Interpreting Kismet (Bombay Talkies, 1943)'. Occasional Paper, New Delhi: Nehru Memorial Museum and Library.

——. 1993. 'Shifting Codes, Dissolving Indentities: The Hindi Social Film of the 1950s as Popular Culture'. Occasional Paper, New Delhi: Nehru Memorial Museum and Library,

Vasudevan, Ravi. 1995. 'Film Studies, the New Cultural Histories and the Experience of Modernity'. *Economic and Political Weekly* 30 (44): 2809–14.

——— (ed.). 2000. *Making Meaning in Indian Cinema*. New Delhi: Oxford University Press.

———. 2010. *The Melodramatic Public: Film Form and Spectatorship in Indian Cinema*. Ranikhet: Permanent Black.

Virdi, Jyotika. 2003. *The Cinematic Imagination: Indian Popular Film as Social History*. Ranikhet: Permanent Black.

Viswanathan, Shiv. 2012. 'Violence as the Other: A Portrait of the Seventies'. *Brunch, Hindustan Times*, 22 July.

Wani, Arti. 2016. *Fantasy of Modernity: Romantic Love in the Bombay Cinema of the 1950s*. New Delhi: Cambridge University Press.

Walder, Dennis. 2011. *Postcolonial Nostalgias: Writing, Representation and Memory*. New York and London: Routledge.

Walsh, Judith. 1995. 'The Virtuous Wife and The Well-Ordered Home: The Re-Conceptualisation of Bengali Women and their Worlds'. In *Mind, Body and Society*, Rajat Kanti Ray (ed.): 330–59. Kolkata: Oxford University Press.

Wexman, Virginia Wright. 1993. *Creating the Couple: Love, Marriage and Hollywood Performance*. Princeton, New Jersey: Princeton University Press.

Williams, Linda. 1998. 'Melodrama Revised'. In *Refiguring American Film Genres: Theory and History*, Nick Browne (ed.): 42–88. Berkeley, Los Angeles, and London: University of California Press.

Index